Client State

Client State

Japan in the American Embrace

GAVAN McCORMACK

VERSO

London • New York

First published by Verso 2007
Copyright © Gavan McCormack 2007
All rights reserved

1 3 5 7 9 10 8 6 4 2

Verso
UK: 6 Meard Street, London W1F 0EG
USA: 180 Varick Street, New York, NY 10014-4606
www.versobooks.com

Verso is the imprint of New Left Books

ISBN-13: 978-1-84467-127-4 (hardback)
ISBN-13: 978-1-84467-133-5 (paperback)

British Library Cataloguing in Publication Data
A catalogue record for this book is available from the British Library

Library of Congress Cataloging-in-Publication Data
A catalog record for this book is available from the Library of Congress

Typeset in Garamond by Hewer Text UK Ltd, Edinburgh
Printed and bound in the USA by Quebecor World

Contents

1

Forever Twelve Years Old?

Japan is the world's second-largest economy, with a GDP greater than those of Britain and France combined, and almost double that of China; yet it is also a nervous, unhappy country. Many of its citizens see their lives as worse than a decade ago and likely to worsen steadily from now on, and the indices of social discontent keep rising. Japan is also the most durable, generous and unquestioning ally of the United States, and one of the world's largest donors of international aid, yet it casts a pale diplomatic shadow. However close it has become to Washington, its opinion is rarely sought or expected to be of interest in global fora, and it is at odds with all its neighbours over issues of history, accountability, resources and territory.

Japan became rich by swallowing its pride, forgetting about national glory and even about national identity and prestige during the decades of the Cold War, concentrating on producing goods of high quality, cheaply, for world markets. It surrendered control over defence and foreign policy to the US in return for the right to protect its nascent industries, and for privileged access to technology, capital and markets within the 'Free World'. By the late 1980s it seemed that the deal had paid off handsomely. Wealth multiplied and hearts thrilled to the prospect of becoming 'Number One' – a prospect that seemed almost within grasp.

For much of the 1990s, however, circumstances forced Japan to shift its gaze inward. The bubble burst, wealth vanished into a 'black hole', and corruption reached epic proportions, eroding confidence in government and business alike. Japan lost a great deal of material wealth, through deflation on a grand scale; it lost status as a development model to the world; and it experienced humiliation by being forced to yield to the US on one policy matter after another, while being sidelined on major issues of regional or global concern. Under Koizumi Junichiro (prime minister from 2001–06) and then under Abe Shinzo (prime minister from 2006), Japan sought a new path. In doing so, it had to rethink the formula of its post-1945 settlement.

General Douglas MacArthur, concluding his spell as Japan's ruler during the US-led occupation (1945–52), declared that, '[m]easured by the standards of modern civilization, they [the Japanese] would be like a boy of twelve compared with our development of forty-five years'.[1] Reflecting a similarly paternalistic view, the early (1942) advice to the US Department of State by Edwin Reischauer was that Japan after the war should be turned into America's puppet, with its emperor functioning on behalf of the US, much as Pu Yi (China's 'last emperor') functioned in Manchukuo until 1945 on Japan's behalf, a 'puppet who not only could be won over to our side but who would carry with him a tremendous weight of authority'.[2]

US insistence on Japan's national uniqueness and fundamental difference from Asia, and its implacable opposition to any moves towards Japanese involvement in an East Asian community, have been fundamental to US policy since the very outset of the occupation.[3] Retained on his throne (and given immunity from prosecution as a war criminal), the emperor would help keep Japan conservative and make it pro-American: the national interest of the US would best be served not by punishing him, but by incorporating him into a new role as the empty (but symbolically rich) centre of the state. When, in due course, the formal apparatus and institutions of political democracy were established, popular sovereignty was therefore balanced and restrained by the emperor, who MacArthur clearly saw as America's man in Tokyo, linchpin of a conservative order.

While the Reischauer suggestion that Hirohito be turned into America's Pu Yi was of course not translated directly into policy, and in retrospect sounds simply outrageous, the basic idea – structured dependence – was nevertheless pervasive and permanent. In Japan today, that pledge has been accomplished: Japan has been turned into a client state, or even, as some would have it, a puppet state. Such an assessment, which until recently would have come only from a critic on the far left, is today the considered view of prominent Japanese conservative politicians, academics and bureaucrats, alarmed at what they see as the radical transformation of their country.

The head of the Liberal Democratic Party's Policy Research Council, Kyuma Fumio, asked in February 2003 about Japan's position as war with Iraq loomed, said, 'I think it [Japan] has no choice. After all, it is *like an American state*' (italics added).[4] Kyuma was to become Director-General of the Defence Agency, later Minister of Defence, in the Abe government from September 2006.[5] Another prominent conservative politician, Gotoda Masaharu, by then in his eighties and shortly before his death, wrote bitterly of Japan as a *zokkoku* – lackey or vassal state – of the US.[6] Sakakibara Eisuke, known as 'Mr Yen' during the 1990s for his power over global currency markets, described the attitude of following the US at all times and under all circumstances as 'depraved ideological conservatism'.[7] The critic Morita Minoru believes that 'Japanese politicians fearful of North Korea want Japan to become another American state . . . for the security of the country, they want Japan to in effect become just another part of the United States.'[8]

The bureaucrats who, 60 years ago and at US direction, put together the formula for the Japanese state, had to resolve certain key issues: the role of the emperor (and accompanying it, the nature of Japanese identity), the role of the military, and Japan's relationship to Asia. Today, those same key questions remain vexed and unresolved, which suggests that the answers adopted then were less than satisfactory.

Once the truly incompatible element in the relationship – the imperial Japanese military – had been eliminated by the US occupation, the principle was incorporation and subordination. The Cold War required that the economic bureaucrats be allowed considerable latitude, and they were successful in creating and nurturing a kind of 'developmental' or 'guided' capitalism, with the phenomenon I have elsewhere described as the 'construction state' functioning as a key mechanism.[9]

Koizumi Junichiro said that he was engaged on a process of 'reform' in Japan equivalent in scale and significance to the transformation from feudalism to modernity in the late nineteenth century, and from militarism to capitalism and democracy in the mid-twentieth century.[10] His successor, Abe Shinzo, likewise built his government around the theme of a clean break with the postwar era, redefining core institutions and values.

Their aims were so far-reaching as to be seen best as revolution rather than reform – though from above rather than below. Though they headed a political party commonly described as 'conservative', through the six postwar decades Japan had had no more committed advocates of radical change. Since Japan was the world's second largest economic power, and Asia's giant, the implications of their agenda were immense. Sixty years is the span of life in East Asia, and the sense that institutions too might have a similar cycle stirred restlessness, and fed a susceptibility to their view.

Their reforms were aimed at transforming Japan itself: its state, its sense of identity and national role, and its postwar democracy. They would dismantle the bureaucratically guided 'capitalist developmental' state associated with the glory days of miraculous economic growth and social inclusiveness and substitute for it a US-style, neoliberal, deregulated and privatized small state. Lifetime employment, corporate paternalism, egalitarian education and universal welfare – the institutions most closely associated with the 1970s Japan of Prime Minister Tanaka Kakuei – would have to go. Crucially, the constitutional pacifist, diplomatically reticent, Cold War-dependent relationship with the US would be reconstituted into a full, subordinate, global alliance, with Japan a dependent nuclear superpower, 'the Britain of the Far East'. Their prescription fused neoliberalism and neo-nationalism, and it had large implications for Japan's regional and global role; its diplomatic, constitutional, and military posture; its corporate, family, and social spheres; and its sense of identity.

Whether the formula was viable was another matter. The Japan of Koizumi and Abe was casting aside its inhibitions in the embrace of market fundamentalism and US hegemony just as the credibility of both was sinking to new depths around the world. Downsizing, deregulating and privatizing the state, they would simultaneously focus national coherence around patriotism, duty, and a proud Japanese identity, while making every effort to give priority to serving the US. Could Japan be simultaneously dependent and assertive?

The diplomatic, economic, and social remaking of Japan was in accord with an American blueprint and designed to serve American purposes, and it therefore required the appearance of nationalism on the Japanese part. Precisely to the extent that Japan was incorporated as a subordinate 'client state', or even a 'vassal state', in the global US Empire, domestically, the gestures, rhetoric, and symbolism of nationalism became necessary. Koizumi in particular played this role brilliantly. His swansong performance on 30 June 2006 of 'I want you, I need you, I love you,' to George W. Bush, while the two were visiting the Elvis museum and shrine, Graceland, in Memphis, Tennessee, was without any hint of humiliation, a true and spontaneous love-song. It was followed just over a month later by his final visit to another shrine, Yasukuni, in defiance not only of all Japan's neighbours but even of the sentiments of the former Japanese emperor, Hirohito. The combination of utter submission to the US with the embracing of 'Japanese' ritual and defiance of Japan's Asian neighbours perfectly represented the contradictions of his government.

This study offers a critical assessment of the way these problems – emperor, identity, the military, relations with the US and with Asia – have been addressed in the early days of the twenty-first century. The term 'embrace' is an echo of the title of John Dower's Pulitzer Prize-winning 1999 volume, *Embracing Defeat*.[11] Dower advanced the thesis that, beneath the surface manifestations of American control and initiative to demilitarize and democratize Japan during its occupation (1945–52), the Japanese people were shaping their own agenda, that Japanese actors were seizing the initiative and gradually substituting Japanese for American priorities, and that the primary subjectivity of the occupation process was therefore Japanese, rather than American. My focus on the early twenty-first century US–Japan relationship leads me to think that, although Japan did indeed 'embrace defeat', accepting the sacrifice of much of its autonomy in return for US protection and incorporation in the US zone of influence, the US retained significant, perhaps decisive, control over it throughout these 60 years and more. The Koizumi–Abe 'revolution' actually meant the liquidation of some important residual levers of Japanese autonomy, and the acceptance of an even higher level of submission and exploitation within the US global empire. The embrace becomes increasingly stifling.

2

The Dependent Superstate

Dancing in the Buddha's palm

Nineteenth-century Japan chose to separate itself from Asia, stressing the non-Asian, unique, racially homogeneous qualities of Japaneseness whose quintessential form was the emperor. It later attempted to build an Asian community, known ultimately as the 'Greater East Asian Co-Prosperity Sphere', but the only gods allowed were Japanese gods, and the Japanese position was absolutely superior; consequently the project lacked credibility. Former Prime Minister Tojo wrote on the eve of his execution in December 1948 that the real cause of Japan's defeat in the 'Greater East Asian' war was its loss of the genuine cooperation of East Asian peoples rather than any material deficiency.[1] In other words, the decisive failure had been intellectual, moral and imaginative. It is sobering to reflect that contemporary Japan seems still unable to secure the trust and cooperation of East Asian peoples.

Identity is the fundamental unresolved question of Japan's modern history. Loyalty to the US was the single, definitive and unambiguous commitment of the Koizumi government, and so far of its Abe successor. Where Koizumi seemed careless of the offence he gave China's leaders by his visits to Yasukuni and showed little interest in repairing the relationship or in pursuing a regional Sino-Japanese – or broader – accord, there seemed virtually no limit to what he was prepared to do to oblige his 'friend', President Bush (even when it involved acting against the clear consensus of Japanese society, as on the dispatch of Japanese Self-Defence Forces to Iraq, and even when the president seemed to feel no such obligation to reciprocate). But such dependence upon the US, giving it such priority over the relationship with the rest of Asia, is best seen not just as a quirk of Koizumi's personal infatuation with George W. Bush but as a natural extension of a dependency deeply structured in Japan's postwar and occupation settlement.

Hirohito's cooperative attitude seems to have especially impressed MacArthur. Although they met on a total of ten occasions, only fragments of their discussion have been revealed. Enough is known, however, for it to be clear that the emperor exercised a major influence in shaping the postwar relationship between the two countries – continuing, in effect, to behave as a sovereign. There is even, therefore, some ground for seeing him as the major architect of the postwar security system, which he may have seen as the new form of 'national polity' (*kokutai*),[2] the necessary accoutrement into the late twentieth century and beyond of the imperial system that at all costs he was determined to maintain.[3] When he took the opportunity of these meetings to urge the US to maintain its forces indefinitely in Japan, bypassing and implicitly criticizing the prime minister, Yoshida Shigeru, on the crucial matter of the terms of a postwar settlement,[4] he was undermining his own defence of his prewar record as simply a constitutional monarch, who could not have intervened to oppose the course to war. From May 1947, he was also transgressing the constitutional limits to his postwar role as a politically powerless 'symbol'. When he told MacArthur that the 'Japanese people's cultural level is still low', that they were too 'willing to be led', and inclined to 'selfishly concentrating their attention on their rights and not thinking about their duties and obligations', concluding that 'the Occupation should last for a long time',[5] and in particular when he expressed his enthusiasm for the longest possible US military occupation of Okinawa,[6] it must have been music to MacArthur's ears. The one thing on which Hirohito had nothing to say was the pain and destruction caused so recently throughout Asia by the rampaging forces under his command or responsibility. On the one occasion – much later, in 1975 – when he faced a direct question about his war responsibility, he replied, 'Not being well-versed in literary matters, I really don't know what you are getting at.'[7]

The belief in the unique, non-Asian, ineffable qualities of Japanese identity, with or without the assumption that the imperial institution is its most concentrated essence, is often taken to be the taproot of Japanese culture. In prewar times, it was codified in the notion of *kokutai*, or national polity, which the authorities of the Japanese state took great pains to enforce as state ideology. In the postwar era, however, the retention of these notions was above all a product of the US Department of War Information (the precursor of the CIA), whose 'Foreign Morale Analysis Division' (FMAD) employed a team of thirty top sociologists, anthropologists and psychologists to conceive of appropriate psychological warfare ('psywar') stratagems to help defeat and subjugate Japan. So successful was this project that its main fruit, Ruth Benedict's *The Chrysanthemum and the Sword*, became one of the greatest ever best-sellers.[8] First published in English in the autumn of 1946, and translated into Japanese two years later, by the late years of the twentieth century it had sold upwards of 350,000 copies in English, and somewhere between 1.4 and 2.3 million copies (in over 100 printings) in Japanese, and it continued to sell.[9] It has to be seen as one of the great propaganda coups of the century. Its insight was to understand that Japan's long-term subordination to US purposes could best be accomplished by propagation of the idea of a deep 'pattern' of Japanese culture as ineffable, emperor-centred, and above all non-Asian. A Japan psychologically distanced from Asia would never be able to form part of an Asian community and would remain tied to the US. After Japan's defeat in war in 1945, it suited the US occupation forces to encourage the persistence in Japan of these myths, because a superior, non-Asian Japan would be incapable of participation in the construction of an Asian community, and would therefore remain dependently tied to the US. The fruits of Benedict's psywar research were first published at the same time as the emperor-centred constitution was adopted – one representing the psychological and the other the legal foundations of the postwar order.[10]

Over time, *kokutai* would be transformed by conservative Japanese and American intellectuals into 'Japaneseness' (*Nihonjin-ron*) theory, thence to reverberate East and West. In one recent formulation, it surfaced in Samuel Huntington's idea of Japan as the world's sole nation-state/civilization, unique and separate from Asia.[11] From time to time there were pointers to the desire on the part of prominent conservative politicians to draw on the residual strength of emperor-centred thinking and insist on it as the core marker of Japanese identity.[12] Gradually, imperial sovereignty was reasserted at crucial points, in particular over time itself. In 1966, the prewar *Kigensetsu*, which attributed the birth of Japan to the mythical emperor, Jimmu, was revived as a national holiday, 'National Foundation Day'. In 1979, the prewar *nengo* system of dating by reference to the reign year of the emperor was revived by law (thus 1945 was known as Showa 20, the twentieth year of the Showa emperor, whose name was Hirohito; and 2007 becomes Heisei 19, the nineteenth year of the Heisei emperor, whose name is Akihito). The sequence of annual holidays was shaped to conform to an emperor-centred sense of Japanese identity, from National Foundation Day (11 February) to the birthdays of the Showa emperor (29 April, a new holiday to commence in 2007), the Meiji emperor (3 November, celebrated under the name *Bunka no hi* – 'Culture Day' – and marked by the ceremony in which the emperor confers the Order of Culture), and the present, Heisei emperor, 23 December (the emperor's birthday). Even the holiday known as Labour Thanksgiving Day (23 November) is based on the imperial rite of *niinamesai*, in which the emperor offers thanks for the first fruits of the rice harvest.[13] In 1990, the constitutional proscription on state support for religious activity was set aside as the full panoply of Shinto rites accompanied the accession of the new emperor. One of the largest organizations of contemporary Diet members is devoted precisely to insistence on the centrality of Shinto, which for most purposes means emperor-centredness (see Chapter 6).

The same separateness that in the 1930s was the intellectual and philosophical barrier to the construction of any greater East Asian community thus continued to function after 1945, and to become the *leitmotif* of both Western scholarship and much of Japanese self-perception. So long as enough Japanese people continued to believe in it, they would be reluctant to embrace any regional community that might warrant its dilution, or even dissolution. Japanese efforts to regain from China the initiative on regional integration are a desperate ploy to do the impossible: to square Japan's emperor-centred superiority with membership of a regional community.

For much of the Cold War, Japan stood with its back turned to Asia. Even though it 'normalized' relations with South Korea in 1965, and with China in 1972, it was not until 1995, during the brief period when the Liberal Democratic Party (LDP) had lost its majority and the Socialist Murayama Tomiichi was prime minister, that a resolution was passed through the Diet expressing deep regret over the suffering Japan had caused to the people of Asia by its colonialism and aggression. Prime Minister Murayama then made a 15 August statement incorporating the same sentiments.

During a certain period in the not-too-distant past, Japan, following a mistaken national policy, advanced along the road to war, only to ensnare the Japanese people in a fateful crisis, and, through its colonial rule and aggression, caused tremendous damage and suffering to the people of many countries, particularly to those of Asian nations.

In the hope that no such mistake be made in the future, I regard, in a spirit of humility, these irrefutable facts of history, and express here once again my feelings of deep remorse and state my heartfelt apology.

In due course all subsequent prime ministers – Hashimoto, Obuchi, Mori, Koizumi and (most grudgingly) Abe – reiterated those sentiments. The 'Murayama statement' was also explicitly addressed to South Korea, and confirmed in a joint statement of the Japanese and South Korean governments in 1998.

The statement was clear enough, but many in government did not accept it, and still have not. The mid-1990s saw the emergence of a plethora of neo-nationalist, revisionist, and reactionary Diet organizations (together with the related organizations that refracted their position nation-wide), all founded precisely to resist the Murayama-era attempt to come to grips with the issues of war and colonialism by unambiguous apology. The 'Diet-members League for the Passing on of a Correct History' was established in 1995, the 'Diet-members Association for a Bright Japan' in 1996, and the 'Diet-members Association for Reflection on Japan's Future and History Education' and 'Japan Conference Diet-members Association' in 1997. The 'History Education' group played a central role in the formation and direction of the powerful national pressure group for the adoption of revisionist texts in history education, *Tsukurukai* (Association for New History Textbooks).

Japan Conference (*Nihon Kaigi*), the country's largest neo-nationalist, historical revisionist movement, is made up of religious (Shinto and Buddhist) groups, major media and corporate leaders, local and national political figures and academics. Its head in 2006 was the former chief-justice of the Supreme Court, Mikami Tatsu. Japan Conference helped orchestrate the movement to have the *Hinomaru* and *Kimigayo*[14] adopted by law as national flag and anthem. It was successful in 1999, and has been at the heart of the push for revision of the constitution and the

Fundamental Law of Education, and for the regularization of Yasukuni as a national war shrine – matters discussed in more detail below. Abe was also a founding member of and adviser to the 'Young Diet-members Calling for Peace, Thinking about the True National Interest, and Supporting Formal Prime Ministerial Visits to Yasukuni', established in 2005. By 2006 it had a membership of around 120.[15]

The League for Shinto Politics, or *Shinto Seiji Renmei* (established 1970), officially rendered into English as 'Shinto Association of Spiritual Leadership', is much older than the other organizations, but it too retains considerable strength. The Association's statement of five basic principles begins: 'We look to the establishment of a Shinto spirit as the fundament of national policy', which is glossed by the explanation that

It is the prayer that the glory of the imperial reign may last forever that constitutes the always-renewed worshipful spirit of the Japanese people. Herein lies the moral view of society and of the state held by the Shinto-believing Japanese people.[16]

Fifty-five years after the end of the war, in June 2000, Prime Minister Mori Yoshiro addressed a group of Diet-members who were members of this Shinto association on the occasion of its thirtieth anniversary. Having himself been a founding member, Mori commended the organization for its 30 years of effort to encourage recognition that Japan was 'a country of the gods centred on the emperor'. The statement must have seemed unexceptional to Mori and to his audience. It was no more than a reiteration of their formal beliefs. Yet it was also plainly the language and the imagery of militarist and fascist, emperor-worshipping Japan; the same words could well have been uttered by any of Japan's wartime leaders, including Prime Minister Tojo Hideki. Such continuity would have been inconceivable in the case of Japan's wartime allies, Germany and Italy. Despite the ruckus that followed the Mori statement, and the Diet interpellations in which he explained himself, little changed, and six years after Mori's speech, in 2006, 223 members of the Diet, including the prime minister, the foreign and finance ministers, and the chief cabinet secretary (Abe Shinzo, its secretary-general), and indeed almost all members of the Koizumi cabinet, were members of this Shinto association.

The sort of Japanese identity which nationalists and neo-nationalists strive to restore, rooted in tradition and blood and distilled in the person of the emperor, is chiefly undermined not by confrontation with the dark recesses of war memory, but by the global market, which de-sacralizes and commodifies everything, including Japanese culture and 'Japaneseness' itself. Movements and organizations such as Japan Conference, and politicians struggling to establish a 'pure' and 'proud' identity through the elevation and sacralization of one or another aspect of the tradition, seem scarcely conscious of the workings of this primary contradiction.

The Shintoists, 'Bright Japan' proponents, and Diet-members concerned with history education share a sense of outrage at the war apology issued by Prime Minister Murayama, and at the attempt to incorporate references to 'comfort women' and the Nanjing Massacre into historical texts. They lament the loss of a distinctive Japanese historical consciousness, oppose the 'masochistic' view of history, and campaign for a return to the values of traditional, imperial Japan. The textbooks they call for (and actually produce and promote) are designed to instil a sense of national pride and 'correct' history – a return to the pure, bright, superior Japanese identity of yesteryear. For them, the fundamental Japanese identity is that of a chosen people, distinct and united around the emperor as its concentrated, semi-divine racial essence.[17] There could be no essential distinction between the postwar emperor system and the emperor system that Japan had enjoyed from time immemorial, in which the state and emperor were one and the same.[18] So long as Japan was superior, a land of the gods, Asians could only be 'third country' people (as Tokyo Governor Ishihara Shintaro put it).[19]

When the new government, under Abe Shinzo was formed in September 2006, eleven of his eighteen cabinet members, four of his five-person prime-ministerial secretariat, his chief and assistant cabinet secretaries, and 210 of his fellow party members in the Diet, belonged to Japan Conference (*Nihon Kaigi*).[20] Abe himself had been a core member of all the groups listed here, and remained deputy secretary-general of the Japan Conference and Shinto Politics groups until he became prime minister. His close political associate, Nakagawa Shoichi, who became chairman of the LDP's Policy Research Council, had been founding president in 1997 of the 'Diet-members' Association for Reflection on Japan's Future and History Education' (with Abe as Secretary-General). Their political careers had been built on vigorously contesting the apologetic view of history embodied especially in the 1995 Murayama statement, campaigning for the revisionist history texts produced by *Tsukurukai* (Association for New History Textbooks), putting pressure on the Japan Broadcasting Corporation (NHK) to delete reference in a documentary it was producing to comfort women and the emperor's responsibility for the war,[21] and denouncing North Korea. Two other members of the new cabinet, the minister for Okinawa and the Northern Territories (Takaichi Sanae) and the special adviser on revitalizing education (Yamatani Eriko), were drawn from the ranks of the 'Japan Future and History Education' group. Otherwise, Abe's brains trust comprised the key figures of 'Shinto Politics' and of other major nationalist organizations, including the *Sukuukai* (Association for the Rescue of Japanese Abducted by North Korea).

Like Ruth Benedict, who constructed her imagined Japanese identity out of what she was told by captured Japanese soldiers, Abe, Mori and their Shinto-believing colleagues imagined a kind of unchanging and perennial Japanese 'pattern'. They failed to understand that the structures and values they believed to be perennial were based on the ideology of militarist Japan that had only become consolidated in the 1930s, which in the postwar era was the subtlest expression of US psychological warfare rather than of an immutable Japanese essence. As Benedict assumed the message she was receiving from captured soldiers of the Imperial Japanese Army was the true, unvarnished expression of a national essence, so Mori looked back nostalgically to the order of his fascist childhood and assumed that it was pristine, and Abe idolized his A-class war criminal grandfather. What they all believed to be ancient tradition was quintessentially modern ideology, since national Shinto and imperial absolutism had been established only in the late nineteenth century.[22] The process of forming and imposing the state religion of Shinto was comparable, in the violence and disruption of its assault on established and traditional religions, to the much later Cultural Revolution in China.[23] Shinto became the frame for the control of the minds and souls of the people, while local deities were driven out as part of a process of establishing modern political absolutism around the emperor, who was in the process made divine (see also the analysis by Umehara Takeshi, in Chapter 6).[24] The persistence of such beliefs on the part of Mori, Abe and their Shinto colleagues was a reflection of the desire for an authentic Japanese story, an essence free from Chinese or Korean continental influences.

Those who watch from Seoul or Beijing as the political stage in Tokyo is occupied by believers in such myths do so nervously. The uniqueness, and implicit superiority, that Mori and his colleagues insist on for a 'land of the gods centred on the emperor' depend on opposition to the 'other' and contempt for the hybrid.

Though at one level this is innocent braggadocio, at another it is analogous to the ideology of ethnic cleansing elsewhere in the world, and to the demagogic and anti-foreign views of neo-nationalist politicians such as Jörg Haider in Austria and Jean-Marie Le Pen in France. As Asia struggles to formulate a sense of shared identity and purpose, to constitute itself as a community for the twenty-first century, Japan's American-imposed identity constitutes a major obstacle. It is underpinned by nostalgia for a strong Japan, by reluctance to concede responsibility for colonialism, aggression, and criminality in the twentieth century, and by a latent resentment of continuing twenty-first-century national subordination, and of the tightening US 'embrace'. The insistence that national history should console and uplift reflects a kind of identity panic.

At the parliamentary level, Diet-members who in the mid-1990s had been associated with the war apologies and the movement for reconciliation with Asia steadily lost ground during the following decade to the Shintoists and historical revisionists. The advent of the Koizumi government in 2001, followed by its return with an increased majority in 2005 and then by the formation of the Abe government in 2006, marked the steady erosion of the apology of 1995, and the revival of the 'non-Asian', emperor-centred Japanese identity to which Mori had alluded in 2000.

In a book published on the eve of his assumption of the office of prime minister as Koizumi's successor in September 2006, Abe referred to himself as 'fearless' and as a 'fighting politician'.[25] As a third-generation LDP politician born with a political silver spoon in his mouth, however, he had no ministerial experience, and his major political commitments until then had been opposition to the war and comfort women apologies, insistence on the prime-ministerial visits to Yasukuni irrespective of the diplomatic cost, the call for sanctions on North Korea, and the vague but emotionally charged insistence on Japan's uniqueness and beauty.[26]

Yasukuni

Throughout his term of office, Koizumi made a point of paying a formal annual visit to Yasukuni Shrine, commencing on 13 August 2001. Yasukuni is the Shinto religious institution devoted to honouring those throughout Japan's modern history who died in the service of the emperor, who is also the high priest of Shinto. In prewar and wartime Japan, it played a central role in generating the ideology of chauvinism and militarism, consoling in advance those being sent to die for the emperor with the assurance that they and their families would be honoured thereafter. A recent study describes its function as one of 'emotional alchemy', turning the grief of bereaved families into patriotic celebration over glorious sacrifice.[27] After the war, Yasukuni continued – though supposedly as a strictly religious institution. The state was constitutionally proscribed from any connection with it (by Article 20), but in the early decades prime ministers, and the emperor himself, continued to pay their respects there to the spirits of the dead. In 1978, however, the spirits of fourteen wartime leaders convicted and punished by the International War Crimes Tribunal as 'Class A' war criminals ('the Fourteen') were added to the shrine's 'deities', and thereafter the Emperor ceased to visit.

From 1983 to 2001, the Yasukuni controversy was perceived as so damaging to Japan's diplomacy that prime ministers refrained from association with it. When Koizumi resumed the custom from his inauguration in 2001, neighbour countries saw his action as an affront, and as tantamount to an attempted vindication of the war cause. He protested that he intended simply to pray for the souls of the dead and reaffirm his commitment to peace, but his statement that 'the peace and prosperity we [the Japanese] enjoy today was built on the sacrifice of the war dead' rankled, since it implied that the Japanese dead were national heroes instead of members of a brutal force engaged in war crimes.[28] It was not until the brief interruption of LDP rule in 1993 that Prime Minister Hosokawa first referred to the war as 'aggressive, wrongful' – a formula then endorsed by cabinet and given formal public status as the Murayama Statement, quoted above.

Subsequent expressions of 'remorse and heartfelt apology' in similar or even identical terms were repeated by Prime Minister Hashimoto in China in 1997, Prime Minister Obuchi to South Korean President Kim

Dae Jung in 1998, Foreign Minister Kono in China in August 2000, and
Prime Minister Koizumi – both to North Korean leader Kim Jong Il in
the Pyongyang declaration of September 2002 and on several occasions
in 2005, including the Asia-Africa Leaders' meeting in April and the
Asian Summit in December. The formal repetitions of the Murayama
statement seemed stilted and formulaic, and it was plain that the words
had been crafted as a means of avoiding the normal moral accompaniment of apology – compensation. But it was not so much this sequence
of apologies, or even their carefully calibrated wording, that drew Asian
attention as the wave of revisionism and neo-nationalism they stirred
among those who fiercely opposed any admission of Japanese guilt or
regret. Their ranks thereafter steadily grew in the Diet and in the
country's media and high-level expressions of pride in the war, and
associated moves to sanitize history textbooks, caused outrage.

In Korea, Koizumi's Yasukuni visit was seen as signalling Japan's
resurrection of hard-line nationalism. Demonstrations broke out in
major cities and Japanese flags were burned; twenty young Korean
men ceremonially chopped off their little fingers and sent them to the
Japanese embassy in protest. Korean Vice Foreign Minister Choi Sung-
Hong summoned the Japanese ambassador to make a formal protest in
which he said, 'It is deeply regrettable that Prime Minister Koizumi paid
respects at Yasukuni Shrine, which is a symbol of Japanese militarism, in
defiance of the South Korean government's repeated expressions of
concern.' He added that the Japanese government should have a correct
sense of history and respect the feelings of the South Korean public.[29]
North Korea also issued words of harsh denunciation. The South Korean
government backed a suit launched in the Japanese courts to demand the
removal of the names of more than 21,000 Koreans who had fought in
the Japanese armed forces from the list of those worshipped at Yasukuni.[30] Koizumi shrugged all of this off.

Constitutionally, Koizumi's Yasukuni commitment was at best dubious. Article 20 (3) stipulated that '[t]he state and its organs shall refrain
from religious education or any other religious activity.' There was no
doubt that the shrine was a religious institution, or that the prime
minister represented the state. When his visit to the shrine was held by a
Fukuoka District court in April 2004 to be unconstitutional, Koizumi
said that he found it inexplicable (and proceeded to ignore it).[31] In
September 2005, when the Osaka High Court returned a similar

judgment, he said he found it 'hard to understand', since he had been intending to 'pray for the war dead and peace'.[32]

As he had dismissed the protests of neighbouring countries, so, with his brusque appeal to common sense, Koizumi dismissed a half-century of constitutional debate, riding roughshod over the principle of the rule of law. The Supreme Court in the following summer threw out complaints against him of unconstitutionality, but it did so on technical grounds, sidestepping the constitutional issue and merely holding that those complaining of Koizumi's actions could not prove that they had suffered damage as a result of it.[33] Still, the embarrassment of the lower courts finding his behaviour unconstitutional while the High Court evaded the issue was plainly a factor in elevating the revision of Article 20 (3) to top priority (see Chapter 6).[34]

During 2006, however, four unexpected interventions punctuated, and transformed, the Yasukuni debate. In February, the editors of Japan's two major newspapers, the *Asahi Shimbun* and the *Yomiuri Shimbun*, normally fiercely opposed, penned a joint statement critical of the prime minister on Yasukuni, among other issues.[35] In May, it was revealed that Koizumi would not be invited to mark the end of his term of office by addressing a joint sitting of the houses of Congress unless he would pledge to cease his Yasukuni visits.[36] In the same month, the Association of Corporate Executives (Keizai Doyukai) criticized the prime minister, expressing business's concern at the continuing friction in Japan's major trading relationship.[37] Finally, in July came the most unexpected and most potentially explosive intervention, from beyond the grave, by the Showa Emperor, Hirohito. According to a 1988 memo by a senior official of the Imperial Household Agency, revealed for the first time, Hirohito had expressed his displeasure with the 1978 enshrining of A-class war criminals, adding 'That is why I've stopped visiting [the shrine]. That is how I feel in my heart.'[38] Public opinion, until then rather evenly divided, swung against Koizumi after these interventions, especially that from the Showa emperor, with over 60 per cent of people saying they paid 'serious attention' to the emperor's view, 57 per cent opposing any further shrine visitation by the Prime Minister, and only 29 per cent supporting the prime minister.[39] Koizumi's resentment was only thinly veiled when, in a press conference on 20 July, he referred to the Showa emperor as 'that person'. As expected, he went ahead anyway with his August visit, declaring his act 'an intrinsic part of Japanese culture' and suggesting that opposition was due to improper Chinese intervention in Japanese affairs.[40]

For Koizumi, the suggestion of criticism from the US government was probably more serious than that from Hirohito. Yasukuni's exhibition hall, in particular, presented essentially the view of prewar and wartime history held by wartime Japanese governments, and the prime minister's determined participation in Yasukuni rituals might be seen as tanta-mount to a repudiation of the obligation under the San Francisco Treaty of 1951 to accept the verdicts of the International Military Tribunal for the Far East (the 'Tokyo Tribunal'). That was not something that Washington could ignore. Consequently, the very item assumed to be the most unambiguously positive aspect of his legacy – the closeness of his relationship with the US – suffered. He could dismiss protests from China and Korea, and ignore that from the late emperor, but explicit criticism from Washington was another matter altogether. Unquestioned loyalty to Bush helped postpone a reckoning on this account, but in the end Yasukuni cost Koizumi dearly, forcing him to substitute for the Congressional ceremony a jaunt in Air Force One with President Bush to Graceland, the Elvis Presley memorial in Memphis, Tennessee.

By the time he left office, many of Koizumi's own senior LDP colleagues, the country's major newspapers, the leaders of the govern-ment's coalition partner, and the Osaka business federation, as well as neighbouring countries including Singapore, Australia and – albeit obliquely – the US, as well as China and South Korea, had all made clear their opposition to the Yasukuni prime-ministerial visits.[41] But such was the spell under which he held many of the Japanese people that when he went ahead with his 15 August visit, framing it as the honouring of an electoral promise and as a refusal to bow to Chinese pressure, the opposition of mid-July (57:29) reversed into support (48:36) in the following days.[42]

Many of those critical of Koizumi, including much of the national media, constructed the Yasukuni problem as though it were merely a matter of how to deal with the problem of the 14 A-class war leaders, but it was more than that. There have been three kinds of proposals for resolving the problem: removal of the Fourteen from the shrine; changing the character of the shrine from a private religious (Shinto) institution to a state institution by nationalizing it;[43] or revising the constitutional clause forbidding state involvement in religious matters –

Article 20 (3) – by creating a 'cultural exception' for Yasukuni and its rituals. The first proposal carried the implication that war responsibility was somehow confined to the Fourteen, absolving the emperor and others, and clearing the way for emperor and prime minister to continue the shrine's 'emotional alchemy'. The second and third, on the other hand, would legitimize and perpetuate present practice by restoring prewar state Shinto practice. Neither opponents and critics of wars past and future, nor the representatives of those who had fallen victim to Japan's aggression, would have any place in such an institution. That Yasukuni was not concerned with the grief of bereaved families was clear from the fact that his insistence on restoring the state-centred institution went hand in hand with the official abandonment, over more than half a century, of the remains of about half of the Japanese soldiers who had died outside the country.[44]

Abe Shinzo, who succeeded Koizumi as prime minister in September 2006, was also a stickler for Yasukuni rituals, whose political career had been built essentially around revisionist, war guilt-denying positions. Although he was a popular figure in Washington, deemed certain to continue Koizumi's uncritical pro-US policies, he was rebuked by the *New York Times* in February 2006 for being 'neither honest nor wise in the inflammatory statements he has been making about Japan's disastrous era of militarism, colonialism and war crimes'.[45] With that shot across his bows ringing in his ears, Abe as prime minister refrained from any early Yasukuni visit, tried hard to make the issue go away, and made conciliatory visits to both China and South Korea his earliest public acts.

Since the end of the Cold War, especially as the impact of globalization deepens, identity politics has been resurgent, and when the question of identity is raised in Japan, the tendency is to return to origins, to what is assumed to be 'real' Japaneseness – to the unique rather than the universal, to 'emperor-centred' identity. It is not just among nationalists, neo-nationalists and those on the right that such thinking is deep-rooted. Generations of Japanese readers respond to Ruth Benedict's thesis as a revelation of 'true' Japaneseness. In the mainstream of Japanese social science scholarship, the most influential of all postwar scholars, Maruyama Masao, shared with rightists (of whom otherwise he was so fiercely critical) the belief in Japanese cultural uniqueness and homogeneity, centred on the imperial institution, where 'ultimate legitimacy always lies'.[46]

Until that emperor-centred identity is subsumed in a new kind of democratic, open and universalist identity, Japan is likely to continue to have difficulty relating to its Asian neighbours. The US prescription for long-term subordination of Japan was the epitome of subtlety: to encourage the fantasy of uniqueness and superiority. The symbols and rhetoric of nationalism function as empty conceits, while the substance of nation is denied. Yasukuni is thus not so much an expression of nationalism as its negation.

Terror

Perhaps the defining political characteristic of Koizumi's office was his joining of George W. Bush's 'global war on terror'. Yet, as Japan stepped up its contribution to the global war, at home a kind of terror slowly spread that had nothing to do with Islam or the Middle East. This terror was homegrown, rooted in the same troubled and unresolved past that Koizumi had so signally failed to settle, and in the present that his social and economic policies had contributed to making more insecure and anxious. His determination to persist with his Yasukuni performance helped stir bitter divisions and resentments both within Japan and in the wider region. Koizumi's air of simple innocence – his 'instinctive, sentimental, impulsive' behaviour,[47] his insistence on dividing people into supporters ('reformers') and opponents ('enemies') and sending 'assassins' to deal with the latter, and his refusal to argue complex issues, sticking instead to emotionally charged one-liners – fed the atmosphere of conflict and tension. Koizumi's term of office was punctuated by a series of violent acts – including assassination, bomb threats and attacks and politically motivated arson – and by stepped-up infringement by the state of basic human rights. There was no Madrid or London bombing, much less any catastrophic '9/11'. But Japanese society too paid a price for its contribution to the 'war on terror', as the following examples illustrate.

Over a ten-month period spanning 2002 and 2003, a group calling itself the 'Punish the Traitors League' was responsible for twenty-three cases of shooting, arson, and bomb attacks across Japan, including attacks on the North Korea-affiliated General Association of Korean Residents in Japan and the Hiroshima Teachers Union, and culminating in a bomb attack on the home of the Foreign Ministry official who had helped arrange the Koizumi visit to North Korea in September 2002.[48] The man arrested for that attack said his motive was anger over the North Korean abductions and at the official. In an apparently unrelated event, a prominent opposition (Democratic Party of Japan) politician, Ishii Koki, was murdered in the street outside his home in October 2003. In due course a petty criminal with links to ultra-nationalist groups was arrested and convicted for the attack. Ishii had been known for his vigorous pursuit of structural corruption and political collusion on the Diet floor.[49] Also in 2002, the statute of limitations expired in the case of the murder in 1987 of an *Asahi Shimbun* journalist in Nishinomiya near Kobe in Western Japan, by a rightist group, which said in a letter, 'We do not accept anyone who betrays Japan. We sentence all *Asahi Shimbun* employees to death.'[50]

In April 2003, as the war in Iraq raged and the question of Japan's participation was being discussed, a 24-year-old Tokyo bookshop worker was arrested for painting 'Opposition to War' and 'Spectacle Society' on the walls of a public lavatory in a Tokyo park.[51] He was held in detention for forty-four days, his papers and books were ransacked, and public security police grilled him on his political background. Far from being contrite, however, the young man asserted that his graffiti were 'an exercise in freedom of expression in a public forum'. It was clear that he had committed a misdemeanour, for which a fine sufficient to cover cleaning costs might have been appropriate. Instead, however, he faced the more serious charge of property damage – a felony subject to long detention – and the investigation focused on the political message, rather than on the act of painting graffiti itself (no other graffiti artist in Tokyo has been arrested in recent years). Found guilty in February 2004, he received a suspended sentence of fourteen months.

In August 2003, a bullet was fired at the office of the Okayama branch of a credit union affiliated with the General Association of Korean Residents of Japan. Two groups calling themselves the 'Nation Building Volunteers' (*Kenkoku Giyugun*) and the 'Korea Conquering Unit' (*Chosen Seibatsutai*) issued a statement, saying: 'We launched the attack in protest against the port visit to Niigata tomorrow by a spyship belonging to the lawless state of North Korea.'[52]

In February 2004, a 50-year-old local government welfare official was arrested under the Public Service Law for having distributed copies of the Communist Party paper, *Akahata*, during his free time in the run-up to

the elections the preceding November. A special taskforce of 200 men
was set up to pursue his case, ransacking his files and possessions, trailing
him, and videotaping him with something approaching a fanatical zeal.
On 29 June 2006, he became the first person in 32 years to be convicted
under a law that, as one commentator observed, would certainly not have
been applied to someone distributing copies of the LDP paper. He was
fined ¥100,000.[53]

In March 2004, a 62-year-old retired schoolteacher at Itabashi High
School in Tokyo was found guilty of having disrupted a school graduation ceremony because he had distributed literature and suggested to
those arriving for the ceremony that they consider not standing for the
anthem ceremony. Prosecutors sought an eight-month sentence, but had
to be satisfied with a May 2006 judgment finding him guilty of
'obstruction of official duties' and fining him ¥200,000.[54] According
to lawyers and supporters of the former teacher, although a metropolitan
assembly member had instructed students in a loud voice to stand while
the anthem played, most had remained seated. He, together with the
principal and the vice principal, then took photos of the scene with their
mobile phone cameras while board officials made audio recordings. Later
the assembly member demanded in an assembly session that the board
find the 'culprit' responsible for the students' behaviour, and a report was
filed with law-enforcement authorities.[55]

Early in 2004, three anti-war activists at Tachikawa in Western Tokyo
were arrested for having posted leaflets in letterboxes at a Defence Agency
residential facility expressing opposition to the dispatch of Japanese
forces to Iraq. The national opinion polls at the time were running at
over 70 per cent opposition to the Iraq dispatch, and their leaflets asked
Self-Defence Force (SDF) members to think deeply about Japan's
decision to support the war:

> SDF officers! Before you say 'because these are orders' [and you
> therefore cannot oppose them], you should think one-by-one
> through what your orders mean. Join us in raising your voice
> against orders that are unacceptable!

The three were held in detention for seventy-five days. They were
subjected to interrogation in exhausting five-hour stretches, their computers and mobile phones were seized, and their homes searched. In

April 2004, Amnesty International labelled the three 'prisoners of conscience'. After the prosecutors called for six-month prison sentences, a district court acquitted them in December 2004, ruling that their act was a political expression protected by the constitution, but the state appealed. A year later, the Tokyo High Court reversed the earlier judgment and found the three guilty of trespass, fining two of them ¥200,000 each and the third ¥100,000. As Omiya Law School's Lawrence Repeta put it:

> This case is crucial. Here we have ordinary citizens being arrested for handing out fliers. This is the most traditional form of free expression. The government must carry a heavy burden to justify a restriction on people expressing their opinions on an important matter of public policy in this fashion . . . they have shown nothing at all to justify their actions.[56]

The Tachikawa Three belonged to one of Japan's oldest anti-war groups, the 'Tachikawa SDF Monitoring Tent Village', which had been campaigning peacefully for twenty-five years on base-related issues, opposing the dispatch of forces from the Tachikawa base to Vietnam or the transfer of base land and facilities being returned to Japan to the SDF. No member of the group had ever been arrested. In fact, the Tachikawa roots of civil struggle for peace and defence of the constitution are even deeper. In the history of Japanese civil society, it was the 1950s resistance by the farmers of Sunagawa (which later became Tachikawa) to compulsory land acquisition that had led to a judgment renowned in Japanese constitutional history – that in which Justice Date Akio found those arrested for opposition activities not guilty because the security treaty with the US against which they were struggling was itself unconstitutional.[57] The Sunagawa/Tachikawa movement grew in 1959 and 1960 into a nation-wide mass popular wave of opposition to the Security Treaty that threw the country into a political maelstrom.[58] A determination on the state's part not to allow citizens ever again to seize such initiative – together with an awareness that the process of military reorganization now underway matched, or even exceeded, that of the 1950s and 1970s – could be discerned in the way the Tachikawa Three were treated. It was just 100 years since the anarchist Osugi Sakae had been imprisoned for four months for offences against the Newspaper

Ordinance when he translated and published a French anti-war article. Four years later, Osugi was framed on charges of a plot to assassinate the emperor, and executed in January 1911. The detention and punishment of the Tachikawa Three held an ominous message of state resolve to crush dissent against the contemporary project of US military reorganization and the transformation of the SDF into a subsidiary US force. The case would have to be studied carefully by civil activists in Okinawa, Iwakuni, and Kanagawa.

In December 2004, a 58-year-old Buddhist monk, Arakawa Yosei, was arrested, and in the first instance detained for twenty-three days, for distributing fliers for the Japanese Communist Party. He was a supporter but not a member of the party, and for forty years had been accustomed to hand out such leaflets without ever having been troubled by the authorities. Prosecutors demanded that he be fined ¥100,000. Eventually, in August 2006, the Tokyo District Court acquitted him of charges of trespass at an apartment building.[59]

In July 2005, a Molotov cocktail was thrown at the home of the president of Fuji Xerox Company, Kobayashi Yotaro, who also happened to be president of the 'New Sino-Japanese Friendship Twenty-First Century Committee' and a notable critic of Koizumi's Yasukuni rituals for the friction they had caused in Sino-Japanese relations.

Also early in 2006, a Tokyo middle school teacher, Masuda Yoko, an author of several books on problems of education, with thirty-three years of teaching experience, was sacked for 'lacking in appropriateness as a teacher'. She had been accustomed to seeking to deepen student knowledge of society through the encouragement of discussion, especially on peace-related issues. Her problems began in 1997. After showing her class a video documentary dealing with the problems of the US marine base at Futenma in Okinawa, the American mother of one student protested to the local education authorities that her daughter was being subjected to 'anti-American education'. The mother launched a defamation suit, ultimately unsuccessful; but Masuda was nevertheless subjected to a pay cut and ordered to attend 'study' sessions at a special centre designed to reinforce discipline and induce the sort of statement of 'conversion' or *tenko* that had been demanded of arrested prewar communists. This 'study' continued over a two-and-a-half-year period. Having then been reassigned to teaching duties, Masuda distributed to her civics class materials designed to encourage discussion of questions of war responsibility, including quotations from a local Metropolitan Assembly politician who had questioned whether Japan bore any such responsibility, and reference to a *Tsukurukai* history text as being the product of a group 'well-known for its historical fabrications'. Again she was reported by parents, who this time took the issue to the right-wing media, including *Sankei Shimbun*, which launched a fierce attack on her.[60] After another six-month session of 'study', during which she was required to show repentance for criticizing prescribed texts, she proved still to be recalcitrant, and was sacked. Nearly 350 public school teachers have been punished by the Tokyo Metropolitan Board of Education for infractions of the flag and anthem rule, commonly meaning their refusal to stand and sing the anthem at school ceremonies. But Masuda became the first to be actually sacked for political reasons.[61]

In June 2006, a representative of a local citizen group in Kanagawa Prefecture, which opposed the base relocation plans for her locality appeared in a televised NHK discussion programme. Among other things, she asked popular nationalist cartoonist Kobayashi Yoshinori, 'What did Japan do in China?' From that same night, she was overwhelmed by abusive and intimidatory telephone calls to her home – 2,000 of them on the first day – and 13,733 abusive attacks addressed that day to her blog (growing to a total of 118,107 over the succeeding five days).[62]

Many have noted the phenomenon of rising levels of violence generated and circulated in the anonymity of cyberspace, in which – typically – young, reasonably well-educated but economically disadvantaged males (the 'new poor') take out their frustration and anger on foreigners (especially Koreans), women, minorities, the elderly, and the poorly educated. One well-known Korean-in-Japan (*Zainichi*) critic and commentator writes of having received tens of thousands of abusive and threatening messages in recent years – up to 630 in a single day. 'By looking down on others,' she suggests, 'such people try to regain their self-confidence.'[63]

The experience she describes is common to citizen activists, especially those who espouse unpopular causes (including anything to do with North Korea). The Tokyo University philosophy professor and prominent citizen activist, Takahashi Tetsuya, speaks of having to be always conscious of the threat.[64] But the most vulnerable tend to be the most victimized. For Korean schoolchildren in Korean national dress, the regular experience of abuse is most likely to escalate into direct physical

violence whenever North Korea-bashing in the media reaches a cres-
cendo over nuclear or abduction issues. On other sensitive matters,
especially concerning the emperor and war responsibility (the Nanjing
Massacre and 'comfort women'), high-level political pressures are occasionally brought to bear against the national media in such a way as to
reinforce pressures emanating from national right-wing pressure
groups.[65] One of the most fearless of Japanese journals, *Uwasa no shinso*
(The Truth of the Rumour), established specifically to challenge taboos,
including the emperor system, had to close in 2005 after repeated
attacks, including a violent physical assault on the editor in June
2000, occasioned by publication of a story about Crown Princess
Masako that did not use the appropriate honorific language.[66]

In July 2006, the Tokyo office of Japan's leading financial newspaper,
Nihon Keizai Shimbun, was fire-bombed, causing minor damage and no
injuries, after the paper had published an exclusive story on Hirohito's
decision to stop attending Yasukuni following the 1978 enshrining there
of Class A war criminals. Reporters without Borders remarked that the
revelation had 'infuriated ultra-nationalist groups, but also Japanese
Prime Minister Junichiro Koizumi'.[67]

On the sixty-first anniversary of Japan's surrender in the Second
World War, 15 August 2006, the violent sub-currents of society
surfaced dramatically, hours after Koizumi's visit to Yasukuni. A right-
wing extremist attacked the Tokyo home of dissenting LDP figure
(and former secretary-general) Kato Koichi, burned the house to the
ground, and then attempted ritual suicide by disembowelment.[68]
Kato, whose 97-year-old mother usually lived in the house but
happened to be absent at the time, had become a vocal critic of
Koizumi, and the most persistent voice for liberalism within the LDP,
advocating unpopular views on Yasukuni, American bases in Okinawa
and North Korea, as well as on the economic consequences of the
neoliberal policies pursued by his party. He had long been the butt of
fierce, commonly anonymous, criticism. He had been subjected to
scurrilous accusations of secret connections with the North Korean
regime in weekly magazines, had the windows of his house smashed in
September 2000, and had been sent live bullets in the mail in
October 2003.[69]

Kato located this new incident in the context of the economic changes
that had produced nearly 20 million 'working poor', an 'irritable' society,

and the 'aggressive nationalism without repentance [of Japan's militarism before and during the Second World War] like, "We did nothing wrong in the last war." '[70] In an extensive interview with the Japanese edition of the web newspaper *Ohmynews*, Kato spoke of the 'floating, rootless society' that was the background to the rise of Koizumi politics:

The biggest problem, in my view, is that individuals are floating, rootless, like balloons cut off and wafted in the breeze. In the cities, they waft about in their hundreds of thousands. In terms of physics, you could see them as free-floating particles, drifting hither and thither, swept this way and that by the winds or by magnetic currents. I am afraid that is the sort of society we have become.

For whatever the reason, family relations have also become attenuated. Fathers do not scold their sons; daughters do not heed their fathers. Reckoning that such is freedom, they retreat to their rooms, to the world of television and computers.

In regional society, this thinning out of human relations has been going on for a long time. So far as the workplace community goes, it used to be the case that section heads and department heads would go drinking with ordinary staff, but these days that has become a rarity. The low level staff say no, and management does not want to ask a second time.

If everybody had their own convictions, it would matter less, but few now have firmly held convictions. That means that freedom is experienced as painful, and people tend to seek someone who can exercise a powerful pull on them.[71]

In such a climate, according to Kato, nationalism was able to exercise an 'extremely powerful magnetic force'.

Despite the fact that silence in the face of terror is commonly taken as tantamount to consent to it, ten days passed before either Koizumi or other top government officials made any comment on the attack on their senior party colleague. Both the prime minister and his chief cabinet secretary, Abe Shinzo, then briefly decried it, but when the prime minister was asked if his own visits to Yasukuni might have stirred up nationalism – thus helping to create the mood in which such crimes could occur – he replied:

It is a fact that certain parties want to stir things up. The mass
media should reflect on why they keep harping on the Yasukuni
problem. Shouldn't it refrain from being stirred up by other
countries, and reporting in such a way as to stir up those
countries?[72]

His instinctive response was to divert responsibility for the outrage onto
the media and onto China.

Eight decades ago, Japan went through a wave of violence – assassina-
tions, coups and attempted coups – which transformed it from a
parliamentary democracy (however tentative and faltering) to a militarist,
fascist, war state. During 2006, the country's leaders and national media
downplayed or turned a blind eye to the slowly rising level of terrorist
violence on the one hand, and to the state pressures to confine and
reduce the space for free and critical opinion on the other, prompting the
Tokyo Shimbun to ask, 'Is it going too far to see in present events a replay
of the collapse of parliamentary politics in the 1930s?'[73]

3

Dismantling the Japanese Model

Until the rise of China as an industrial power around two decades ago, the word 'Japan' was often thought synonymous with 'growth' and 'miracle'. It seemed that Japan had mastered the techniques of industrial organization and that its unique 'developmental capitalist' state was outshining the Anglo-American market economies, and would probably continue to do so. The mood of the times was captured in Ezra Vogel's *Japan as Number One*. Time, of course, has proved otherwise. At the heart of Japan's then system was a mechanism commonly known as the 'construction state' (*doken kokka*), or occasionally as 'public works state', which reached its fullest flowering under Prime Minister Tanaka Kakuei (1972–75).[1] That system was modified and criticized, but not until the government of Koizumi Junichiro did it come under full, frontal attack. His attempt to adopt in its stead Anglo-American capitalism brought the wheel full circle.

At the heart of the construction state lay the Post Office, whose actual postal services were much less than its enormous savings and insurance wings. The Japanese Post Office is unique, in that it handles not only the management of 25,000 post offices and the nation-wide postal delivery system, but also a savings and life insurance system. In that latter capacity it sits atop the world's largest pool of funds – a total of around ¥350 trillion (over $3 trillion), made up of ¥230 trillion in postal savings and ¥120 trillion in insurance funds (30 per cent of the Japanese life insurance market). In scale, that is roughly two and a half times Citigroup or twenty times Germany's Postbank (the banking subsidiary of Deutsche Post).[2] In many remote communities the post office is the central social institution, a non-market node for social exchange. People entrusted their savings to it in preference to private banking institutions

despite the low interest (less than 1 per cent) because of its security and
its low fees.

People also had the vague sense that they were contributing to a kind
of national development fund. The bureaucrats of the Finance Ministry
channelled the population's savings and insurance funds into a wide
range of semi-public bodies – constructing highways, airports, bridges,
and dams under the over-arching national plan. The system concentrated
resources on the building of national infrastructure while also redis-
tributing wealth, both between regions and between social strata. The
Post Office thus became a core component of the Japanese bureaucratic
developmentalist state. It also served the LDP, especially the Tanaka
faction, by vote-gathering and influence-peddling. The system provided
lucrative *amakudari* (post-bureaucratic retirement) positions in the semi-
public development corporations for faction-favoured cronies who
moved from managing the flow of funds to enjoying the benefits of
the flow. The LDP political machine gained widespread public acceptance. The engine for growth that it seemed to provide, and the benefits
it brought to many sectors of society, helped legitimate it. It delivered
growth, redistributed wealth, and provided a welfare system that was
under-funded by European standards, but that still offered something of
a social safety net. It was a variant of Keynesianism, inclusive and
effective, and under it Japan enjoyed its heyday of lifetime employment,
universal education and health provision, corporate welfare, and the
company loyalty system. This was the Japanese model of development,
benevolently guided by bureaucrats whose overriding concern was
supposed to be the public benefit. Most people felt they were middle
class in those years.

But the system had two large weaknesses. It was based on the
assumption that growth would continue, outpacing and swallowing
debt, and it could not respond when growth slowed and then stopped
and debt ballooned. It lacked any mechanism for socially or fiscally
responsible accounting, or any means of shifting track so that resources
could be diverted from saturated areas of social need (roads, bridges, and
so on) to emerging ones (welfare, care of the elderly, and so on). Under
Tanaka and his successors, the *doken kokka* also spread a web of power
and corruption throughout the country, substituting interest representation – brokering – for politics in the strict sense. Public infrastructural
needs were mostly well satisfied by the 1980s, but resources, de-linked

from need, continued to flow, producing thereafter what might be called *extra*-structure. Especially from the late 1980s, a steady flow of unnecessary, useless, environmentally destructive and grossly inflated projects emerged from the planning rooms of the Ministry of Finance and Ministry of Construction. The bureaucrats, in turn, were responding to insistent US pressures – following the trade disputes of the 1980s and articulated most clearly in the 'Structural Impediment' talks with the US (see below, p.47ff) – to prime the Japanese pump by expanding domestic demand. In June 1990, Japan promised to spend ¥430 trillion on a ten-year Public Works Investment Plan – a sum that it increased in 1994 to ¥630 trillion (to be spent in the period 1995–2007).[3] Public debt ballooned. Reflecting on the process in 2002, Gotoda Masaharu, a politician who had been at its centre, said:

> Tanaka created mechanisms that funneled public works funds and subsidies from the central government to local governments and small businesses. He pushed legislation through the Diet, including road-related legislation, to set up the necessary mechanisms – public corporations – with a variety of special accounts, subsidies and other funds with strings attached to implement specific projects . . . Public works projects carried heavy weight in fiscal policy, and they were implemented mainly by public corporations and local governments . . . In the period of Tanaka politics, the goal was to achieve national development and prosperity . . . to create mechanisms that allowed everybody to enjoy the benefits of prosperity. The basic thinking was that the overall level of wealth should be raised through government spending.[4]

For all its flaws, it was, as one critic put it (and as Gotoda would presumably have agreed), a 'pastoral capitalism', in which effort, discipline, skill and care were rewarded and a sense of social solidarity nurtured – by contrast with Anglo-Saxon 'wild capitalism', in which reward and effort were de-linked and the speculative spirit dominated.[5] But the important point was that, as Gotoda himself admitted, it no longer worked. As he put it, late in 1998, 'all [Japan's] systems are malfunctioning'.[6]

In the 1990s, the economy matured, while growth slowed and eventually ground to a halt. Over time, the manipulation of the system to serve the advantage of those within the 'golden triangle' (bureaucrats, politicians, and representatives of the construction and finance sectors), and to serve political as well as public purposes, fatally weakened it. The system became the butt of public and media outrage.

As corruption, incompetence, soaring public debt, the proliferation of bridges to nowhere, and the concreting of the country's rivers and coast discredited the system honed by Tanaka, its (and his) enemies within the LDP became more confident. Casting himself as a radical reformer who would, if necessary, destroy the LDP to fix the problems, Koizumi in 2001 seemed a breath of fresh air. He won his party unprecedented power while blaming it for the mess the country was in. Where support for the government of his predecessor, Mori Yoshiro, had fallen below 10 per cent, under Koizumi it suddenly soared to around 80 per cent.

Koizumi's plan called for the existing Post Office entities to be split into four corporations, with full privatization to take place over a ten-year period to 2017. Even then, government would still hold over one-third of the total value of stocks through a holding company. When a vote on his postal privatization bill was defeated in the Upper House of the Diet on 8 August 2005, 37 members of his own party having either abstained or voted against it, he dissolved the Lower House and called an election. The only constitutional provision for confrontation between the Houses of the Diet – under Article 59 (2) – was for the bill in such circumstances to be remitted to the Lower House, where it would pass into law provided it secured a two-thirds majority. Because Koizumi knew that was impossible, he opted instead to punish the Upper House as a whole, and rebels within his own party in the Lower House for rejecting his bill by dissolving the Lower House. He then travelled the nation on the stump, sticking doggedly to the single point that the election was about reform and reform meant privatization of the Post Office, presenting the electorate with a simple yes-or-no choice.

It was not that the Post Office was somehow inefficient or a cause of widespread dissatisfaction. On the contrary, it was generally regarded as a remarkably well-run institution. Koizumi offered little explanation of the need to privatize it, other than the mantra that he repeated ad nauseam: *kan kara min e* ('from public to private') – meaning that anything in the public sector that might possibly be privatized, should be. In other words, his decision was ideologically driven.

Denouncing those who had voted against him as rebels, he dismissed them from the party, and sent so-called 'assassins' – including a number of high-profile, glamorous women with no political experience – to contest their seats. Throughout the campaign, he behaved as though he were acting a role in a samurai period drama, likening himself to Oda Nobunaga – hero of the late sixteenth-century civil war who, according to a recent book, uttered the words 'I have decided to rid the world of this trash' as he stormed up Mount Hiei in 1571, burning Enryakuji Temple to the ground and killing hundreds of rebellious monks in the process. At other times, he likened himself to Galileo, implying that the need to privatize the Post Office was akin to recognition of heliocentricity; like Galileo, he was ready to die if necessary. He also had his own personal and political revenge motive: to right what he saw as the wrong done in 1972, when his original mentor in politics, Fukuda Takeo, a former Finance Ministry bureaucrat, had been defeated in a savage political turf war with Tanaka Kakuei that had been dubbed the 'Kaku-Fuku War'. The country was spellbound by the drama.

By coincidence, the election campaign coincided with the performance in a Tokyo theatre presented by the great Shakespearean director Ninagawa Yukio, in which all of Shakespeare's 37 dramas were combined into a single magnificent spectacle. Like Ninagawa's, Koizumi's theatre combined comedy, tragedy, romance and history: the electorate stirred with excitement over the assassins, the idea of dying for a cause, and the promises of 'reform'. By polling day, abstentions were down to 32.5 per cent – lower than in any election since 1990.

It was the idea of 'reform' in general that swayed the electorate, rather than the specifics of the complex postal plan – much less any general belief in the virtues of privatization. Although he campaigned as though the Post Office bill was indispensable to national salvation, in an unguarded moment Koizumi admitted that he himself had not even read the bill. In the event, he did the unthinkable, securing an even bigger majority than in 2001, by promising again to do more or less the same – 'reform', and attack all vested interests who stood in his way. It is difficult to think of any other example of a head of government after four years winning a resounding triumph by presenting himself as leader of a crusading force of reformers. With this triumph, the proponents of the distributive, egalitarian principles of the Kakuei state were decisively worsted.

Elections

Elections since 1994 have been based on a system that replaced Japan's old multi-member electoral constituencies with a mixture of 300 single-member, first-past-the-post seats and 180 filled by proportional representation. In the proportional section of the election, Koizumi's LDP won the votes of 25.8 million people (38.18 per cent of those who voted, roughly three points better than Tony Blair a few months earlier). Overall he gained 61 per cent (296) of the seats, while his coalition partner, the Buddhist Komeito (Clean Government) Party, with 8.9 million votes (13.25 per cent of the electorate), took an additional 31 seats, giving his government a two-thirds majority – 327 seats in a 480-seat House. But despite the national swing to the LDP, without the support of Komeito's religious votes, few of the LDP candidates would have had sufficient support to carry their single-member urban constituencies. By contrast, the main opposition party, the Democratic Party of Japan (DPJ), despite its 21 million votes (likewise in the proportional representation section) representing 31 per cent of the electorate, saw its representation slashed from 177 to 113 seats. Its share of votes in the single-member constituency section declined by only 1 per cent, from 37 to 36 per cent; but its share of seats was halved, from 35 to 17 per cent. The Japan Communist Party (JCP), with 7.25 per cent of the national vote, got 1.9 per cent of seats (none at all in the single-member seat section), maintaining its previous nine seats, and the Social Democratic Party (SDP, formerly the Japan Socialist Party), with 5.5 per cent of the vote, secured 1.5 per cent of seats, improving its representation from six to seven. Seventeen ex-LDP 'rebels' and one other independent were also successful, and now sit in the remotest corner of the parliamentary chamber, either as independents or under the banner of one or other of the small new parties.[7]

The outcome was indeed one of the great triumphs of modern Japanese political history; but the LDP was far from gaining the support of a majority of the electorate – indeed, it has not won that since 1963. Its victory owed much to the vagaries of the electoral system. Table 1 illustrates how the LDP has benefited from the 1994 electoral reform.[8]

Table 1: LDP electoral performance 1996–2005

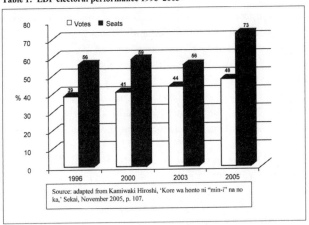

Source: adapted from Kamiwaki Hiroshi, 'Kore wa honto ni "min-i" na no ka,' Sekai, November 2005, p. 107.

If the overall number of votes (in the small electorates) was simply translated into seats on a proportional basis, the LDP in 2005 would have won 183 seats to the DPJ's 149, and the JCP and SDP would have won 35 and 27 seats respectively. When the *Asahi shimbun* totted up the numbers of votes cast in the single-member constituencies, it found that the combined government (LDP and Komeito) vote, at 33.5 million, was around one million votes *fewer* than the aggregate opposition vote.[9] The government parties dramatically recovered their electoral strength in the great urban concentrations of the Tokyo to Fukuoka belt. In the previous (2003) election the LDP had been able to win only five of the 128 seats contested – this time it won 104 of them.[10] The election delivered a landslide *of seats*, but scarcely the decisive electoral shift in favour of Koizumi and his policies that was widely reported.

The situation was complicated, however, by the fact that Koizumi's major opposition party, the DPJ, while opposed to the specifics of his postal privatization bill, supported the principle. Consequently, although the staging suggested huge choice, in fact the electorate had little choice. It was neoliberalism under Koizumi, or neoliberalism under the DPJ's Okada Katsuya. The DPJ, currently the main opposition party, is a hybrid, unstable coalition that assumed its present form in 1998, made up of formerly 'left' and 'right' factions from the existing parties (both the LDP and the Japan Socialist Party) that coalesced in the political turbulence of the mid-1990s. In 2003, the DPJ even enjoyed a measure of financial support from the Keidanren business federation, seeking additional leverage for its 'reform' demands. It was intent on cutting any residual links with unions, on privatization and deregulation, and on revision of Article 9 of the constitution. In 2005, failing to grasp that Koizumi had made the election a plebiscite on a single matter, it paid the price. Presenting complex problems and choices of policies, it actually offered no alternative policy option, little critical insight into the sort of society Koizumi was bent on creating, and no compelling alternative vision.

Beyond the DPJ the opposition benches also accommodate a number of smaller but still significant parties. The Japan Communist Party's vote has fluctuated between about 2 and 8 per cent throughout the postwar era. The Social Democratic Party (SDP), as the Japan Socialist Party, until 1994, used to gain the votes of around 15 per cent of the electorate, but from the mid-1990s shrank to a shadow of its former self after the fateful choice made by its then leader, Murayama Tomiichi, to accept the constitutional legitimacy of the Self-Defence Force (SDF) and endorse the US–Japan security treaty and the *Hinomaru* and *Kimigayo* as national flag and anthem, thereby abandoning principles regarded as central by many party members. Despite its subsequent identity confusion, however, the SDP was able to weather the Koizumi hurricane, even slightly increasing its parliamentary representation in the September election, by insisting on the principles of peace and constitutionalism. Together with the communists and social democrats, making up the opposition to Koizumi's coalition, were the postal rebel independents and several small new parties. One of the paradoxes of Japanese political terminology is that political conservatism – resistance to the changing of basic institutions – is to be found in the ranks of communists and social democrats rather than so-called 'conservatives'.

No recent Japanese election campaign, and few anywhere, had hinged so much on image. Koizumi's bouffant hairstyle, swashbuckling image, passionate and monosyllabic soundbites, gripped the nation's attention. He impressed people as 'more anti-LDP' than opposition leader Okada who, in dark suit and tie, looked the quintessential salaryman, and whose speeches were as dull as they were earnest. When asked what was his favourite karaoke song, Okada replied that he did not 'do' karaoke,[11] which was tantamount to confessing that he was an alien. Misreading the Koizumi campaign and its media grammar, Okada was swept away in a wave of clever images and soundbites, and resigned shortly after the election. After a brief interim, he was replaced at the party's helm by the veteran politician, former cabinet secretary of an LDP government, Ozawa Ichiro.

Through the summer leading up to the election, Koizumi was at the centre of a well-honed government campaign to promote informality and cooler summer dress under the name of 'cool biz', discarding a jacket and wearing open-necked striped or floral-patterned shirts that symbolically distinguished him from the conservative LDP image. Koizumi had not only marked his accession to the prime ministership in 2001 by releasing a CD introducing Elvis Presley songs, but had burst into an impromptu rendition of 'I Want You, I Need You, I Love You' when meeting Tom Cruise in 2003, and again on visiting the Elvis museum, Graceland, in the company of George W. Bush in 2006.

Table 2: Election of 11 September 2005

Party	Single member	Proportional representation	Total
LDP	219	77 (25,887,798 / 38.18%)	296 (+59)
DPJ	52	61 (21,036,425 / 31.02%)	113 (-64)
Komei	8	23 (8,987,620 / 13.25%)	31 (-3)
JCP	0	9 (4,919,187 / 7.25%)	9 (0)
SDP	1	6 (3,719,522 / 5.49%)	7 (+1)
PNP	2	2 (1,183,073 / 1.74%)	4 (+4)
NPJ	0	1 (1,643,506 / 2.42%)	1 (+1)
Shinto Daichi	0	1 (433,938 / 0.64%)	1 (+1)
Others	18		18 (+59)
Totals	300	180 (67,811,069)	480

Source: see Table 1.

Abbreviations:
LDP – Liberal Democratic Party
DPJ – Democratic Party of Japan
Komei – New Clean Government Party
JCP – Japan Communist Party
SDP – Social Democratic Party
NPJ – New Party Japan
PNP – People's New Party

The swing towards the LDP was most pronounced in just those urban districts of Tokyo and Osaka, among youth and women, where the DPJ had in recent years been making most headway – even securing 2 million more votes than the LDP in the proportional representation section of the November 2003 election. In 2005, however, in their fear and anxiety, people turned for change to a party that had been in almost unbroken power forty-nine of the past fifty years, and to a prime minister who had been in office for more than four years – accomplishing little, but looking and sounding decisive. Who better to entrust with the task of smashing the LDP than the leader of that party?

Koizumi wagered everything on postal reform, despite indications that the proportion of the public who had begun by agreeing with him on its importance had been infinitesimal. Remarkably, the election passed without discussion, let alone serious scrutiny, of the implications of his plan for future delivery of services – especially in remote areas – of the prospect of higher charges and increased risks, or of the likely consequences of opening the national savings to global market forces. Most likely few especially cared whether their mail was delivered by public servants or private companies, but the security of their savings and insurance was another matter. Koizumi was careful not to raise it during the campaign, and opposition leaders and the media failed to make it an issue.

The claim that privatization would invigorate the Japanese economy also seemed improbable. The precedent of the privatization of the Japan National Railways – carried out in 1987 and involving the freezing and then slow expansion of the former national body's enormous debt, even as all its assets were sold off – was scarcely mentioned in the privatization push. There were other examples that might have been material for a debate on privatization that did not occur. Once the taxi industry had been liberalized, in 2002, the number of operators rose by almost one-fifth (to 8,800), drivers found themselves working substantially increased hours (averaging over 200 per month) because of competition, their income shrank, and the number of accidents they were involved in increased by about 50 per cent.[12] Private banks already had more funds than lending outlets, demand was weak, and major corporations had plenty of cash. Why would fully privatized institutions choose to put their funds in zero- to low-interest government bonds (of which they now hold around ¥105 trillions worth)? And yet they were in a bind. If they stopped doing so, either the bonds might collapse in price or their interest rate rise precipitately. As privatization approached, a senior executive from Toyota was appointed to head the new postal body, and Toyota management principles and pressures began to apply. Work pressures were intensified; global positioning satellite systems were introduced to track mail delivery staff movements; deaths from exhaustion and overwork (*karoshi*), or suicide, rose; and in postal branches the fear of closure and retrenchment spread.[13]

The kingdom

Outside the Koizumi theatre, in the streets where the neoliberal script had to be lived, all was far from well. It is true that the economy resumed growth early in 2002, that most of the banking system's 'bad debts' had by then been cleared, and that the period of expansion was by mid-2006 'on track to become the longest in Japan's post-war era'.[14] But the accomplishment was ambiguous, and had been won at great cost.

While he talked incessantly of small government, the shifting of public sector tasks to the private sector, and deregulation, he poured vast sums of public money into rescuing and shoring up private banking institutions; and – although he did indeed slash public works expenditure, from around 8 to 9 per cent of GDP to about half that figure[15] – he continued public works projects for the construction of new express rail lines, dams, airports, and highways (with ¥5 trillion or more to be spent on a new Tokyo–Nagoya expressway alone).

The 'restructuring' that he enthusiastically promoted meant the loss of many jobs, the further gutting of the already enfeebled traditional Japanese employment system, the reduction of salaries,[16] increases in social security payments, and reductions in benefits for many. More than half of all households, according to a government survey, described their situation as 'painful' (*kurushii*).[17] Working people's wages fell steadily under Koizumi, 2005 marking the seventh consecutive year of such decline,[18] and the ranks of the poor grew steadily.

Over 1 million households subsist on welfare,[19] and two or three times that number are without resources or reserves and *should* be on it.[20] Around one household in five has no savings, according to the Bank of Japan.[21] Anxiety is becoming widespread, and people are beginning to fear the possible collapse of the national pension system. Facing an insecure future, young people are turning away from marriage, and the society itself is signally failing to reproduce.

Table 3: Koizumi's reform: some fruits after four years (2000–04).

	2000	2004	
National Income	372	361	(in ¥ trillion)
Employee salaries	271	255	
Private Corporate Income	44	50	
Individual Enterprise Income	19	18	
Recurrent Corporate Profit	36	45	
(of which large enterprises)	25	33	
(middle/small enterprises)	11	12	
Average salary, regulars	4.61	4.39	(in ¥ million)

In short, national income fell by ¥11 trillion, employee salaries fell by ¥16 trillion, and corporate profits rose by ¥6 trillion (mostly in large enterprises). Over 3 million regular jobs were lost, partly compensated by the gain of 2.3 million 'irregular' (insecure, low-paid) jobs, and average salaries – even for 'regular' employees – fell slightly.

Source: adapted from Yambe Yukio, 'Jittai naki keiki kaifuku o yomitoku,' *Sekai*, March 2006, p. 125.

Table 4: Households on welfare 1990–2005

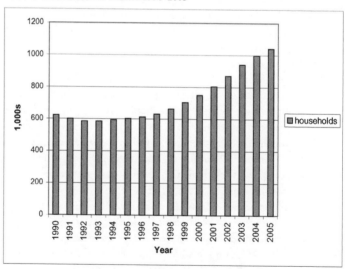

Source: Ministry of Health, Labour and Welfare
Asahi Shimbun, 7 October 2006

Table 5: Ratio of non-regular employees/workforce

Source: Ministry of Internal Affairs and Communications *Shukan Kinyobi*, 29 September 2006.
Hiratate Hideaki, "'Waking pua" no genjitsu,' Shukan kinyobi, 29 September 2006, pp. 20-22.

By 2006, the labour market had been subject to successive waves of
liberalization over two decades, with Koizumi presiding over only the
latest and most drastic stage. A 1986 Labour Dispatch Law allowed,
supposedly as a short-term measure, the employment on a temporary
basis of technical staff with high-level skills. In 1995, however, the
National Federation of Employers' Associations (Nikkeiren) drew up a
plan to extend this model to the national labour market – a step that it
insisted was essential for competitiveness in the globalized economy.[22]
Under the ' "Japanese Management" for a New Era'[23] design – in place
of the traditional system of lifetime employment, age-based promotion,
company welfare, and in-house training, sometimes referred to as
'corporate socialism' – labour rights should henceforth be confined to
a small group of career management and administrative staff, numbering
around 10 per cent of the labour force. A second group of between 20
and 30 per cent would comprise high-level technical specialists on fixed-
term contracts, enjoying performance bonuses but no entitlement to
automatic promotion, while the majority – 60 to 70 per cent of workers
– would fall into the insecure employment sector, paid by the hour,

without seniority benefits, promotion or welfare entitlements.[24] The labour market would come to be triangular in shape, with 'traditional' labour rights confined to a small minority at the apex, while most would remain stuck throughout their lives in the base. Employers demanded such terms as their price for competitiveness under conditions of globalization, and Koizumi and his colleagues were happy to oblige.

The LDP, as the party of capital, proceeded to implement this vision. In the decade to 2004, 4 million manufacturing jobs were shed,[25] many of which were not replaced, being either permanently shifted offshore (mainly to China) or transformed into quasi-jobs, to be 'outsourced', done by temporaries, *freeters* (casual workers aged between 15 and 34 years, hired from labour supply companies), or robots.[26] As the 'labour dispatch' system was extended under Prime Minister Obuchi in 1999 to other, specialized sectors, and under Koizumi in 2004 to manufacturing and construction, the social consequences were dramatic. By April 2006, more than one-third of the workforce was in the category of contract labour – insecure, temporary, enjoying few rights, and with little chance of advancement. Between 1995 and 2006, the ranks of 'irregulars' grew by 6.62 million, or from 21 to 33 per cent of the labour force,[27] most of whom were earning around ¥6,000 per day, or approximately 120,000 per month.[28] The manpower supply business boomed.

One in three workers, reconstituted as members of a 'reserve army of labour', found themselves on the poverty line, able to be moved about, exploited, and casualized or sacked to suit corporate convenience, with no provision for health or welfare, earning about half the salary of regular workers – or over a lifetime about a quarter. Stripped of security, welfare and hope, they became the new, or working poor. While higher education was to become increasingly the preserve of the class at the apex of the triangle, for those at its bottom – the 'no-hopers', as they were cynically designated by neoliberal reformers – patriotism and obedience would be of primary importance. The constitutional entitlement under Article 25 (1) to a 'wholesome and cultured living' would be emptied of meaning.

Within the general category of the 'irregular', *freeters* drifting from one low-paid temporary job to another doubled in the decade to 2004, to more than 4 million,[29] and were expected to grow to 10 million by 2014, with the middle-aged component (35 and over) growing to constitute one in five.[30] In comparative OECD terms, Japan has 15.3 per cent of its population below the poverty line, as against the OECD average of 10.8 (and 17.1 in the US).[31] Another group, 2.13 million aged between 15 and 34, are not in school or employment, and therefore are described as NEET (not in employment, education, or training).[32] An estimated 1.2 million young people retreated from all contact with the outside world into the confines of their own rooms – modern hermits or *hikikomori*.[33] For those who, for the moment, retain jobs, stress and anxiety levels rise, since for the most part they have reduced job security and income, and increased anxiety over future pension entitlements and tax burdens.[34] The official figure for unemployment (3.13 million) remains relatively low, but only because shame or helplessness deter many from registering for it.[35]

Until recently, those graduating from university, especially from the graduate school in one of the country's major universities, could expect comfortable absorption within the middle class. As of 2005, however, 20 per cent of graduates were working part-time or in casual employment – a figure that had risen sharply in recent years.[36] The country's graduate schools were turning out over 10,000 new doctorates each year (by 2003), following a proliferation of graduate schools in the 1990s under Ministry of Education guidance. But as demographic pressures hit the universities, undergraduate enrolments shrank and mergers were common. One estimate was that there were, at most, 3,000 jobs annually in regular universities or research institutes, leaving 7,000 with very uncertain prospects, serving as part-time lecturers or cram-school tutors, which they were likely to do indefinitely. In 20 years' time, Yamada estimates, Japan would have over 100,000 middle-aged doctors – super-qualified *freeters*.[37]

The sense that things were going from bad to worse was widespread – in the economy, employment and working conditions, education, crime, security, morals and ethics, and even international status. A Cabinet Office survey in 2004 found that 60 per cent of people expected their future to worsen over coming decades.[38] In 1997 the suicide rate leapt from around 22,000 per year to over 30,000, where it has stayed ever since – higher than any other nation on earth.[39] In 2004 it was over 32,000 (90 per day), roughly double the US rate, and the increase came especially from the ranks of middle-aged and elderly males, for economic reasons.[40] Furthermore, for each successful suicide, there may be as many as ten failed attempts.[41] To spend time in Japan in recent years has been to hear all too often the chilling announcement on the train or subway about a delay due to a *jinshin jiko* or 'accident involving a human body'. Equally shocking is the fact that, while Japan has the longest life expectancy of any country in the world, four in ten people reportedly 'do not wish to lead a long life'.[42] The Japan that in the 1970s and 1980s was known for its astonishing degree of worker commitment and identification to the corporation, the land of the corporate warrior, is now the OECD country with the *lowest* levels of corporate loyalty,[43] and one of the highest levels of income inequality.[44]

For these reasons, what voters in early twenty-first-century Japan were most concerned about was not the Post Office but pensions and welfare (52 per cent), the economy and employment (28 per cent), and foreign affairs and defence (9 per cent), with just 2 per cent for postal privatization (at the time when Koizumi insisted it was the number-one issue.[45] Shortly before the September 2005 election was called, the *Yomiuri shimbun* reported that postal privatization was ranked sixteenth among seventeen priorities, indicated as a priority by only 7 per cent of those responding. Only as the parliamentary crisis built towards the election, however, and Koizumi stepped up his campaign, was a small majority in favour of privatization detected[46].

Irresponsible bureaucratic mismanagement of public pension funds erupted into a full-scale political crisis in 2004, when it was revealed that the Ministry of Public Health and Welfare's welfare enterprise, 'Green-pia', had invested public pension funds so recklessly in a proliferation of public and concert halls, sports and recreation facilities, and that around ¥3 trillion ($27 billion) had been lost.[47] The national Diet struggled simultaneously to cover up the scale of the disaster, to reassure those with pension entitlements, and to adjust to the prodigious losses of public wealth by adoption of a new Pension Law that would increase contributions and reduce benefits. Several key political figures, including the leader of the opposition, resigned when forced to admit that they had neglected to pay their premiums. Koizumi himself conceded that he too had not bothered paying his (compulsory) premiums for nearly three years, but he dismissed it airily as a trivial matter that had happened a long time ago (around 1970). When pressed to explain his delinquency, while for nearly three years on the payroll of a company for which he did no work, he replied with the words of a popular song: 'there are many different ways of living', adding, 'there are also many different kinds of companies, and different kinds of employees'.[48] In response to his bold decision to threaten a national election if his bill were defeated, public attention shifted miraculously from the scandals of Greenpia and pensions, including his own cavalier attitude to his obligations, and his popularity surged.

Japan is recognized by the OECD as the most indebted of all modern states. Under Koizumi, the national debt had spiralled, heading for ¥ quadrillion (a truly mind-boggling figure – a 1 with fifteen zeros) by the end of financial year 2006, or 21 years of tax revenues at their present level of 46 trillion.[49] At 170 per cent of GDP (by the relatively conservative OECD figure), this debt was the highest in the OECD and the highest in modern history, and Koizumi had contributed more to inflating it than any of his predecessors.[50] The fiscal crisis called for either increased revenue or reduced expenditure. But tax rates, both corporate and individual, have been steadily reduced, so that by 2004 they were the lowest in the OECD, at 21 per cent, with income tax constituting a mere 6 per cent of GDP (as against 12.1 in the US and 10.6 in France).[51] In slightly more than a decade, tax revenues shrank as a source of state revenue by about half, from ¥26.7 trillion in 1991 to ¥13.8 trillion in 2004, while the consumption tax, introduced at 3 per cent in 1989 and raised to 5 per cent in 1997, steadily grew in importance.[52]

The idea that significant savings could be made by cutting the number of public servants was commonly to be heard during the discussions on postal privatization, but Japan is scarcely over-governed. Ordinary government expenditure amounts to only 37 per cent of GDP, against an OECD average of 41 per cent, and there are only 35 public servants (including local ones) per 1,000 of population, compared to 73 in the UK, 80 in the US, and 96 in France.[53]

As for possible cuts in welfare, the welfare budget is already among the lowest in the OECD. Gross public social expenditure, including public pensions, was 16.9 per cent in 2001, twenty-fifth among OECD countries, and marginally above the US.[54] The mass retirement of the baby boomer generation (around 2007), in the context of rapid ageing and a declining birthrate, means that expenditure will rise vertiginously. The welfare budget, at ¥32 trillion in 2004, already equal to more than three-quarters of national tax revenues (¥42 trillion), was growing steadily as the population aged. Soon, the country's entire tax revenues would have to go to meet welfare obligations, and then continue to grow until they reached approximately twice those revenues by 2025.[55] That was inconceivable, of course, and consequently Japan's level of expenditure on health as a percentage of GDP[56] seems bound to be targeted for a significant cut.

Already public works expenditure has been slashed (by approximately 25 per cent over the five years to 2006),[57] and the 'Big-Boned Measures' (*Honebuto no hoshin, 2006*) announced by the government in mid-2006 called for slashing a further ¥11–14 trillion from government expenditure over the coming five years. Welfare and education would have to bear a large portion of that. The *Asahi shimbun* commented that '[i]f things remain as they are, the government will be unable to offer our children and grandchildren the current level of social welfare and education we now enjoy'.[58] Such was the scale of the problem, however, that even draconian cuts in expenditure would merely arrest the growth in debt, without even beginning actually to restore fiscal health. As the society ages and the welfare burden rises, at unprecedented rates, expenditure has to be slashed, and taxes (meaning almost exclusively consumption tax) raised.

The prime minister's Council on Economic and Fiscal Policy (CEFP) is clear that pension entitlements will have to be further cut, and social insurance payments raised.[59] The same advisory panel suggested in October 2005 that it might also be appropriate to raise the consumption tax from its current 5 per cent to 19 per cent.[60] As public services and social protections are degraded, the mass of citizens will be encouraged to buy social protection from private finance and insurance houses.[61]

With the over-65s in its population surpassing 20 per cent in 2005, Japan was leading the OECD into the unfamiliar territory of a 'super-aged' society.[62] Population actually began to decline the following year. The precise figures were dependent on many variables, but on current trends would fall to around 90 million by mid-century, and perhaps half of that by end of century. The projections looked so grim that one recent minister of health and welfare remarked in 2002: 'If we go on this way, the Japanese race will become extinct.'[63]

For many women, in particular, the system fails doubly: regular jobs fade into temporary ones, and marriage prospects shrink as numbers of males without salaries increase. The bureaucratic/political analysis tended to attribute the declining birthrate to increased opportunities for women's participation in an equal society, but others attributed it to social impoverishment, describing Japanese youth as 'increasingly un-happy compared with their parents' generation', and attributing their refusal to bear children to the belief that 'their offspring will experience yet greater hardship and unhappiness'.[64]

The UN estimates that, for Japan to maintain the same productive population (those aged between 15 and 64) as in 1995, it would have to admit 600,000 immigrants each year, at least until mid-century. At that rate, roughly one in three of the population would be an immigrant. Mid-way through the first decade of the century, with the ideology of Japanese uniqueness still strong, a mainly closed social structure, and positive resistance even to the admission of political refugees, such a prospect is unimaginable. Currently Japan's foreign worker population is extremely low, at about 1 per cent (about three in ten of whom are illegals), as against 12 per cent in the US and between 6 and 8 per cent in France and Germany.[65]

The Koizumi era was especially notable for the emergence of 'a new class of urban poor [and] the proliferation of young workers drifting from one low-paid job to another without prospect of escape'.[66] The political events of 2005 were rooted in deep social malaise, and books analyzing the transformation of Japanese society in terms of the disappearance of the 100 million-strong middle class, and of the widening split between the super-rich and the marginal masses (winners and losers, *kachigumi* and *makegumi*) became bestsellers.[67]

The empire

Beyond the kingdom, however, lay the empire. Postal privatization had been pressed upon Japan by the US for decades, high on the Washington wish-list of Japanese policy changes. Following the Plaza Agreement of 1985, when despite massive yen revaluation the US trade deficit with Japan continued to grow, Japan was assumed to be deriving unfair advantage from the 'difference' or closedness of its social and economic system. Negotiations to level the bilateral playing field began in 1989, under the name 'Structural Impediment Initiative' (SII). To soften the implication of peremptory US intervention in Japan's internal arrange-ments, the Japanese Foreign Ministry deleted the word 'impediment',

and simply translated it as 'structural negotiations' (*kozo kyogi*). At the
second meeting, the US side presented a list of over 200 demands for
reform – covering everything from the budget, tax system, and joint
stockholding rules, to the request that the Japanese stop working on
Saturdays. It was described by one senior Japanese official as tantamount
to a 'second occupation'.[68]

Negotiations in similar vein, to remove 'impediments' to the US share
of the Japanese market, resumed under various names thereafter, and
Washington presented Tokyo with an annual 'Statement of Desired
Reforms'. Plainly such a document, emanating from any other government, would have been seen in Tokyo as an intolerable intervention in
Japan's internal affairs; but in fact few in Tokyo saw anything offensive
about it. Koizumi, as post and telecommunications minister from 1992,
became directly involved.

Koizumi's personal stake in attacking party and factional enemies
coincided with the US government's view that Japan's Post Office, like
its bureaucratically regulated banking and insurance system, constituted
a trade barrier – an 'impediment' – to be dismantled. Just before he
took office as prime minister the 'Armitage Report' (see Chapter 4)
included the admonition: 'Deregulation should be accelerated.' The
incoming Bush administration found Koizumi a more than willing
partner. One of his first priorities upon assuming office was the
agreement with George W. Bush to reopen bilateral negotiations under
the title 'US–Japan Regulatory Reform and Competition Policy Initiative'. Their scope was breathtaking, including 'telecommunications,
information technology, energy, medical devices and pharmaceuticals,
financial services, competition policy, transparency, legal reform, commercial law revision, and distribution': in short, just about everything.[69] Koizumi's popularity in Washington reflected appreciation for
the enthusiasm with which he embraced his mission of transforming
Japan to meet American requirements.

No measure was more persistently and more passionately urged
upon Japan than postal privatization, especially with regard to the
insurance component of the postal system. Japan's $120 trillion
government-run insurance business was the world's second largest,
after that of the US itself, and roughly equal to the GDP of Canada.
American insurance demanded access.[70] The office of the USTR (US
Trade Representative) insisted that privatization be implemented 'based

on market principles only', and that the Japanese government withdraw completely from postal savings and life insurance.[71] In the October 2003 'Reform Request', Japan was urged to draw up a plan by the following autumn. Because of the political difficulties, however, little progress was made during that year, and when Koizumi met with Bush in New York in September 2004 he found himself facing embarrassing direct questions from the president about it. When Koizumi replied, 'I will do my best' (*shikkari yatte ikitai*), it was tantamount to an absolute commitment, and the president duly expressed his satisfaction.[72] A month later, Robert Zoellick, then US Trade Representative and shortly to become Deputy Secretary of State, wrote to Japan's Finance Minister Takenaka Heizo, who had just taken up the additional post of Minister for Postal Privatization. He renewed the pressure, declaring US enthusiasm and readiness to help pursue postal privatization and, in a handwritten note, commended Takenaka for the splendid job he was doing, offering detailed advice as to how he should proceed and 'looking forward to working together with him'.[73] When the question was later raised in the Diet of whether Zoellick's letter might have constituted US government intervention in a sensitive and contentious Japanese matter, Koizumi merely expressed his satisfaction that Takenaka had been befriended by such an important figure. His government accepted without question the US prerogative to make demands on core financial and economic policy. Koizumi's government had already contributed enormously towards stabilizing the US economy by its purchases of US treasury bonds and notes, and postal privatization was a prospect for the Bush administration to relish – a further, large step in sustaining Washington's Iraq mission and related imperial policies.

As the Koizumi government cleared the obstacles to privatization, US private investment institutions looked forward to gaining access to the giant Japanese pool of savings. According to the *Wall Street Journal*, Citigroup expected US treasuries, European bonds and Japanese and foreign stocks to be 'the big winners'.[74] While about 50 per cent of the population in the US owned stocks, and 36 per cent traded them, in Japan around 10 per cent owned and 3 per cent traded them. 'It's . . . a big space for us to grow into', as one broker put it.[75] As the US finance and insurance sectors looked forward to 'growing into' the newly opened spaces, the next target, featured consistently on the annual 'Desired

Reforms' list, appeared to be the medical services sector (including pharmaceutical products and services).[76]

Reform! Reform!

Koizumi emerged from the September election with a parliamentary dominance without precedent since that of the wartime governing party, the Imperial Rule Assistance Association. The paradox of his triumph is that it was born of *déclassement*, anxiety and fear, bordering on desperation, rather than support for a true agenda of economic, social and political reform. Koizumi attracted mass support, and was even seen by some as a saviour, because of the image he projected of stern and steely determination. His support seems to have been especially strong among precisely the inhabitants of the emerging world of un- or semi-employed youth. In the drabness and desolation of their world, Koizumi sparkled and was seen as 'really cool' (*kakkoii*).[77] Responding to his cries of 'Reform! Reform!', people ignored his responsibility for bringing on the crisis and the reform agenda itself. They longed for him to wave a magic wand to restore the secure world of the 1970s, blind to the fact that he was pledged to destroy precisely that world and its certainties.

Koizumi's theatre offered multiple illusory effects. Although 30 per cent of Koizumi's candidates were second- or third-generation politicians (Koizumi himself was third-generation), one in six of them were ex-bureaucrats; and before, during, and after the election Koizumi depended on the support of a religious party (New Komeito). The LDP nevertheless presented itself as a 'new' force, struggling mightily under a reformist, vigorous, iconoclastic leader against entrenched, 'conservative' and bureaucratic interests. Excited over the prospect of smashing the LDP, people forgot that Koizumi was its latest avatar.

In the 1980s, Prime Minister Nakasone (Yasuhiro) desisted from worshipping at Yasukuni Shrine when he saw the anger it provoked in neighbouring countries and the potential harm it caused to the national interest. But Koizumi, before becoming party chief (and prime minister), had promised the politically powerful Veterans Association that he would make a formal annual visit. He kept his promise, making six visits during just less than six years in office, dividing national opinion over how to remember the past and mourn the Japanese dead, and encouraging a narrow nationalism and defiance of the opinions of neighbouring countries that steadily crippled Japanese diplomacy. Yet within Japan his gesture had the air of bold insistence on principle, and of refusal to kowtow to China or Korea. Despite the political cost, his support in the Diet and in the country remained strong.

Another part of the freshness and appeal of the Koizumi campaign was that he seemed to have made the LDP the party of women. Yet Koizumi's pre-2005 election parliament included only 7 per cent female MPs, ranking it 101st in the world.[78] His LDP colleagues were wont to make outrageous statements – defending gang rape (by university club members) as an indicator of male vigour, 'close to normal', in just one example – without drawing any recorded protest from Koizumi.[79] His LDP presented far fewer female candidates for the election (26 out of 346) than the DPJ, had no policies for improving women's conditions, and was committed to revising the guarantee of equality between the sexes in Article 24 of the constitution. The few female assassins ('ninja in lipstick') it thrust onto the national stage were unlikely to make much difference to the party's male-dominated structures.[80]

The issues of greatest importance to Japan were those not mentioned in the campaign: ecological crisis, diplomatic isolation, chronic indebtedness, population decline and ageing, abandonment of the traditional employment system, rising child crime figures, rising suicide figures, and deep social pessimism. Koizumi's 'reform' prescription was for privatization and deregulation – in other words, neoliberalism – on the one hand, and for deepening dependence on the US (including a Japanese force in Iraq),[81] more patriotism and more national pride – in other words, neo-nationalism – on the other. Revising the constitution and the Fundamental Law of Education, substituting Hayekian, neoliberal, American principles for the Keynesian *doken kokka*, redistributive, 'Japanese' way, under Koizumi, the once broad-church LDP was becoming a narrow – in some respects fundamentalist – clique. Absolute priority to servicing the alliance with the US, plus deregulation (*kisei kanwa*), rationalization (*gorika*), and restructuring (*risutora)* were the dogma, and there was no room for dissent or criticism. Cuts in taxation levels on the wealthy and on corporations, and reduced investment in the public sector,[82] in the context of the deepening national fiscal crisis, made it inevitable that the consumption tax would have to be raised substantially soon after he left office.

Talking of newness and reform, Koizumi brought his party to the brink of the realization of the long-held dreams of its most reactionary wing – revision of the constitution and Fundamental Law of Education, and a 'normal' great power military posture. What he meant by 'getting rid of factions', or 'destroying the LDP', was getting rid of *other* factions – exorcizing the Kakuei ghost from the LDP machine. He may have reduced the power of the *zoku* or sectoral 'tribes' (agriculture, posts, construction, and so on), but only at the cost of delivering the party as a whole to unprecedented levels of influence by Japanese business, whose confederations united in a chorus of support for his neoliberal 'reform' agenda.[83] What former LDP leaders had been restrained from attempting by the realities of Diet politics or the factional balance within their own party, Koizumi could now contemplate without inhibition. Former prime ministers and LDP elder statesmen looked at the state of parliamentary democracy and saw Koizumi presiding over a time of 'extremely conspicuous decline', in which there was minimal serious debate (in the words of Miyazawa Kiichi) – no medium- or long-term strategy, no philosophy, just performance (according to Nakasone Yasuhiro).[84]

While Koizumi's neoliberal enthusiasm was unbounded, the LDP 'rebels' – described by the *Economist* on 8 September 2005, days before the election, as 'recalcitrants' belonging to 'the ferociously anti-reformist wings of the party' – tended to hold to 'wet' social and political views, and to take seriously the party's original (1955) platform statement about ensuring that 'the construction of a welfare state is successfully completed'. Like Kamei Shizuka, the former head of the party's Policy Research Council, these recalcitrants took pride in the fact of the system of free healthcare for the elderly and a 60 per cent income for retirement (instituted by Tanaka Kakuei in 1973, and only cut – to 50 per cent – by Koizumi's 'pension revolution' in 2004).[85] For Kamei, wealth creation had to be balanced by its redistribution to the regions, and the provision of a safety net – in sharp contrast with Koizumi's dry, modernizing – in his own word, 'ruthless' – mission. Kamei was also committed to a strict constitutionalist position on peace and security, and absolutely opposed to Koizumi's dispatch of the Self-Defence Forces to Iraq.

The Koizumi campaign worked hard to paint Kamei and other opponents of postal privatization as reactionary proponents of corrupt special interests, virtual traitors. Despite being purged from his party, however, Kamei was able to fight off his 'assassin', Koizumi's favourite, the internet millionaire Horie Takafumi. Horie was arrested and indicted for corrupt business practices just a few months later. For Kamei, the Koizumi triumph was a bubble, setting Japan on the road to ruin, and the Yes or No of the election was a Yes or No to Japanese subordination to the US, and to the casting adrift of Japan's regions and of its poor and weak.[86]

The boldness of Koizumi's attempt to smash and rebuild his party is plain, but its success was not assured. To smash is much easier than to rebuild. Party membership declined steadily,[87] and 'reform fatigue', reflecting a desire to stop or slow the 'reform' agenda and pay attention to its social costs, was pronounced among those still left in the party when Abe Shinzo took over.[88] While purging it of most of its liberalism, Koizumi's politics relied heavily on populism – and populism, as one right-wing critic put it, is the enemy of conservatism. Its attempts to articulate and manipulate popular demands and resentments always carry the risk of turning into a storm beyond control – especially populism like Koizumi's, which stressed destruction and prided itself on ruthlessness (*hijo*).[89] Anxious right-wing thinkers thus lament that Koizumi was attacking Japaneseness itself, substituting dry, even ruthless market reductionism in place of the 'wet' notions of social solidarity and *giri* (duty, obligation) and *ninjo* (affection, humanity) – the thick, social web of relationships on which the LDP and Japan had grown and thrived.[90] Nishio Kanji, a key figure in textbook revision and author of neo-nationalist texts on Japanese history, wrote bitterly and contemptuously of Japan as a drifting state hijacked by Koizumi with bread and circuses.[91]

Koizumi's assault on his party could be compared to Mao Zedong's launch thirty-five years earlier of the Great Proletarian Cultural Revolution against the party and system of which he was the head. It was, if anything, even more paradoxical in its outcome, in that, by rousing the Japanese masses to overthrow the LDP, and sending out assassins against enemies, he succeeded in delivering power to his party on an unprecedented scale. Yet, having won a huge 'pro-reform' victory, the party apparently wanted nothing so much as to arrest that 'reform' process, and the softened tone of the incoming Abe government indicated a desire to address such concerns.

Koizumi was aided by the fact that, throughout the Cold War years, with the help and encouragement of Washington, the forces of Japan's civil society – labour unions, students, and citizen movements – had been neutralized, perhaps more comprehensively than in any other capitalist society.[92] While around 7 million workers were affiliated with the national Rengo labour federation, three and a half times that number – around 25 million part-time and fixed-term contract employees, *freeters*, NIITs, the unemployed and the welfare-dependent – had no representation.[93]

'Reform' in recent Japanese politics is the more keenly desired the more it is frustrated, manipulated, and denied. The 'reform' wave that began in the late 1980s, and was fed by anger and disgust at the corruption of LDP rule exposed in the Recruit[94] and other scandals, gave rise to a new electoral system in 1994. But that 'reform' can now be seen not, in fact, to have reduced corruption, and rather to have frustrated the desire for reform. Sidelining the broadly social democratic and communist parties of the opposition, it created merely the simulacrum of a two-party system, comprising two rival wings of a single conservative party, both sharing a consensus on the priority to US demands for security 'cooperation', the regularization of Japan's military forces by revision of the constitution, and neoliberal social and economic policies.[95] In the second great wave of reform, born of the gloom and stagnation of the late twentieth and early twenty-first centuries, Koizumi thrived on his ability to channel and focus popular fears and hopes by manipulating them into the single issue of postal reform.

On 14 October 2005, the Upper House voted 134:40 for the very same Post Office bill that it had rejected by 125:108 just two months earlier, on 8 August. All but one of the rebels, including some who had vowed to resist 'to the death', meekly offered their necks to the party authorities for punishment, hoping for leniency and reinstatement at the earliest possible opportunity. Eleven of them were in fact reinstated as one of the early acts of the Abe government, late in 2006.

4

Japan in Bush's World

An alliance 'second to none'

Nobody in Japan doubts the importance of maintaining close ties with the United States. If there is one lesson above all others that Japan learned from the twentieth century, it was that alliance with the global superpower – Great Britain in the first two decades of that century, and the US for the last five – offered the best assurance of stability and prosperity. Whether that lesson from past experience was applicable in the twenty-first century, however, was open to question. How the treaty relationship was to be reconciled with the pacifist constitution was also problematic, at best. Despite its constitutional pacifism and popular sovereignty, the Japanese people were the last to be consulted when the postwar treaty relationship was initiated in 1951, when it was revised in 1960, or when it underwent its greatest transformation, in 2005–06.

The US–Japan relationship is often described – especially on ceremonial occasions – as 'second to none' in importance. Between them the two countries – bitter enemies until sixty years ago – account for about 40 per cent of global GDP, and for 40 per cent of the United Nations budget. America has 'no closer ally', as US President George W. Bush put it in his message to commemorate the 150th anniversary of the opening of relations in July 2004.[1] It was so close, in fact, that, in one of his more egregious bloopers, the president could even forget that they had once been enemies, telling the Japanese Diet in 2002 that 'for a century and a half now, America and Japan have formed one of the great and enduring [sic] alliances of modern times'.[2]

Ceremonial rhetoric aside, however, what 'alliance' can there be with a superpower? A decade ago, Zbigniew Brzezinski – national security adviser under Jimmy Carter, and a senior foreign policy adviser under both the Reagan and first Bush presidencies – spoke in brutally realist terms of a world divided into three kinds of countries: vassal, tributary, and barbarian. The 'three grand imperatives of imperial geostrategy', he said, were 'to prevent collusion and maintain security dependence among the vassals, to keep tributaries pliant and protected, and to keep the barbarians from coming together'.[3] Japan, though a world-class power, was a US 'protectorate'.[4] No single power could ever be allowed to supplant the US's role of 'decisive arbitration', or superpower; consequently China had to be reined in. As the US's East Asian agent, its vassal, Japan would be expected to help keep the 'barbarians' under control.[5]

Throughout the Cold War, Japan's policy had been to cooperate with both the US and the UN, and with the general framework of international law. Under George W. Bush, however, once the US decided to go to war in Iraq in defiance of the UN and international law, that became virtually impossible. Forced to choose, Koizumi's Japan chose the US. It was, as Koizumi put it in February 2004, of overwhelming importance for Japan to show that it was a 'trustworthy ally', because if ever Japan were to come under attack it would be the US – not any other country or the UN – that would come to its aid.[6] His reference to a possibility of attack did not need to be spelled out. When he declared Japanese support for the US-led war on Iraq, and when he sent Japanese forces to aid the occupation in January 2004, it was not Iraq that was in Japanese sights so much as North Korea.

When Bush and Koizumi met in Kyoto in November 2005, the president praised Japan as 'a good friend in spreading freedom and democracy', while Koizumi, for his part, declared that, 'To the extent that relations between the US and Japan are good, we can build good relations with the countries of Asia, including China and Korea.'[7] Few agreed, however, and the contrary seemed more plausible: ties with neighbour countries were at a nadir, while – and perhaps because – those with the US were at an apex.

From Cold War to 'Guidelines'

When the postwar US–Japan relationship was formed – initially one between occupier/conqueror and occupied/defeated – it was predicated

on Japan being separate from Asia, content to be in satellite orbit around
the US. During the Cold War, decades passed before Japan slowly turned
its attention to 'normalizing' relations with Asia; even then it followed
the US lead, maintaining the assumptions of difference and separateness
from Asia and of the primary importance of the US. Questions of
colonialism and war responsibility, long shelved, only came to demand
serious attention in the parliaments and public opinion of the region –
and in Japanese courts – after the end of the Cold War.

Though the Japanese media celebrated the warmth of the Bush–
Koizumi relationship, the term 'treaty relationship' was in fact first
used only in 1981 – and when then-Prime Minister Suzuki used it, it
caused an uproar. His foreign minister had to resign and, by saying
that his statement 'had no military implications', Suzuki made the fuss
worse. In the quarter-century that followed, the terms of the treaty did
not change, but the relationship did: it was revised *in practice*. It
remained profoundly unequal, but it was inconceivable that any
Japanese minister could ever deny that it was actually an alliance,
or that it had very large military implications. It was only under
Koizumi, however, that it came to be accepted without question that
Japan was America's Asian ally. If ever there was an alliance accomplished by bureaucratic stealth, this was it.

From its foundation in 1955, the ruling LDP committed itself to the
American goal of abolishing Article 9 – its constitutional 'peace clause'–
in order to respond better to both nationalist pressures and American
designs. The US had regretted almost from the start its 1946 decision to
insist on Japan adopting Article 9. At the time, however, it had been
necessary to reassure Japan's neighbours, including Australia, that there
was nothing to fear from a Japan which, at American insistence, would
retain at its masthead the same emperor who had just led it through
fascism and war. But as Japan's industrial recovery and integration with
the US proceeded, the desire to turn it into an active partner grew, and
the popular commitment to pacifism proved a formidable obstacle. The
SDF grew in size and sophistication of equipment, and the US became
increasingly dissatisfied with Japan's passive support, which was limited
to hosting and paying for the bases.

Through the late decades of the twentieth century, the US government served notice repeatedly that the limited and essentially one-sided
character of the 1960 Security Treaty relationship with Japan would no

longer do: a higher level of cooperation was required. Japan was assigned an active and leading role in dominating and regulating a US-dominated world order on the eastern periphery of the Eurasian landmass, similar to the one played by Britain in the West.

Compatibility with Washington's purposes during the long Cold War was never especially difficult to achieve – nor, for that matter, demanding. While the US prosecuted wars in Korea, Vietnam, and the Gulf, in which its bases in Japan – especially Okinawa – played a major role, the Japanese military role (that of the SDF) was passive and subsidiary. Successive prime ministers agreed that it would be 'absolutely impossible' for Japanese forces ever to function outside Japan.[8] The idea that US forces were in Japan to defend it against communist aggression was widely accepted, and for over half a century from August 1945, no Japanese soldier either killed or was killed in battle.

A hiatus followed the end of the Cold War, when many in Japan anticipated that 'victory' – the collapse of the Soviet Union and the end of any military threat it posed – would mean a renegotiation of Cold War relationships somewhat along the lines of the transformation that was taking place in Europe. But that expectation was short-lived. The Cold War relationship was indeed renegotiated, but in the direction of intensified military preparations and commitments, culminating in a 2005/06 agreement to the fusion of command and intelligence between Japanese and US forces.

In 1991, even though it bankrolled the Gulf War to the tune of $13 billion, Japan was roundly criticized for having done too little, too late, because it declined on constitutional grounds to participate in the multinational force. Tokyo was shocked at the criticism – even traumatized, in the view of some commentators – and has ever since struggled to overcome the 'handicap' of its constitution.

In 1992, a Peace Keeping Organization Law was adopted, followed by a series of laws to justify SDF peacekeeping missions to post-conflict Cambodia, Mozambique, the Golan Heights, and East Timor. Although confined to road-building, or the construction and running of hospitals and refugee camps, these missions involved a steady widening and loosening of the official interpretation of Article 9, in the sense that a force whose only justification was the defence of Japan against direct or indirect threat, was committed, however innocuously, in various global theatres.

In the late 1990s, Japanese security complacency was shattered – first in 1998, when a North Korean rocket flashed through its skies and fell into adjacent Pacific waters, and then in 1999, when the Maritime Self-Defence Force (MSDF) engaged for the first time in its history in the unilateral exercise of force against the so-called *fushinsen* – intruding 'suspicious-looking ships' which sped across Japanese waters and disappeared in the direction of North Korea when chased. Although the naval action was in apparent breach of the law defining when such force might be legitimately used,[9] more than 80 per cent of the population approved, finding the action to be either 'appropriate under the circumstances', or even inadequate.[10] The mood in hitherto somnolent Japan had changed, as a direct result of fear and anxiety over North Korea.

In accordance with the new US security doctrine defined by the Nye Report (the 'East Asian Strategy Review') of 1995, the presence of US forces in the region was described as the 'oxygen' making economic growth and prosperity possible. Consequently a 100,000-strong US force was to remain stationed in Japan and Korea 'for the foreseeable future'. The bases – far from being liquidated, as people had come to hope (especially those in Okinawa) – were to be upgraded and freed from the restrictions on their use. The general principles of the Nye Doctrine were subsequently affirmed at the Clinton–Hashimoto Summit of April 1996, with its 'Joint US–Japan Statement on Security' fleshed out in the 1997 'Guidelines for US–Japan Defense Cooperation',[11] and carried through into legislation with the 1999 'Regional Contingency Law'. Japan's role was reactive: to adopt the necessary legislative and administrative steps to reinforce its own military capacities, to ease the legal and constitutional constraints on them, and in general to ensure that the Nye Doctrine was carried out.

Despite the insistence of Prime Minister Obuchi Keizo (July 1998–April 2000) that the new arrangements not go beyond the existing Security Treaty, their effect was a major de facto revision and expansion of Cold War cooperation agreements.[12] The official position was that 'rearguard support' (*koho shien*) would not amount to belligerence on Japan's part, and therefore would not involve it in any hostilities – but that was nonsense, of course. The conservative nationalist, Gotoda Masaharu, objected: 'What sort of distinction can there be in modern warfare between the frontline and the rear?'[13]

The transformations underway were enormous, but, perhaps for that reason, public scrutiny and debate were avoided. On both sides of the Pacific, the memory remained fresh of what had happened in 1959–60, when debate over revision of the Security Treaty had thrown the country, under then Prime Minister Kishi Nobusuke, into chaos – calmed only by his resignation (after a forced passage of the legislation through the Diet). What did it mean for Japan to pledge to provide 'rear support' for the US in the event of 'situations in areas surrounding Japan'? The wording of the crucial phrases was a study in ambiguity. Unlike the United States–Japan Security Treaty, which applied to 'the Far East and its surrounds', the new agreements were declared to have no geographic sense, only a 'situational' one, applying to 'situations likely to affect the peace and security of Japan'. 'Situation', nowhere clearly defined, seemed to mean something very close to 'war', while 'rear support' meant the free use not only of base facilities and supplies, but also of Japanese roads, ports, hospitals and airfields. Under the 'Guidelines' – in post-Cold War, constitutionally pacifist Japan – the level of preparedness for war far surpassed that of the Cold War period. Japan had signed up to support US efforts to institute a new, post-Cold War global order.

Even under pressure in the National Diet, the Japanese prime minister would not say what sort of *situation* was contemplated; but Washington made quite plain that the context was an intensification of readiness for a second Korean War. In the spring of 1994, when war with North Korea was planned under something called 'Operation 5027', and came very close to actuality, American estimates were for a 90-day war costing $1 trillion, and resulting in at least 1.5 million casualties (52,000 from the US military, 490,000 from the South Korean military, and about 1 million Korean civilians), plus almost unimaginably extensive physical devastation of the Korean peninsula, north and south.[14] Such a catastrophe was only averted at the last minute. The revision of the security relationship with Japan pursued since then was designed to regain for the US the sort of freedom of manoeuvre, and of use of facilities in Japan, for an anticipated 'Second Korean War' that it had enjoyed during the first (1950–53). The 'Guidelines' agreements were meant to ensure that, in such an event, Japan would be thoroughly integrated into the war-fighting machine.[15]

The acceptance of this subordinate role in military and strategic matters consolidated Japan's position as a reliable dependency. That process required a simultaneous stress on nation, and coincided with a growing reliance on the symbols of national identity, as if that identity were sovereign and indivisible. Thus the flag and anthem law was adopted in 1999, upgrading and giving legal sanction to the symbols of national identity.[16] The philosopher Tsurumi Shunsuke wrote at the time of the feeling that he was witnessing the making of a *fin de siècle* opera, grander even than Verdi's celebration of Italian nationalism a century before, with the Japanese and American flags waving and anthems blaring across the stage as the great spectacle evolved and 'the Japanese people were united again, as once around the ideals of the Meiji state, *but this time in the service of the United States*' (italics added).[17] The pomp and triumphalism of the late nineteenth century were turning, at the end of the twentieth, into a theatre of the absurd.

The American demands were welcomed as opportunity for Japanese rightists to pursue their own agenda. Senior defence officials floated the balloon of Japan possessing a right to preemptive attack, and even its own nuclear weapons (see Chapter 8). They apparently believed that Japan's peace constitution no longer ruled out either a unilateral Japanese act of war against a neighbour state or possession of nuclear weapons. However, the American pressure on Japan was designed to remove inhibitions on its contribution to US purposes, but not to turn it into a potentially autonomous nuclear power. The officials who had gone too far were shunted aside, therefore, while the process of subordinate integration of Japanese and US forces proceeded.

Maturity: Japan onto the playing field

The 1997 Guidelines arrangements committing Japan to 'rear support' in 'situations' in Japan's 'environs' were not enough. According to the Japanese government's understanding, Japan possessed an inherent right of collective self-defence but was constitutionally prohibited from exercising it: Japanese forces could only participate in multilateral operations subject to the rule of non-involvement in combat or areas where combat was underway. The next Washington objective was to remove this constraint. That strategic objective was clear even before the events of 11 September 2001, but it took that shock and the escalating East Asian tension over North Korea to bring it close to realization.

On the eve of George W. Bush's accession to the presidency, a 'bipartisan group of then-former government officials, foreign policy and national security analysts, and interested scholars' concerned with the relationship with Japan met in Washington under the auspices of the Institute for National Security Studies, and the leadership of Richard Armitage and Joseph Nye.[18] Two of their number were soon to become Deputy Secretaries in the George W. Bush administration: Richard Armitage at the State Department and Paul Wolfowitz at the Department of Defense. Recommendation 3 of their report, entitled 'The United States and Japan: Advancing toward a Mature Partnership',[19] referred to Japan's prohibition against collective self-defence as 'a constraint on the alliance', and offered the special relationship between the US and Great Britain as the model for a future relationship, with Japan becoming the 'Britain' of East Asia. Throughout the Bush administration, it may be that no goal has been pursued with such unswerving consistency and conspicuous success as that of developing what Armitage and Nye called the 'mature relationship'.

To achieve that 'maturity', and 'in the interests of closer and more efficient security cooperation', Japan would have to lift its prohibition against collective self-defence, since that was 'a constraint on alliance cooperation'. It should also take steps to 'improve its economy', by which was meant that it should open its markets: 'there must be greater transparency in accounting, business practices, and rule making . . . Deregulation should be accelerated . . .'. As one prominent American critic noted at the time, the strangest aspect of the report was that 'roughly half of it is filled with suggestions for what Japan must do'.[20]

Although noting that the Japanese were 'averse to radical change, except in circumstances where no other options exist', the Washington group was setting comprehensive goals for its government, implying that indeed Japan had 'no other options'. They assumed without question the prerogative to decide what was best and necessary for Japan, and it is unlikely that they were troubled by the thought of how they would respond were Japan to counter with a similar 'report' urging Americans to 'change their constitution on matters of defence, consume less, save more, and send US Marines home'.[21] The fact that 'maturity' in the relationship would be reached to the extent that Japan submitted to the US agenda was a pointer to how *immature* the relationship really was.

In similar vein, an influential Rand Corporation report, in June 2001, spelled out that it was fundamental that Japan 'continue to rely on US protection', and that any attempt to substitute for it an entente with China would 'deal a fatal blow to US political and military influence in East Asia'.[22] Recommendation 3 of the report's Executive Summary went on to urge: 'Support efforts in Japan to revise its constitution, to expand its horizon beyond territorial defense, and to acquire capabilities for supporting coalition operations.' For Washington, the thought that Japan might one day begin to 'walk its own walk', intent on becoming the 'Japan of the Far East' rather than the 'Britain of the Far East', was a nightmare. It was destined, therefore, to become a 'partner' able to render full military, political and diplomatic support on a global scale. For that, a comprehensive reordering of its institutions was necessary.

These recommendations became the kernel of the Japan policy of the Bush administration. Within days of the 9/11 attacks on the US, Richard Armitage – by then deputy secretary of state – issued the blunt advice that Japan would have to pull its head out of the sand and make sure that the Rising Sun flag was visible in the coming Afghan war.[23] Ten days later, Koizumi spoke the following words on the White House lawn:

> I'm very pleased to say, we are friends. Had a great talk, friendly. And I convey what I am thinking. We Japanese are ready to stand by the United States government to combat terrorism. We could make sure of this global objective. We must fight terrorism with a determination and a patience. Very good meeting. Fantastic meeting.[24]

His excitement over the 'great talk' and 'fantastic meeting', and his friendship with the president, were oddly out of keeping with the gravity of the occasion and the immensity of the commitment (still to be ratified by the Japanese parliament) that he was making. In due course Japan adopted an 'Anti-Terrorism Special Measures Law', and sent a flotilla of 24 naval ships to the Indian Ocean, which over time provided about one half of the fuel needs of the allied war force in the Afghanistan War. The dispatch of the SDF to the Indian Ocean was an important step in the direction of the objective, repeatedly insisted upon by Washington, of participation in 'collective self-defence'. It meant a commitment to back the US in this and future wars, and to do so not just financially (as had been the case in the Gulf War).

Crucially, it meant Japan's entry into the war against terror and submission to American strategic leadership.

Apart from the very substantial constitutional issues surrounding the Japanese involvement, the coalition's attacks were of dubious legality.[25] Military action under Article 51 of the United Nations Charter, the 'self-defence' clause, could only be justified in the immediate wake of an attack, and not before the machinery of the Security Council could be activated. Even then it is required to be necessary, proportionate, not inspired by vengeance, and not harmful to civilians – conditions that certainly were not met in Afghanistan. Although the 'threat or use of force as a means of settling disputes' was proscribed by Japan's constitution, the Maritime Self-Defence Force's state-of-the-art Aegis frigate, equipped with missiles and torpedoes, sailed off to the Indian Ocean as part of the international force for Afghanistan.

For Japan to move, with minimal public debate, to support the US war, sidelining the UN, was crucially to modify its postwar diplomatic principle of a UN-centred foreign policy. When the US withdrew from the World Court in 1986, in protest against being found guilty of 'unlawful use of force' (the mining of harbours and funding of the Contras – in effect terrorism) against Nicaragua,[26] or when it engaged in the sporadic, decade-long bombing of Iraq and the 1999 bombing of Yugoslavia – almost certainly illegal acts – Japan had simply turned a blind eye.[27] Washington's rejection of the Kyoto Agreement on Climate Change and the International Criminal Court, and its secession from the Anti-Ballistic Missile Treaty, were further signs warning Japan that the US was increasingly becoming a country above (or outside) the law. Richard Perle, a key figure in the Reagan administration and an adviser to the Bush administration, told a conference in Toronto in May 2001, four months before 9/11, that the US 'should not be bound by any international agreements that would restrict its unilateral capacity to ensure American security. The friends of the United States should have no worries about a "Pax Americana" – he used the term – since America's intentions are benign.'[28]

One prominent Japanese scholar wrote: 'The United States, which claims to be the world's policeman, has been acting on its own values, logic and interests since the end of the Cold War, ignoring the United Nations and other international circles. It is the United States that is becoming a rogue state.'[29]

Iraq: down to the 'baseball diamond'

In March 2003, the 'coalition of the willing' went to war against Saddam Hussein's Iraq. From early April, once the war proper was over, Koizumi came under heavy pressure to make good his promise of unconditional support. Armitage urged that Japanese 'boots on the ground' be committed to the occupation of the country,[30] following up with advice that Japan should 'quit paying to see the game, and get down to the baseball diamond'.[31] At their tête-à-tête in Texas in May, Koizumi gave Bush his pledge to send the boots required, and also pledged to speed up the review of 'missile defense' – a project dear to the Bush administration. In return, for the first time, Bush declared his 'unconditional' support for the Japanese position on the families of the North Korean abductees – that North Korea would have to satisfy Japanese demands before there could be any easing of sanctions on that country (see Chapter 5). It was, as a senior LDP official admitted, a deal: Japanese forces sent to Iraq in exchange for US support for Japan's position on North Korean issues.[32] While formal diplomatic statements referred to weapons of mass destruction and, later, the cause of Iraqi democracy, in the Japanese domestic political context the key point was that troops had to be sent to Iraq because the US forces in Japan were essential to defence against North Korea, and therefore Japan had to satisfy American demands.

Upon his return to Japan from Texas, however, Koizumi dithered in the face of formidable domestic opposition, and the pressure was renewed. An anonymous Defense Department spokesman put the message bluntly to his Japanese counterpart: 'Why don't you shape up?'[33] Armitage admonished Japan's special ambassador to the Middle East, Arima Tatsuo: 'Don't try to back off.'[34] Armitage also offered the gratuitous advice that 'I have come to believe it necessary for the Japanese Cabinet Legislative Bureau [responsible for interpreting the constitution] to take a flexible interpretation' of the right to participate in collective security.[35] In other words, it was simpler for Japan to do the US's bidding by the device of interpreting away the remaining content of Article 9, rather than go to the trouble of revising it, as Armitage had earlier urged. He was to repeat this advice, favouring a 'flexible' interpretation of the existing words early the following year.[36]

In July, the Special Measures Law for the Reconstruction of Iraq was adopted. As the Japanese deliberations continued, David Kay – the former senior investigator in the search for Iraqi weapons of mass destruction – concluded that it was 'highly unlikely' that there were any such weapons. Unshaken, Koizumi told the Diet on 25 November 2003: 'I believe President Bush is right and he is a good man.'[37] A Foreign Ministry official remarked of the Kay Report: 'It is like being betrayed and bitten by a pet dog you trusted.'[38] In the high diplomacy of the US–Japan relationship, the intervention of truth and independence of mind was tantamount to the ravings of a mad dog. It was early 2004 before units of all three of Japan's Self-Defence Forces (air, sea, and land) left for Iraq.

When the SDF marched off, with substantial armed force, to the Iraq war, they were entering uncharted constitutional waters. Even the most hawkish of previous prime ministers had in the past insisted that any overseas troop deployment would be 'absolutely impermissible'.[39] In taking this major step, the Japanese government was flouting its own previously held interpretation of its constitution. It also lacked legal justification (a Security Council resolution) or moral pretext (WMD). 'Trustworthiness' outweighed constitution, law, and morality.

As he watched Japan scramble to comply with the various demands, adopting an Iraq Special Measures Law and sending off the SDF – supposedly on a humanitarian and reconstruction mission – to Samawah in Iraq's Al Muthanna province, Armitage remarked that the US government was 'thrilled' that Japan was not 'sitting in the stands any more', but had come out as 'a player on the playing field'.[40] Japan was seen to be at last overcoming its war and defeat syndrome, moving from 'pacifism in one country' to assume a diplomatic and military role in the region commensurate with its status as the world's second-largest economy, overcoming its inhibitions about the possession or exercise of military force, and behaving appropriately as an advanced, industrial democracy tied closely to Washington.[41] Both the US and Australian governments had long abandoned any sympathy for the pacifist aspiration they had once cultivated in Japan.

When the decision was ratified in the House of Representatives at the end of January, the government relied on a special investigative mission to Iraq, which had reported that security problems were minimal, and the SDF could safely go to Samawah. It later transpired that this report had been drafted by bureaucrats even before the group left Tokyo in mid-September, and that it had been further edited before being submitted to the Diet in January by the removal of details that might have sounded negative.[42]

Still, opposition in the parliament and the country was such that the vote had to be postponed until after midnight, when the chamber was boycotted en masse not only by the main opposition party, the Democratic Party of Japan, which protested that the law was unconstitutional, but even by some of the most influential members of the ruling LDP itself. Three of the party's top figures – the former head of its policy planning committee, Kamei Shizuka, and two former secretaries-general, Kato Koichi and Koga Makoto – rejected Koizumi's justification for war. Former Posts and Telecommunications Minister and Parliamentary Deputy Defence Minister Minowa Noboru even launched an action in the Sapporo District Court to have the troop dispatch declared unconstitutional.[43] When the Japanese ambassador to Lebanon, Amaki Naoto, wrote to the prime minister protesting that the troop dispatch would breach both the Japanese constitution and international law, he was summoned to Tokyo and peremptorily sacked.[44] Former Deputy Prime Minister and LDP *éminence grise* Gotoda Masaharu described the war as 'a one-sidedly aggressive war by the US and UK on the basis of manufactured intelligence'.[45]

constitutional qualms were overwhelmed by a flood of sentiment. The Japanese people were slowly won over by their determined prime minister, and by the barrage of media messages to the effect that the SDF men and women were 'engineers', not really soldiers, and that their operation was purely humanitarian (*jindo fukko shien* or 'humanitarian and recovery assistance') – somehow divorced from the war and occupation. Koizumi described the SDF men and women as the 'pride of their families, the pride of Japan and the pride of the Japanese people', and the media enthusiastically portrayed the hometown boys (and some girls) in boots as heroes, lavishing attention on their every move: training in Hokkaido's snow for the Iraq desert, performing rituals of regimental colours, waving farewells to their tearful families and crowds of flag-waving supporters. Colonel Bansho Koichiro, the SDF commander, became a media favourite for his rough, homespun sincerity, and was to be seen day after day giving friendly speeches in halting Arabic discussing how to revive the local hospital, or presenting gift sheep to a local community. Where popular opposition to the decision to send the SDF to Iraq had been running at between 70 and 80 per cent in early-to-mid-2003 (before, during and immediately after the main hostilities), by early 2004 Koizumi had performed the remarkable political feat of turning that around, so that a small but absolute majority was in favour.[46]

Despite sporadic shelling of their camp, and a steady decline in security conditions throughout the country, the SDF survived the war unscathed. Even as public opinion in the US and Britain turned against the war, one after another country abandoned the 'coalition of the willing', and Poland's president expressed anger at the US and British deception on which the war had been based, suggesting that an apology was in order, in Japan support for Japanese troops rose steadily as they carried out their mission in a tiny sliver of Iraqi territory. A few shells were fired at their encampment, doing little damage, and – alone among political leaders who had supported the war – Koizumi's domestic support did not suffer. When eventually, in mid-2006, Japanese land forces were withdrawn (leaving the air SDF contingent), his popularity was still riding high.

As in Afghanistan, Prime Minister Koizumi was fulsome in his words of support for the Iraq war, did his best to help finance it, ignored questions of legality, cooperated in sidelining the UN, and sent a Japanese military ('self-defence') unit to take part in the occupation. Yet, as was suspected then and has come to be well known since, that war was without Security Council warrant, was launched on a false pretext, and was conducted in defiance of international law from its origin, down to – most infamously – the institution of a global regime of torture and illegality that stretched from Guantánamo to Abu Ghraib. The dispatch from Japan of forces whose sole legal warrant was as the 'minimum necessary force for the protection of Japan against direct or indirect threat' to assist in war and occupation in Iraq took Japan a long way from its constitutional pacifism. But Japanese forces could still not operate like the British, and in their 'humanitarian' role they had to be protected – first by mercenaries, and later by British and Australian forces. Washington was not satisfied, and the pressure for further military 'reorganization', and revision of the constitution was therefore stepped up.

Until its collaboration with the British–American force in Iraq, Japan had enjoyed respect throughout the Middle East as a non-Western, economically advanced power, which had been a nuclear victim, and was neutral on the Israel–Palestine question and constitutionally opposed to the use of force to resolve international disputes. By sending its armed forces as part of the US-led 'coalition of the willing' it took sides – inadvertently inviting the hostile attention of the enemies of the US throughout the region.

Koizumi defended the dispatch by saying that the intervention would be confined to humanitarian and reconstruction work exclusively in 'non-combat' areas, and would not use force. 'I am sending the SDF', he said, 'because there is no security problem . . . the security situation in Samawah is completely safe and there is no risk'.[47] For the US authorities under which the SDF served, however, all of Iraq was a combat zone. Koizumi conceded that the situation was so dangerous that Japan should not entertain any other presence in Iraq than that of a well-armed military unit; but he still argued that Samawah was a non-combat zone in the sense that there were no hostilities being conducted by 'states or quasi-state organizations'. It was a casuistry worthy to rank with the lies and manipulations practised in the US and elsewhere to justify the war.

In the first half of the twentieth century, 7 million Japanese soldiers marched off to distant battlefields with shouts of 'banzai!' ringing in their ears. Not one of them had ever been sent, officially, on a mission of 'aggression'. Like Colonel Bansho's, their task was always honourable: to resist the aggression of others (the Russo-Japanese War of 1904–05); to fulfil duties to allies (the Boxer war in China of 1900 and Second World War); to help the people of a neighbour country (the Russian people against the Bolshevik revolution, 1918–25); to defend Japanese lives and property against bandits, terrorists and warlords and help construct an order of justice, peace and prosperity (in China, and later Southeast Asia, from 1927 to 1945). Only long after the event did history render a different, much harsher judgment. Many Japanese scholars today gloomily suspect that the same will be true of the Koizumi dispatch to Iraq.[48] One influential thinker described the US operations in Iraq as an aggressive war comparable to Japan's invasion of China that had started in 1931 – both, he argued, characterized by defiance of international society and the belief that military superiority would be decisive. In his view, Iraq was America's Manchukuo – a base from which to try to transform the Middle East, as Japan had once thought to transform the whole of China, and just as likely to mark the beginnings of imperial decline.[49]

Constitutional and legal niceties were of little interest to the Iraqi residents of Samawah. They generally welcomed the Japanese troops, hoping at least that they would bring with them jobs, clean water, electricity, better medical facilities, and better roads. Some locals expressed disappointment that Japan had sent them soldiers rather than the corporate forces of Toyota or Sony; but at least the Japanese SDF presence was preferable to an American or British one. The Japanese force – around 600 soldiers, two-thirds of whom were devoted to security or administration – were from the start part of the occupying force, serving its overall goals and sharing the responsibility for the chaos that slowly engulfed the country. They functioned in a tiny area (roughly 1 per cent) of the country, housed in 'one of the most formidable military camps planet earth has ever seen' – an isolated fortress, secure behind its own moat and barricades, with its own karaoke bar, massage parlour and gymnasium.[50] The operation, whose initial mission was to supply 80 tons of fresh water daily to 16,000 people, together with some assistance in refurbishing local schools and hospitals, was fabulously expensive, costing approximately ¥40 billion ($360 million) in its first six months. By contrast, the French Agency for Technical Cooperation and Development (ACTED), an NGO, provided services in gas, water, health and sanitation (including a seven-times-greater supply of water than the Japanese in Samawah – 550 tons daily) to 100,000 people in Al-Muthanna province, at a fraction of the annual cost (just over half a million dollars – approximately ¥60 million). The NGO provided a low-cost, low-profile and high-impact operation, the money going mostly on the hiring of tankers, and virtually all the labour being provided by local Iraqis. The Japanese SDF operation had a high cost, a high profile, and low impact.[51] Political purpose trumped economic sense or humanitarianism.

When an Iraqi provisional administration was installed in June 2004 – in accordance with UN Security Council Resolution 1546 – Koizumi described the new resolution as 'a victory for America's righteous cause', and promised that the Japanese troop commitment would continue under the multinational force. Strictly speaking, participation in any multinational *force* was constitutionally forbidden, so Koizumi stressed that it was subject to four conditions: non-use of force, confinement to non-combat areas, adherence to constitutional limits, and operation under Japanese command.[52] The words 'unified command', clear in both the resolution itself and in Secretary Colin Powell's accompanying letter to the Security Council, were rendered not by the precise Japanese equivalent, but by a vague, unfamiliar and equivocal term meaning 'joint command headquarters'.[53]

Although official Japan thus supported war and occupation, much of Japan's civil society opposed it, and tried to address humanitarian concerns in a completely different way. While the soldiers in their impregnable five-star encampment maintained their supply of water to Samawah, but otherwise remained mostly invisible, three young Japanese were taken hostage in April 2004. One was a volunteer returning to Baghdad to resume work with abandoned street children; another was a student investigating and publicizing the health effects of depleted uranium; and the third was a journalist committed to photographing and making known to the world the struggles and suffering of the Iraqi people. Held for a week, from 7 to 15 April, they were in due course released through the good offices of the Islamic Clerics Association. A second group – two journalists seized on 14 April – was released three days later.[54] These representatives of Japanese civil society and their families became victims – even before their release – of a government and media campaign to legitimize the official SDF mission, and to discredit them as reckless and irresponsible. Their detention may even have been prolonged by Koizumi's use of the term 'terrorists' to describe their captors, or Foreign Minister Kawaguchi's television message (broadcast on Al-Jazeera) calling for the release of the abductees, but arguing that they and the SDF were engaged on the same humanitarian mission. Japan's official stance contrasted sharply with that of its civil society. The families and support movement of the abductees desperately insisted on that difference, even as the government sought to blur it in order to legitimize the SDF operation.

During the detention crisis, government and major media groups treated the abductees' families and support groups coldly and with suspicion, and Prime Minister Koizumi refused to meet them. The national media, taking its cue from government ministers and spokes-persons, took up the cries of 'irresponsibility' and 'recklessness', and accused the abductees of causing Japan trouble and expense. The telephones, faxes and websites of the families were bombarded with abusive and intimidating messages. Responsibility for their plight was shifted onto the victims, and attention directed away from the nature of the occupation that official Japan supported. By the time the first group of three abductees had returned to Japan, the barrage of hostile criticism compounded – if it did not actually precipitate – a state of shock, so that they arrived home exhausted, humiliated, and, apart from mumbled words of apology, silent.

Although the three Japanese civilians were thus pilloried, it was they who had striven to put into practice the principles of the constitution – specifically its rejection of the role of armed force in resolving international disputes – while Koizumi was actively subverting it. Following these incidents, NGOs reported that their security had diminished, and that Japan's moral standing as a country of peace had been squandered, by the dispatch of the Japanese army (as Iraqis saw the SDF).[55]

By the time the Ground SDF was withdrawn from Iraq, in mid-2006, the US had lost more than 2,500 soldiers, most of them after hostilities had been declared over three years earlier; the Iraqi civilian casualty toll was almost certainly to be counted in six figures – one credible estimate put it at 655,000.[56] Having provided medical assistance on 267 occasions, supplied 54,000 tons of water, and repaired 27 bridges, 88 kilometres of road, 34 schools and 27 medical facilities, Japanese forces withdrew in mid-2006.[57] In the chaos and misery that overtook Iraq, however, the local good works performed by the Japanese forces were a minor blip; Japan's uncritical support for the war and occupation was much more important.

Alone among the countries that joined the 'coalition of the willing', there was never any serious political debate in Japan – even when the lies on which the war had been based were revealed. There was no parallel in Japan for the exposure in the 'Downing Street Memo' of the corruption and deception that had led to war, or for the steady decline in Blair's political fortunes as his unconditional submission to the American cause became known.[58]

Transformation and realignment

However momentous for Japan had been its participation in the Iraq war and occupation, it was still far too limited and passive to satisfy Washington. Japan still had a long way to go to become like Great Britain. At the February 2005 talks in Tokyo, this goal for Japan, enabling its forces to play a key role in overseas missions in the 'Arc of

Instability' stretching from Japan itself to the Middle East and North Africa through the coming century, was restated by a Defense Department official'.[59] In fact, the reorganization of the global military posture conducted under Defense Secretary Rumsfeld, designed to reduce American forces while increasing their mobility and capacity for fast response, and to shift more of the burden onto allies, went beyond cooperation between the US and Great Britain to envisage a measure of role-sharing and burden-sharing that amounted in essence to a *merger* of the US and Japanese forces. The significance of this was momentous, but public, media and parliamentary interest were low, attention focusing instead on the theatrics of Koizumi's Post Office privatization.

The reorganization of facilities and command in Japan – and Korea – was designed to establish special forces bases and to secure multiple routes for deploying those units in case of emergency. Reduction of the burden on host communities such as Okinawa was a secondary consideration. Japan and Korea were to be incorporated in an 'Alliance of the Willing' – not precisely on the same level as the UK and Australia, but nevertheless so as to play a crucial role in addressing future incidents of terror or disaster, and in containing China and North Korea.[60] The negotiations culminated in an interim agreement of November 2005, with a final document adopted the following May.

The Interim Agreement on the Realignment of US Forces in Japan, signed by the foreign and defence ministers of Japan and the US on 29 October 2005 and approved by Cabinet in Tokyo two weeks later, projected the comprehensive realignment of US forces in the transformation of the Cold War security relationship – in which, at least nominally, the defence of Japan had been the major priority – to a military alliance of partners in support of US regional and global objectives. The Japan agreement took longer to reach than similar agreements between the US and any other parts of the world, and was perhaps the most important, since it had the effect of converting the limited cooperation of the 1951 and 1960 versions of the security alliance into a true military alliance;[61] 'interoperability' and 'joint operations posture' were key phrases.

Under the Interim Agreement, the US and Japan agreed on 'common strategic objectives' and 'global challenges'. They would cooperate in the fight against terrorism, the Proliferation Security Initiative (PSI), Iraq, ballistic missile defence, and disaster relief operations. The principal goal of the alliance was defined as 'Defense of Japan and responses to situations in areas surrounding Japan, including responses to new threats and diverse contingencies.'[62] From a limited alliance for the defence of Japan against invasion or attack, the alliance became a comprehensive and global one for the war against terror.

The Japan Ground Self-Defence Force's 'rapid reaction force' would be moved to Camp Zama in Kanagawa prefecture, where it would share facilities and coordinate activities with the headquarters of the US Army's First Corps, to be transferred there from Fort Lewis in Washington State. The Japanese Air Self-Defence Force's headquarters would be merged with the headquarters of the US 5th Air Force at Yokota Base outside Tokyo. The Marine Corps' 'crisis response capabilities' would be reinforced by redeployment of its forces between Hawaii, Guam, and Okinawa, with a substantial force – 8,000 US Marines – transferred from Okinawa to Guam, and a major new base constructed in Okinawa by the Japanese government for the Marines, substituting for the existing base at Futenma, whose return had been promised for nearly a decade.

The costs would be staggering, and the Japanese government would foot much of the bill – eventually contributing – as agreed in April 2006 – $6.09 billion of a total bill of $10.27 billion. Even that was to be only a portion of the overall estimated cost of the ongoing reorganization, for which Japan was to pay another $26 billion over ten years.[63]

As Japan had paid through the nose for the Okinawa 'reversion' of 1972, and has continued paying to maintain the American bases there ever since, now it would pay to secure the 'reversion' of one base and the construction of another to replace it, plus a vast sum for unspecified other costs to support the continuing US occupation of bases in Japan, and the 'war on terror' generally. Furthermore, although the transfer out of Okinawa of 8,000 Marines might seem to offer the prospect of a reduced military burden, the agreement made clear that Japanese forces were expected to replace the Americans under the 'joint operations posture' and 'interoperability' principles. The precedent set in the 1970s of Japan paying exorbitantly for the return of Okinawan facilities (see Chapter 6) was by 2006 well established. This time, as in 1972, little would be returned (less than 10 per cent of Okinawan base land), and much would have to be provided anew.

The detailed plans for base relocation and the 'roadmap' for achieving all the agreed objectives were adopted six months later, on 1 May 2006.

A target date of 2014 was set for completion of the FRF (Futenma Replacement Facility) and the transfer of the Marines to Guam.[64] The deployment of missile defence systems – both the latest 'X-band' radar system at the SDF base in Aomori, Hokkaido, and of Patriot Pac-3 at US bases and facilities – would be accelerated. Missile defence costs alone were expected to rise beyond ¥1 trillion.

The upshot of the 2005/06 reorganization was a further qualitative change in the US–Japan security relationship. The Cold War arrangements, initially confined to the defence of Japan against external threat – an imagined Soviet invasion – and widened under the 1995 Defence Plan and 1997 'Guidelines' to 'situations' in the 'vicinity', were now transformed to a preventive alliance directed at stabilizing the entire world – by bringing it into accord with Washington's prescriptions. Operational plans drawn up in 1984 (*Japan–US Joint Strategic Plan 5051*) had assumed a Soviet invasion of Hokkaido, while in 1995 they had envisaged the dispatch of Japanese troops for a Middle East crisis (*Japan–US Joint Strategic Plan 5053*), and in 2002 a crisis (i.e. war) on the Korean peninsula (*Japan–US Joint Strategic Plan 5055*). All had been drawn up secretly, and presumably equivalent plans were being drawn up to meet the newly agreed common strategic objectives of 2005/06.[65] To complete the new agreement, new 'strategic plans' (presumably also secret) might be required, as well as further Japanese legislation, including constitutional revision, and perhaps legislation governing regular arrangements for the SDF to serve around the world. While most attention in Japan focused on the details – the implications for Futenma or Iwakuni or Camp Zama – it was the overall frame of shared values, structured assimilation, and the common US–Japanese geostrategic posture, which deserved it.

The strategic objective of the George W. Bush administration has been clear from the start: permanent global dominance. No state was to be allowed to grow to the point of ever challenging overwhelming US military superiority, backed by its insistence on the right to a nuclear first strike, set out in the Nuclear Policy Review of December 2001. The February 2006 statement of the *Quadrennial Defense Review* singled out China as having the greatest potential to present a competitive threat, and identified the consequent need for a greater military presence in the Pacific, and stepped up integration with allies to help prevent the threat from eventuating.[66] The lesson for Japan was that the US's 'unique relationships with the United Kingdom and Australia, whose forces stand with the US military in Iraq, Afghanistan and many other operations' were the 'models for the breadth and depth of cooperation that the United States seeks to foster'.[67] The head of the US Pacific Command (PACOM), Admiral William Fallon, told the Senate Armed Services Committee in March 2006 that both Japanese and South Korean forces were to be incorporated in a system of 'trilateral military cooperation', to deal jointly with rising Chinese power and influence, North Korea's possible collapse, and terrorist threats in Southeast Asia.[68]

By accepting the sharing of strategic objectives with a superpower that was committed to global hegemony, preemptive war and nuclear weapons, Japan was emptying of residual meaning its constitutional commitment to pacifism, and negating Article 6 of the Joint Security Treaty with the US, under which the US military presence in Japan was tied exclusively to defence of Japan and the Far East.[69]

The confrontation between Tokyo and the regions (whose autonomy is supposedly guaranteed under the constitution) steadily sharpened as the new arrangements were revealed. The local governments designated by the plan to play an increased military role in the future US–Japan alliance's burden-sharing arrangements immediately opposed it. Iwakuni, in Yamaguchi prefecture, was designated to become the most important military base in East Asia, with 120 warplanes, increasing from 57, plus naval and other units.[70] It conducted a plebiscite, which recorded opposition running at an overwhelming 87 per cent. In April 2006 a leading opponent of the planned 'reorganization' was elected mayor of the city, receiving more than twice as many votes as his conservative opponent. In Okinawa, everyone from the governor down was outraged. The supposed 'reduction of burden' was going to mean a massive concentration of military force in the north of the island – on its fragile coral, marine, and forest environment. War was to determine the semi-permanent identity of the island. Nation-wide, an *Asahi Shimbun* poll found that 84 per cent of people thought the government 'had not adequately explained the realignment'.[71] It would be more accurate to say that it had done its best to avoid explaining it at all.

Anger was by no means confined to local groups whose towns and villages were being incorporated in war plans without their consultation, but was strong even on the part of mainstream conservatives. Nonaka Hiromu, Chief Cabinet Secretary under Koizumi until 2003, expressed his 'anger and sadness' over the striking of such a deal by a handful of bureaucrats without consultation with the Japanese people (or any of the local governments of the regions, whose future was to be so profoundly affected), and at the 'haggling like banana sellers' over whether the new base at Henoko (the FRF) should have one or two runways.[72] Military critic Maeda Tetsuo saw the arrangements in the context of the mounting pressure to bring about 'regime change' in North Korea – in other words, to bring the Pyongyang regime to its knees by surrounding it with overwhelming force and serving it with ultimatums. He noted that, while the US was confident that it did not face any direct threat from North Korea, it was Japan that would suffer the greatest consequences from any North Korean collapse or war on the peninsula.[73] Sharpened military confrontation with China – Japan's putative enemy from 2004 – was implicit in the new arrangements; and in any clash over Taiwan Japan would have little say, but would bear the heaviest consequences.

A completely different view of the outcome was expressed, not surprisingly, by Richard Armitage. Reassessing his 'Armitage Report' in 2006 (having retired from government the previous year), he expressed himself well satisfied – delighted that Japan had done what he had advised, showing the flag in the Indian Ocean and getting its 'boots on the ground' in Iraq. Already, he thought, his goal had been accomplished: the US–Japan relationship was on a par with the US relationship with Great Britain.[74]

Japan as Great Britain

What might it mean to become a 'Great Britain'? Britain, of course, has long been close to the US, sharing a common language, close economic ties, and alliances against fascism in the Second World War, communism during the Cold War, and 'global terrorism' since 2001. The chain of more than thirty US military in Britain played a key role in each of these struggles, and especially in the wars in the Gulf, Afghanistan and Iraq. The largest airbase – Lakenheath, 30km northeast of Cambridge, with a complement of 5,000 service personnel – is larger than Brize Norton, the largest British base. It and other bases up and down the country, many of them known officially as British RAF sites, host US bombers, missiles, nuclear weapons caches, nuclear attack submarines, missile defence systems, and communications and intelligence gathering systems.[75] Britain also provides the US with strategically crucial bases in the South Atlantic (Ascension Island) and the Indian Ocean (Diego Garcia).

It has always been clear that the primary consideration for the base structure is the defence of the US. The US Air Force, having begun plans for atomic war on the Soviet Union just one month after the destruction of Hiroshima,[76] steadily built up its forces in Britain, designed only to deter attacks on British cities, not to defend them.[77] At the height of the Cold War, it was assumed that Britain would be devastated in nuclear exchanges with the Soviet Union – 'forty atom bombs would cripple the country, 120 would utterly destroy it'[78] – while the US would suffer much less, or, if all went well, even remain intact. With the transition from Cold War to the Global War on Terror, the scenario of large clashing main armies and massed bombers in all-out nuclear exchanges collapsed – but the base system remained, as a war-fighting system to which the defence of Great Britain remained tangential.

The inner workings of the relationship have always been shrouded in secrecy, but the more it is exposed, the clearer it becomes that it has been characterized by secret deals, cover-ups, and lies. To take only the most recent and egregious example, the 'Downing Street Memo', published in May 2005, revealed the high-level deceptions practised by the allies in 2002, including the tailoring of intelligence to suit a predetermined policy opening the way to war on Iraq, in the absence of any legal justification.[79] It is hard to imagine the US having fought the war alone, in defiance of the UN and all the major world powers; British support, in both planning and execution, was almost certainly indispensable. By 2006 it was possible to make a provisional assessment of what the alliance had wrought. The considered view of sixteen US intelligence agencies, including the CIA, was that the US (and presumably therefore the UK too) had been made less safe, and that the war was deepening the chaos of Iraq and 'breeding a deep resentment of US involvement in the Muslim world and cultivating supporters for the global jihadist movement'.[80]

One might wonder why Japan should seek to follow such a model. When Prime Minister Nakasone used the term 'unsinkable aircraft carrier' to describe Japan in 1983, volunteering the whole Japanese archipelago to the US as a bulwark against Soviet and/or Chinese communism, he was following the British path and thinking primarily of the defence not of Japan, but of the US. His offer, however, had an unfortunate ring, since the word 'unsinkable' had once applied to the Japanese battleship *Yamato* – in April 1945 the world's biggest, at 72,000 tons, but which nevertheless sailed to war only once. It was quickly sunk, taking with it almost 4,000 Japanese lives.

The 'benefit' of the alliance to Tony Blair and previous British prime ministers has nevertheless been thought incalculable. As a close ally of the global superpower, Britain earns a seat at the global 'top table', and can continue to believe itself a great power. Weapons technology – including nuclear weapons technology – and access to global arms markets and shared intelligence are thought to be priceless benefits. By 2006, however, Blair's popularity had sunk into the 20 per cent range, and the British people were finding the price too heavy. Discontent was growing with the alliance, the war, and Britain's servility; Blair's belief that being close to the centre of power enabled him to influence it no longer held water. The unrehearsed exchange picked up by the microphones at the St Petersburg G8 meeting in July 2006, showing President Bush treating Blair with contempt, seemed to many to encapsulate the relationship.[81] Japanese leaders, in rushing to emulate the British, could expect in future to be required to do much more for the alliance. The remarkable thing was that Blair suffered so much, and Koizumi not at all, for their enthusiastic embrace of the American cause.

In future much more was to be required of Japan; an 'even stronger Japan–US relationship' was necessary to cope with the emergence of China.[82] Not only was Japan to be assigned a huge burden of the ongoing costs of stationing US forces in Japan and relocating some of them to Guam, but, according to US Ambassador Thomas Schieffer, it would be expected to step up its defence spending and to take on 'an *equal role*' (italics added).[83] If he intended that to be taken in anything like a literal sense, Japan was to be asked to step up its defence spending by about ten times.

Under Koizumi, the US officials who, like Richard Armitage, descended upon Tokyo every so often to lecture and importune their Japanese opposite numbers on everything from the need to get troops on the ground in Iraq and revise the constitution, to that of privatizing the Post Office or importing American beef, were acclaimed as 'pro-Japanese'; yet it is hard to escape the feeling that they functioned rather as proconsuls, advising and instructing, while seeing Japan still as an imperial dependency, rather like General MacArthur a half-century earlier, who was acclaimed as a benevolent liberator even while treating the Japanese people as children.

The Japanese case for being a 'peace power' rather than a 'great power' is seldom heard; and when it is, it is heard almost exclusively from citizen groups and NGOs, not from the government. With the moral authority of its constitutional pacifism, with no enemies in the Islamic world and no involvement in the historic disputes and wars of the Middle East, and with the reputation of a nuclear victim country, Japan might have chosen to play a mediating, conciliating role – perhaps in formulating a 'Marshall Plan' for regional development, education, and welfare. Its credibility in an independent mediating role might also have been strengthened by the fact that collective madness and desperation were phenomena of which it had some relatively recent experience – the suicide bomb itself being a Japanese invention, and an instrument of Japan's Second World War planning. It might have played a significant and constructive role, mobilizing doctors, nurses, teachers, engineers, experts in locating and removing mines – ultimately serving the same goals of human rights, democracy, and justice that US leaders invoke, but doing so in a distinctive way as befitting its international position and its history. In the process, the Japanese flag might have come to be seen as a symbol of peace and cooperation. Instead it chose to ally itself totally with the US, and to give increasing primacy to the 'threat or use of force' as means of settling international disputes, despite its constitutional ban on them.

Five and a half years after Richard Armitage and Joseph Nye had set out their agenda for making the relationship 'mature' – when President Bush and Prime Minister Koizumi met for the last time in the context of a formal state visit, and the relationship was celebrated as 'one of the most mature bilateral relationships in history',[84] – the choice of words was surely no accident. The objective set out on the eve of the first George W. Bush administration had been accomplished. It was a singular American diplomatic triumph. Armitage's satisfaction with the relationship of which he had served as so central an architect was understandable, given that the US had no more compliant or generous ally – whether it was 'showing the flag', putting 'boots on the ground', providing massive infusions of cash, putting the major military force in East Asia under US command, or building brand new bases.

In truth, however, the relationship was so unequal as to warrant comparison with the treaties under which Japan had been incorporated into the global system in the nineteenth century. At no point in the extensive discussions – as they were reported in the Japanese or English media, or in the documents spun off from them – was there any trace of a distinctive Japanese strategy or vision. The governing principle was the simple one articulated by Koizumi:

> The United States is an irreplaceable ally of Japan and provides a vital deterrence that defends the peace and security of our nation. The United States also plays an indispensable role in securing the peace and security of the Asian region surrounding Japan . . . It is Japan's duty, and it is all too natural, that Japan should provide support as much as it can.[85]

Think 'billions'!

Apart from the large diplomatic and military costs that Japan was required to meet under the terms of its 'alliance', it also had to pay a very substantial direct financial subsidy for the US empire. The principle of such subsidy began in the 1970s with the 'reversion' of Okinawa. Japan was then booming, and the US was reeling from the effects of the war in Vietnam. The subsidy has continued and grown since then, however – even though, by the early twenty-first century, Japan itself was in dire financial straits.

Long before the advent of the Koizumi administration, Finance Minister Takemura declared, in 1996, that the country was in a state of 'fiscal crisis'. Late in 1999, when he found himself issuing a record ¥84 trillion in new national bonds, Prime Minister Obuchi described himself, with perverse pride, as 'king of the world's debtors'. Two years later Koizumi took the helm, promising drastic reform. Under him, the level of public debt soared to 170 per cent of GDP – higher than any state in modern times.[86] In his first four years he issued more than three times as many new bonds as had Obuchi, to a value of around ¥250 trillion. In 2006 the OECD pronounced Japan's debt level to be unsustainable. That should have merited Koizumi assuming the title of 'king of debtors' far more than Obuchi, yet he was acclaimed as a national hero.[87]

Japan is not only the world's biggest debtor, but also its greatest holder of foreign currency reserves, to a value of some ¥90 trillion yen (roughly $800 billion dollars) by 2006, overwhelmingly held in US dollars. It has significant assets, in other words, as well as liabilities, but its assets (under this head) cover only about one-eighth of its national debt. Furthermore, its dollar holdings could not be liquidated without triggering a global economic collapse, so they are really only assets in an abstract sense – perhaps best seen as a kind of taxation to sustain Washington's fiscal, military, and even cultural supremacy. Where other countries – notably China – have begun to balance their dollar holdings with euros, Japan shows little inclination to follow suit.

The paradox of the global financial structure is that it is precariously poised atop 'twin peaks' of Japanese and American debt – each of similar height. Public debt in the US at the end of August 2006 was approximately $8.5 trillion dollars,[88] and in Japan around ¥1 quadrillion (a one with fifteen zeros), or roughly $9 trillion.[89] The seriously ill Japanese economy takes every possible step to prop up the equally ailing US economy, pouring Japanese savings into the black hole of American illiquidity in order to subsidize the US global empire, fund its debt, and finance its over-consumption.[90] Japanese support has become the sine qua non of Washington's global, superpower strategy and status. According to Taggart Murphy,

> It was Japan that unleashed the floodgates of its burgeoning financial wealth in the early 1980s to finance the so-called Reagan Revolution – America's first experiment in steep tax cuts without concomitant spending reductions. It was Japan that pumped credit into the international system in the weeks after Black Monday – 19 October 1987 – when the US stock market lost one quarter of its value in a few hours. It was Japan that largely financed the first Gulf War . . . kept buying dollar securities right through the Asian financial crisis, 9/11 and the invasions of Afghanistan and Iraq . . . Japan continues to play the central role it has for 25 years now in supporting the global value of the dollar – and by extension, US hegemony.[91]

The benefit in this relationship is twofold: on the one hand, Japan satisfies Washington's need to sustain a huge inflow of funds to offset its deficits (and maintain consumer demand), and, on the other, keeps its manufactured exports competitive by preventing a sudden rise in the value of the yen. Since the Bush administration has chosen to plunge ever deeper into debt while maintaining tax relief for the rich, its trade deficit grows at around ¥100 trillion each year, and its fiscal deficit by about half of that amount, so the inflow of Japanese (and Chinese) funds must be maintained and even increased. US fiscal irresponsibility is in the long term unsustainable, but nowhere is confidence in it higher, and readiness to support it stronger, than in Tokyo.

Quite apart from these general, structural subsidies, Japan also pays staggering amounts in direct financial support to the US, much of it under the rubric of 'sympathy budget' (*omoiyori yosan*), more commonly known in English as 'host nation support'. Once the Japanese subsidies had begun, with the 'price' paid for the return of Okinawa in 1972 (see Chapter 7), there seemed to be no way of stopping them. Japan now subsidizes the approximately 40,000 US troops stationed in Japan to the tune of around $150,000 per head every year.[92] Chalmers Johnson insists that, whatever the strategic point, the economics of such a relationship are simply too attractive for the Pentagon to consider relinquishing it.[93]

The War on Terror in its Afghanistan and Iraq manifestations also entailed specific financial obligations for Japan. Its so-called 'rear support' for the anti-terror coalition included meeting the oil needs of allied ships in the Persian Gulf.[94] Subsequently, in addition to sending units of both ground and air Self-Defence Forces to Iraq as part of the 'coalition of the willing', asked for additional aid for rebuilding Iraq, and told that 'billions' was the appropriate unit for consideration,[95] Koizumi promised $5 billion – roughly five times the amount offered by the EU on behalf of the whole of Europe, or by Saudi Arabia.[96] In addition, under further pressure from Washington, the Japanese government indicated its readiness to forgo recovery of a large part of the debt owed to it by the government of Iraq.[97] Japan was by far the largest creditor, owed just over $4 billion.[98]

Japan has also promised to build for the US Marine Corps a brand new base complex in northern Okinawa, likely to cost at least an additional ¥1 trillion ($9 billion), to foot much of the cost of US force reorganization in Japan (several trillion more), and to purchase hugely expensive missile defence systems. The initial estimates for the latter called for ¥500 billion ($4.5 billion) over five years, but that soon doubled.[99] The Rand Corporation estimated that a basic system, capable of intercepting 'only a few North Korean missiles', would cost approximately $20 billion, and a full coverage system more than the national defence budget.[100] By 2006, Japan had spent around ¥600 billion on development,[101] towards an ultimate price tag expected to be around ¥2 trillion ($18.5 billion).[102] The best scientific and military opinion seemed to be that the systems (a combination of advanced radar (FPS-XX), SM-3 equipped Aegis destroyers, and Patriot Pac-3 anti-missile land-based batteries) might or might not work.[103] Under controlled test conditions, when the military knew in advance the size, speed and timing of their incoming missile, it worked for the Pentagon in September 2006, after the expenditure of around $100 billion.[104] However, the remark by Japan's former Defence Agency director-general, Ishiba Shigeru, that even a 40 to 50 per cent success rate would make them worthwhile, sounded more threatening than reassuring.[105] Furthermore, even if the Patriot system did work, its protection would be confined to places within a 15km radius of the batteries – meaning that the capital and major (US) base complexes might be protected, but not the rest of Japan.[106] Whatever the ultimate cost, the missile defence commitment integrated Japan ever more firmly under Pentagon control, stirred China's distrust, and threatened to provoke a regional missile race.

Washington has no other ally or customer in Japan's league of open-pocket generosity. Even as it squeezed health, education, and overseas aid programmes in the face of its fiscal crisis, and Koizumi spoke of nothing being sacrosanct from his reforming broom, such alliance 'taxes' clearly were sacrosanct. Come what may, Tokyo would honour its commitment to the US empire.

Japan's gross national debt itself also owes much to the peculiarities of its relationship with the US. During the trade and exchange disputes of the 1980s, the US insisted that Japan prime its pump and expand domestic demand, and the high priests of the Japanese construction state were happy to see this as justification for the fantastic boondoggle in debt-funded public works that brought the country to the brink of collapse. Responsibility for this disaster, and for the crisis in public finance, can scarcely be laid directly at the American door, but it was nevertheless the desperate attempts to prime the Japanese pump, taken at US insistence, that fed the corrupt, collusive public works system.

Koizumi inherited the system, and by his policies helped it cover up its criminality and shift the losses onto the public, adding substantially to Japan's debt mountain. His 'reform' agenda offered no clue as to how he would ever reduce it.

Both Washington and Tokyo insist that Japanese generosity – the 'sympathy' budget; the war subsidies; the 'reorganization' sums agreed in 2006; and the purely financial measures to shore up the dollar, such as the well over ¥30 trillion (around $250 billion) poured into the markets during 2003 and 2004 in the struggle against an ebb-tide of weakening demand for US Treasuries, bonds and stocks[107] – was spontaneous. Public support for it has never been measured, but it is fair to say that it is tolerated in grudging recognition that such 'taxes' are the price of trustworthiness, and the guarantee of US military backing in the event of a showdown with North Korea. On the US side, the denial by a 'senior White House official' that the US president would ever think of Japan as 'just some ATM machine' (that needed no secret number to operate) was so bizarre as to suggest that perhaps that might be precisely how he saw it.[108]

If Japan had indeed become what Armitage described as a 'player', there could be no mistake as to who was the captain and coach of its team, and no doubting the deadly seriousness of the game. Remarkably, the intervention in Japan's domestic affairs by the issuing of peremptory US advice and instruction did not become an issue. Armitage and others were regarded not as bullying proconsuls, but as friends of Japan. Armitage made clear in another context, talking to an Australian audience, that what he meant by 'alliance' was a relationship in which 'Australian sons and daughters . . . would be willing to die to help defend the United States. That's what an alliance means.'[109] Neither Armitage nor, for that matter, Koizumi had yet spelled out that 'bottom line' for Japan.

Asianism vs. Americanism

From its turbulent twentieth-century experience, Japan draws the lesson that it is most successful when allied to the global superpower – Britain in the first two decades, and the US in the last five. Such an alliance was the guarantee of security and prosperity, while the diplomatic isolation of the 1930s led to war and devastation, and was thus to be avoided at any cost.

The payment of subsidies to the dominant imperial power was therefore well worth it. These assumptions are so deep-rooted as to be difficult to contest, even though the circumstances of the security relationship with the US have fundamentally changed since the end of the Cold War.

Together with this assumption, Koizumi inherited the nineteenth-century paradigm of turning away from Asia. 'Asia' was then thought of as synonymous with backward, uncivilized, colonized (or likely to be colonized). Japan therefore insisted on its non-Asianness, its 'European' or honorary European status. In the twentieth century it adopted two different strategies for addressing Asia: in the first half of the century, as the quintessential Asian 'elder brother', with a manifest destiny to rule; and in the second half as a US-protected, 'Western' state. Both poses attempted to combine Asianness with non-Asianness, and both tended to arouse suspicion on the part of Japan's neighbours. The result is that Japan remains an outsider in Asia. As long as it preserved its psychological distance from its continental neighbours, Koizumi's Japan saw no option but to return the American embrace; that embrace in turn tightened, further blocking it from reconciliation and cooperation with Asia, and thus emboldening the US to tighten it further. In particular, as long as Japan's 'North Korea problem' (see Chapter 5) remains unresolved, and as long as the distance from China over issues of history and identity – most explicitly over Yasukuni – is not bridged, dependence on the US will continue.

This means, however, that if the North Korean problem were resolved, and if Japan could reach an accommodation with its neighbours based on a return to the understanding of history it briefly reached in the mid-1990s, then East Asia could be rapidly transformed. With relations normalized between Japan and North Korea, and between North and South Korea, Japan and China could commit themselves to a political partnership to match the economic ties that already link them so closely. The comprehensive incorporation of Japan within the US's global hegemonic project would become unnecessary, and Japan could shift its policy priority from that of being a trustworthy ally of the US to one of attending to its own multiple problems, and becoming a trustworthy member of a future Asian commonwealth.

In the 'Pyongyang Declaration' of September 2002 – for the first time since the ignominious collapse of the Greater East Asian Co-Prosperity Sphere in 1945 – Japanese and North Korean leaders joined in announcing a shared commitment to the building of a 'North-East Asia' of peace and cooperation.[110] That hope was quickly stymied, but it was not at all surprising that – as a conservative Japanese politician with a traditionalist heart, an eye to history and a desire to leave his mark on it – Koizumi also heard and was swayed by the siren song of Asia.

Though he was commonly seen as a nationalist, Koizumi's nationalism was more pose than substance. Faithful to Washington on almost everything, he had to disguise himself with strong Japanese national accents and postures: the more he served foreign purposes, the more important it was that he look and sound like a nationalist. What his nationalist pose disguised was therefore a form of neo- or pseudo-nationalism, located not on the level of policy and substance but on that of rhetoric and symbolism. Combining structural dependence with rhetorical bombast, it might be described as 'comprador', or 'parasite', or 'dependent'.[111] Leaders such as Koizumi and Abe, together with other prominent figures like Nakamura Shingo[112] and Ishihara Shintaro (governor of Tokyo),[113] express the nationalist aspiration in distorted and sublimated form, while they proceed to entrench and deepen national subordination under the terms of the Guidelines and the ongoing 'reorganization'. Nationalist dance and song are therefore mere pirouette and bluster within the palm of the 'Great Buddha' in Washington – the controversial gestures such as the prime ministerial visits to Yasukuni Shrine a sign not of a reviving nationalism so much as of an attempt to compensate for an abandoned one.[114] Political and military subordination *require* the accompaniment of nationalist rhetoric and symbolism.

However Japan addresses the dilemmas of regional and global policy, Washington's blueprints for the twenty-first century require of it a new level of subordination and integration, necessitating revision or substantial reinterpretation of the constitution and comprehensive neoliberal restructuring of its social and economic institutions. As the confrontation with North Korea sharpened, that process gained momentum. In the twentieth century Japan derived great benefits from serving the empire loyally and unquestioningly, and the costs were acceptable. The blueprints for the twenty-first century call for a new level of subjugation, and the cost rises steadily.

Buddies for ever?

The spectacle of George W. Bush and Koizumi laughing and joking together – the closest of buddies – is familiar from the photographic record of their meetings over five years. Together they rode the presidential golf cart, swapped baseball jokes, and visited Graceland. It is hard to know whether this reflected the warmth of mutual respect between equal partners, or that between a master and his faithful servant. Koizumi would never dare to offend Bush's Washington by taking a 'French' or 'German' stance on major issues; yet neither did he seek or expect to be taken into Washington's councils in the manner of, say, Britain's Blair. He was rebuffed on two occasions that we know about: in response to his suggestion late in 2004 that Bush respond to North Korean leader Kim Jong Il's overture for a meeting, and to his request in 2005 for Bush's help with the Japanese quest for a permanent seat on the UN Security Council. In the former case, he was met with a 'stony silence';[115] and in the latter, he was treated to an extensive lecture on the need for Japan to relax restrictions on the import of American beef.[116] It may well be that nowhere in the world did Bush have so unreservedly faithful and uncritical a follower. Commonly celebrated in Washington and Tokyo as 'mature' and 'equal', the relationship rested on US unilateralism and condescension.

The opportunity – presented by the end of the Cold War, the collapse of the Soviet Union, and by the end of LDP rule and of the '1955 system' – to seek a new path for the new century, seems to have been lost in Japan. A new order may be emerging in the wake of 9/11, but much about it looks familiar. Japan commits much to this new order, and is under heavy pressure to commit more in future. Its immense wealth and power contrast sharply with the sense of fragility, isolation, and vulnerability that hangs in the air. Japan's antennae continue to face firmly across the Pacific, as it strives to accommodate an ever more demanding Washington. Meanwhile, the displaced energies of the would-be nationalists are concentrated on causes such as the project to create a 'bright' history and a 'proud' Japanese identity by a return to the certainties of an earlier time.

Although the US–Japan relationship is conventionally represented as one in which Japan benefits from shelter under a US umbrella, the US no longer just 'protects' Japan (by maintaining a chain of bases through which American power is projected throughout Asia); it now demands more but offers less. With the 'War on Terror' solidifying as a state of permanent global martial law, Japan finds itself committed – indirectly but crucially – to an unfamiliar fundamentalism: a system responsible for multiple breaches of international law; for torture, assassination, and indiscriminate attacks on civilian and religious targets; for nuclear intimidation and preemptive war.

In the 1930s, it was the failure to resolve fundamental questions of national identity and relations in the region that had opened the way to war. In the 1990s, powerful political, bureaucratic and corporate forces in Japan combined to urge an answer to these questions by a formula combining obedience to the US with the construction of an exclusivist, proud, and pure Japanese history and identity. Such a formula is plainly contradictory. It makes little sense, as right-wing critic Nishibe Susumu puts it, to 'protect Japan's culture by becoming a 51st US state'.[117] Today there is no sign of the military fascism and expansionist aggression of the 1930s, but 'dependent nationalism' nevertheless threatens the region indirectly, encouraging the focus on windy rhetoric and manipulated symbols rather than on Japan's own ongoing structural subordination, and blocking the sort of deep engagement in the construction of a shared past and future with Japan's Asian neighbours that is needed to balance the trend towards unipolar American hegemony.

5

Japan in Asia

The year 2005 was the sixtieth year of the East Asian cycle, a time of completion and renewal. Commemorations of the events of sixty years earlier loomed large: in particular, the collapse of Japan's East Asian empire, which had spelled liberation for the region. But in sharp contrast with Europe, where representatives of the former enemy states of the Second World War gathered to commemorate the collapse of Nazi Germany and mourn the victims of war, Asia's commemorations were separate: Asia celebrated liberation and victory; Japan mourned defeat. It was inconceivable that representatives of the Japanese state could be honoured guests at commemorative events – in Nanjing, Harbin, or Beijing, or in Seoul or Pyongyang. The year that followed was steeped even more in unresolved resentment over the past, irritation over the present, and rivalry over the future. Despite the official proposition that the relationship with Asia would be just as good as that with the US, in fact the more that the latter was tightened and militarized, the wider and deeper became the gulf separating Japan from its Asian neighbours.

As the countries of the region struggled to find the formula for a European type of commonwealth that would give political expression to their economic interrelatedness, the twentieth-century legacy of imperialism and war continued to bedevil their efforts. For an East Asian community to be realized, Japan's historic rift with Asia would have to be healed; but during Koizumi's term of office it widened.

Japan's relations with both South Korea and China had rarely, if ever, been worse since they had been normalized, in 1965 and 1972 respectively. In the 1990s, with South Korea in particular, an entente seemed on the verge of blossoming. Prime Minister Obuchi issued a straightforward apology, President Kim Dae Jung declared the wish to set aside past differences, and a 'partnership for the twenty-first century' was declared. The two countries jointly hosted the World Cup in 2002, and a wave of enthusiasm swept over Japan for Korean culture – especially cinema, the slight, bespectacled figure of the movie star Bae Yong Jun becoming the most popular Korean in more than a millennium of contact between the Korean peninsula and the Japanese archipelago. But the promise was not fulfilled, and under Koizumi fierce contests raged over the legacies of wartime, including contention over both the facts of history and the necessity of apology, Koizumi's ritual visits to Yasukuni Shrine, and territorial sovereignty (over Dokdo Island, known in Japan as Takeshima).

Similar issues aggravated the relationship with China, with perhaps even more momentous implications. Along with Yasukuni and war history, China and Japan were at odds over territorial sovereignty and resource access in the East China Sea (especially the islands of Diaoyu/Senkaku, and possible oil and gas reserves in adjacent waters). With Koizumi dubbing China's protests over his Yasukuni visits improper Chinese intervention in Japan's affairs, and refusing to consider rethinking his position, summit meetings between Japan and China were suspended during his five years of office. From 2005, despite the closeness of their economic links, for defence and strategic purposes China began to be thought of as a potential enemy.[1] Abe Shinzo launched his government in 2006 with brief conciliatory visits to Seoul and Beijing, but gave no sign that he had seriously addressed the deep problems of identity, history, and territory.

The quest for a permanent Japanese seat on the UN Security Council became a major diplomatic initiative under Koizumi. The case was somewhat tarnished by his statement to the Japanese Diet that he looked for Japan's defence not to the UN but to the US – especially in light of Japan's participation in the US-led 'coalition of the willing' in Iraq despite its failure to gain endorsement for such action from the Security Council, and despite the evident displeasure of the Secretary-General Kofi Annan. Still, such participation was considered the ultimate badge of superpower status, which Koizumi set great store by gaining. As Japan concentrated its diplomatic energy on securing the permanent seat, China worked to block it. When the heads of all Japan's diplomatic missions around the world were recalled to Tokyo in 2005 to coordinate the last stages of the campaign, the result was a signal diplomatic humiliation. Only a handful of Asian countries (Afghanistan, Bhutan, the Maldives) voted with Japan.

No other advanced industrial state was at odds, as was Japan, with *all* of its neighbours, or so unable to win their support on what should have been a simple issue of principle: that as a global power, paying more than 19 per cent of the UN's budget (setting aside the US, more than all other permanent members of the Security Council put together), constitutionally committed to pacifism, it eminently deserved a Council seat. Perversely, however, the case that Japan was most reluctant to make – that it deserved such a seat because it was a country constitutionally committed to pacifism – should have been its strongest.

In 2001, speaking at a nationally televised 15 August meeting to commemorate the fifty-sixth anniversary of Korea's liberation from Japan, Kim Dae Jung said that the South Korean people 'earnestly hope that Korea–Japan relations run on a right course on the basis of a firm historical consciousness'. He went on,

> Many conscientious Japanese citizens watched with apprehension the distortion of history and their prime minister's paying tribute at the controversial war shrine . . . To our disappointment, however, some people in Japan are attempting to distort history, casting dark clouds over Korea–Japan relations again . . . How can we make good friends with people who try to forget and ignore the many pains they inflicted on us? How can we deal with them in the future with any degree of trust? Those are questions that we have about the Japanese.[2]

It was as severe a comment as had ever been made by a Korean leader about Japan.

In March 2005, Kim Dae Jung's successor as president, Roh Moo-Hyun, made it clear that, after forty years of so-called 'normalization' with Japan, the relationship was still far from normal.

> In order for the relations between the two countries to develop, the Japanese government and people needed to make sincere efforts to make the truth of the past known, and offer sincere apologies[,] and if necessary, pay compensation. Only then can we be reconciled.[3]

While Japan under Koizumi and Abe inclined towards positive embellishment of its history, and affirmation of the mid-twentieth-century war with Asia as a just struggle for 'Greater East Asia' – as it is presented in the museum attached to Yasukuni Shrine – South Korea proceeded in the opposite direction, towards a purge of the collaborationist strain from its history. In 2004 the Korean National Assembly adopted a 'Special Law on Truth Concerning pro-Japanese anti-Korean Activities during the Forcible Japanese Occupation', and set up a special committee to investigate the 'anti-national' activities of collaborationist Koreans. The following year, it adopted a 'Basic Law for Truth and Reconciliation'.[4]

Surveys showed that 90 per cent of people in South Korea did not trust Japan,[5] and a mere 6 per cent of people in China entertained 'friendly sentiments' (*shitashimi*) towards it.[6]

In 2006, the Japanese cabinet adopted a resolution declaring the tiny Dokdo/Takeshima islet, occupied by South Korea from 1954, part of its national territory since the mid-seventeenth century, thus implying that South Korea was illegally occupying it. South Korea, for its part, stepped up its defences in the waters around Dokdo, and President Roh denounced Japan's claim as 'provocative behaviour' by an 'ultra-nationalist Japan seeking to justify its history of aggression'.[7] When Japanese cabinet members responded to the launch of missiles by North Korea in July 2006 by raising the possibility of a Japanese preemptive strike against the launch facilities, South Korea's presidential spokesman, Jung Tae Ho, described it as a 'grave situation' in which Japan was trying to 'justify armed actions on the Korean peninsula', thereby revealing its 'natural inclination to invade'.[8]

Koreans recalled bitterly that Japan's 'opening' to the West, and its transformation from feudal to modern state in the 1850s and 1860s, was followed almost immediately by a debate over Korea that became known as the *Seikanron*: should Korea be treated as an equal, or should it be attacked and subdued? It seemed to Koreans at the beginning of the twenty-first century that little had changed save that North Korea had been substituted for Korea.

North Korea

The 'black hole' at the heart of the booming North-east Asian region – the obstacle to the emergence within it of any community of shared purpose, strategic vision, and prosperity – is undoubtedly North Korea: the unresolved legacy of Korean nationalism, Japanese colonialism, and the Cold War. Long neglected and reviled by Japan, during Koizumi's prime ministership it became a determinant of major tactical and strategic decisions by Japan relating to its own future and that of the region (including the decision to send its troops to Iraq).[9] As one of Japan's leading Korea scholars, Okonogi Masao, put it, 'No specialist envisages a preemptive North Korean attack. There is virtually one scenario – a preemptive US attack'.[10] Yet, while the specialists saw North Korea as a porcupine, stiffening its quills defensively[11] – or even as a snail, retreating into its shell in fear of any external contact[12] – the Japanese mass media and many politicians painted it as a tiger.

The North Korean regime was certainly anti-Japanese – it could hardly be otherwise, since it had been born out of anti-Japanese fascist guerrilla resistance of the 1930s. Its first leader had had a large price placed on his head by the Japanese authorities; and his son and successor, seventy years later, was still calling on the people to model themselves on the spirit of the partisans of the 1930s. That could not change until relations between past colonial ruler and the nationalist resistance movement were normalized.[13]

When the Cold War ended, there were moves to create a new order in East Asia. The veteran LDP figure and former deputy prime minister, Kanemaru Shin, led a multi-party Japanese delegation to North Korea in September 1990, and succeeded in the adoption of a tripartite declaration on normalization – adopted by the LDP, the Japan Socialist Party, and the Workers Party of Korea. It registered a Japanese apology, and expressed a desire to compensate for the misery and misfortune caused by thirty-six years of Japanese colonialism and the 'losses incurred' over the forty-five years since then, as well as a readiness to open diplomatic relations. North Korea, too, was keen to 'come in from the cold'. A 'cross-recognition' formula was devised, whereby China and Russia would normalize relations with South Korea while the US and Japan did the same with North Korea. But Japan's leadership lacked the resolve to pursue such a diplomatic initiative: its resistance to any compensation for post-1945 'losses' to North Korea; South Korean governments' negative attitude towards Japanese approaches to North Korea (until the advent of the Kim Dae Jung administration in 1998); suspicions over the North Korean nuclear programme; and – not least – US pressure, combined to block any progress. Nonaka Hiromu, a key LDP power-broker through the subsequent decade, writes in his memoirs of the 'cautioning' from the US that followed the Kanemaru initiative.[14] In effect, the US continued to exercise a veto on any independent Japanese diplomatic initiative through the first post-Cold War decade, while the situation surrounding North Korea steadily worsened. Kanemaru himself was arrested on corruption charges in November 1992. Not until the advent of the Koizumi administration in April 2001 did the logjam again shift.

Faced simultaneously with the rise of China as a great economic power and of South Korea as a mature and dynamic civil democracy, Japan under Koizumi pursued contradictory, even schizophrenic, strategies: fleetingly (as on his occasional visits to Pyongyang) as a partner in the construction of a regional community based on phenomenal economic growth and democratic institutions; but also, and with greater frequency and consequence, as a dependent and subordinate deputy in a militarized global US empire. While he kept up his annual visits to Yasukuni, outraging Japan's Asian neighbours, and cooperated with apparent conviction in the US's post-9/11 missions in Iraq and elsewhere, he also pursued the normalization of relations with North Korea as his personal political mission, and declared his faith in the future of the Northeast Asian region as a community. In other words, while on the one hand taking steps to lock Japan more firmly into dependence within a US-dominated global order, and using hostility towards North Korea as a fulcrum, on the other he took tentative steps towards resolving that very North Korean issue – surely aware that accomplishing that, or even moving significantly towards it, would be to shake the frame of US hegemony over Japan, and by extension East Asia generally.

With the Iraqi sector of the 'Axis of Evil' disposed of, in a fashion, by the overthrow of Saddam Hussein in 2003, the focus shifted to North Korea. Iraq had no weapons of mass destruction, but by most accounts (including its own) North Korea either had them or was in the process of gaining them. How to deal with this situation became perhaps the crucial question of Japanese foreign policy and of the US–Japan relationship.

North Korea exercises a powerful hold over the Japanese imagination, but the shadow that it casts is disproportionate to the reality. Despite its nominal constitutional pacifism, Japan's annual military expenditure is twice as large as North Korea's GDP; and its own GDP is roughly 200 times greater than that. The North Korean economy is on a par with the poorest of Japan's forty-three prefectures – Okinawa. While North Korea has a 1.1 million-strong army – numerically worthy of a superpower – its exercises or manoeuvres are rarely reported. Many units spend their time foraging and farming for subsistence; equipment mostly dates from the 1950s; and shortages of fuel are so severe that pilots can only practise for a few hours each year. Japan, for its part, has become a military superpower in all but name.

In March 2003, Japan launched two reconnaissance satellites – one optical, the other radar-based. A third followed in September 2006, and a fourth was planned for early 2007. Cumulatively, they were capable of scanning the surface of the earth with a resolution of about one metre, and there was no doubt in anybody's mind that the earth they would be scanning most intently would be that of North Korea. Were North Korea to reciprocate by sending spy satellites into the skies above Tokyo or Osaka, a Japanese preemptive strike to get rid of them would certainly have followed quickly.

Japan's printing presses produce a steady flow of books and articles about North Korea, the overwhelming majority of them hostile. One – a comic-book account of Kim Jong Il as violent, bloodthirsty and depraved, published in August 2003 – sold half a million copies in its first few months, probably more than all the other books in *all* languages *ever* written about North Korea.

Koizumi both benefited from and played his part in feeding the national paranoia. His controversial Yasukuni visits and ambiguous statements about Japan's militaristic past confirmed his nationalism, while his devotion to George Bush demonstrated to Washington a reassuring orientation towards their alliance. Alone among the world's political leaders, however, Koizumi visited Kim Jong Il twice – in 2002 and 2004 – on his own initiative, and with at best the reluctant consent of Washington. He could do this with impunity both because his fidelity to Washington seemed beyond doubt, and because (from January 2004) the boots of Japanese troops were planted firmly on the ground in Iraq, and multi-billion-dollar Japanese financial support was propping up the Bush world.

The summit of apology – 2002

Whereas the Bush administration began in 2001 with the famous denunciation of North Korea as part of the 'Axis of Evil', Koizumi began his administration with a search for a breakthrough in Japan's bilateral relationship with the same country. In October 2002 he went to Pyongyang, apologized for 'the tremendous damage and suffering inflicted on the people of Korea during colonialism', and accepted in return the apologies of North Korean leader Kim Jong Il for the abduction of thirteen Japanese citizens in the 1970s and 1980s, and for sending what the Japanese described as 'mystery ships' on spying missions into Japanese waters. Both then joined in signing the 'Pyongyang Declaration'. For a brief moment, there was a real promise of historic reconciliation.

But the Japanese media and political leadership thereafter focused exclusively on the crimes committed by the other side, ignoring both the crimes for which Japan itself had apologized and the North Korean desire to come in from the cold that had accompanied its apology. By admitting and apologizing for criminal actions, North Korea was doing something unprecedented in the history of modern states, and something that was undoubtedly painful and difficult. Such a step might have been welcomed as a sign of the desire to turn over a new leaf, but instead it aroused Japan to denunciation and calls for punishment – while the Japanese apology was never again to be mentioned. It was as if the 'harm' caused by Japan over thirty-five years of colonial rule was as nothing compared to the harm it had suffered through the abductions.

Even before Koizumi alighted from his plane on return from Pyongyang, he had been sabotaged by his government in Tokyo. Despite the agreement he had made with his counterparts that the five abductees sent back to Japan in the wake of his visit would return to Pyongyang after one to two weeks to work out their long-term future in discussion with their families, his government (in the person of Deputy Chief Cabinet Secretary Abe Shinzo, playing Brutus to Koizumi's Caesar) decided that under no circumstances would they be allowed to go back.[15] Implementation of the agreement that had just been reached in Pyongyang was blocked. As Abe put it, 'In Japan there is food and there is oil, and since North Korea cannot survive the winter without them, it will crack before too long.'[16] With the Japanese media overflowing with hostility towards

North Korea, Koizumi committed Japanese forces to the American cause
in Iraq – not because the Japanese public believed the war justified or the
prognosis good, but because, as he explained, in a crunch with North
Korea it was the US, not the UN, that would come to Japan's aid.[17]
Every abduction is of course a major, violent crime, and Pyongyang is
undeniably obliged to restore, to the best of its ability, the human rights
of the victims of its criminal acts of the 1970s and 1980s. But the
Japanese refusal to trust it to make restitution in accordance with the
formula agreed between the leaders of the two countries was a calculated
insult.

Elsewhere in Asia, the hubbub in Japan – in which the North Korean
regime's abductions came to be seen as the crime of the century, and the
Japanese the ultimate victims – had a painful air of unreality, since
'abduction' in modern East Asian history meant primarily the Japanese
seizure of tens – if not hundreds – of thousands of Korean men and
women before and during the Second World War to work in Japan or
elsewhere in the Japanese empire. Their labour – including that of so-
called 'comfort women' – was forced or coerced. In a speech of March
2005, addressing the specific issue of North Korean abductions of
Japanese citizens in the late 1970s and early 1980s, South Korean
President Roh said:

> I fully understand the Japanese people's anger over the abduction
> issue. In the same light, Japan must put itself in the Koreans' shoes
> and understand the anguish of our people who suffered thousands
> and tens of thousands times as much pain over such issues as
> forced labour and comfort women.[18]

Some of his words were identical with those used six weeks earlier by the
North Korean Foreign Ministry (on 17 January 2005), which 'ask[ed]
Japan to show remorse and face the harm caused by its imperialist control
in the past', and referred to the abductions as an 'unfortunate incident' in
the context of a hostile relationship, and 'not more than one thousandth
or one ten thousandth of the pain Japan in the past inflicted on
Koreans'.[19] The coincidence of language and sentiment between South
and North Korea was striking. If the wounds of Japanese colonialism
were still only partially healed in South Korea – despite forty years of
'normalization' and with millions of citizens of both countries making

mutual visits each year – the depth of such wounds in North Korea, where there had been hardly any contact at all, could only be imagined.

Two winters passed without Pyongyang 'cracking'; and it took a second Koizumi visit, in May 2004, to break the stalemate that resulted from the Japanese breach of its Pyongyang promise. Acrimony deepened as both sides struggled to gain the moral upper hand, each demanding 'sincerity' of the other, and insisting on its own.

Koizumi's second visit was seen in Pyongyang as a kind of new apology. North Korea accepted that the return of the abductees was permanent, and agreed that their families could leave North Korea to join them. For his part, Koizumi agreed to reopen negotiations and provide humanitarian aid. Afterwards, asked his impression of his North Korean opposite number, Kim Jong Il, he told the Diet, 'I guess for many his image is that of a dictator, fearful and weird, but when you actually meet with him he is mild-mannered and cheerful . . . very smart [and] quick to make jokes'.[20] He added that Kim Jong Il was so keen to talk with George W. Bush that he had asked Koizumi to provide the music so that they could sing together until their throats were sore.[21] Later, upon relaying this promise to President Bush, Koizumi was greeted with a stony silence.[22]

Koizumi's pledge to restore trust between Japan and North Korea, so that 'abnormal relations can be normalized, hostile relations turned to friendly relations, and confrontation to cooperation',[23] and to strive to normalize relations within his remaining two years of office – if possible within a single year[24] – contrasted sharply with the view of Bush, who declared that he loathed Kim and found him 'evil'; and that of Vice President Cheney, who in December 2003 said that 'you do not negotiate with evil, you defeat it'.

But like his first visit, in 2002, Koizumi's second visit roused fierce opposition. A coalition of pressure groups, emerging in the 1990s around the issues of proud, pure Japanese identity, and rejecting as 'masochistic' the apologies for colonialism and war issued by the Murayama government, united in hostility to North Korea and staunch support for the US. So powerful did this movement become that it was, in effect, beyond the capacity or courage of the media to examine or criticize.[25]

The national movement comprised three main strands: the National Association for the Rescue of Japanese Abducted by North Korea (*Sukuukai*, or the 'Rescue Association'); the National Association of

Families of Japanese Abducted by North Korea (*Kazokukai*, or 'Families Association'); and the Association of Diet-members for the Japanese Abductees (*Rachi Giin Renmei*). All believed in exercising maximum pressure, and if necessary even in direct military intervention to rescue the abducted – and all functioned with the backing of powerful media and corporate interests, and within a neo-nationalist frame alongside the *Tsukurukai* association for new history textbooks, the various associations for revision of the constitution and the Fundamental Law of Education, and nation-wide movements such as *Nihon Kaigi*. For all of these, North Korea and the abduction problem served as a rallying call. Jointly, these groups pushed Japan steadily in neo-nationalist directions, isolating and negating dissent while deepening its submission to US global designs. However unlikely it might have seemed that the overthrow of the Pyongyang government would create conditions conducive to happy family reunions for the abductees' families, that was what they called for – and their influence on government was extremely strong. No politician identified more closely with these various causes than Abe Shinzo. Indeed, without their support it is likely that Abe might never have become prime minister. As the political mission to overthrow the Pyongyang regime supplanted the humanitarian one of resolving the abduction problem, Japanese policy was wrenched away from the tentative attempts at normalization by Koizumi, and brought roughly into line with that of Vice President Cheney and the Washington neoconservatives insisting on regime change in Pyongyang. Over the last two years of Koizumi's government, it was not Koizumi but Abe who had had effective control over North Korea policy.

Cumulatively, the agenda of these organizations was to turn the clock back to the days of the family- and emperor-centred, disciplined, loyal Japan; to focus anger, frustration and resentment on North Korea (for which the only satisfactory outcome could be 'regime change'); and to require unequivocal support for the US. While stressing the symbols of national identity and brandishing them as sacred and indivisible markers of identity, they positively embraced deepening military and strategic national subordination.

As the drama of the abductees' families unfolded before the Japanese nation, major television channels, newspapers and journals catered to – and in turn cultivated – a mass market of hostility, fear, and prejudice. Children commuting to and from Korean schools in Japan were easy targets. One in five Korean schoolchildren in Japan reported various forms of abuse, both verbal and physical – sometimes their clothes were slashed with box-cutters while on the subway or on the street.[26] North Korean-affiliated organizations and individuals were subjected to abuse or threats; some targeted individuals received up to 633 abusive messages, including emails, in a single day.[27] When a time bomb was left at the residence of the Foreign Ministry official who, in 2001–02, had tried to negotiate a diplomatic settlement with Pyongyang, Tokyo's popular and powerful governor, Ishihara Shintaro, promptly gave his assessment: 'He got what was coming to him.' When challenged, he said that he had not meant to support terror, but added that Tanaka 'deserved to die 10,000 deaths'.[28]

Ironically, as Hokkaido University political scientist Yamaguchi Jiro noted, those intent on overthrowing Kim Jong Il's regime in fact resembled it – especially in their desire to control the media and impose an ideological orthodoxy in the name of the nation as an organic, family unit.[29]

Abductions

The success of Koizumi's second mission hinged on a reinvestigation of the cases of the eight missing abductees – in particular that of Yokota Megumi, abducted on her way home from a badminton game as a thirteen-year-old schoolgirl in 1977. In North Korea, in 1986, she had married a Korean man, had given birth to a daughter the following year, and was said by Pyongyang to have committed suicide when suffering depression in either 1993 or 1994. Pyongyang's account of her life and death was judged in Japan to be completely unsatisfactory.

Kim Chol Jun, Megumi's former husband, became an important witness. In December 2004 he handed over to Japanese officials what he said were the remains of his wife, which he said he had dug up after the initial burial in order to cremate them.[30] Upon investigation (by mitrochondrial DNA analysis), the Japanese government concluded that the remains were those of two unrelated people, and accused North Korea of deliberate deception. It said that there was 'absolutely no evidence' to support North Korea's claim that the eight abductees said to have died – including Megumi – had actually done so. Believing therefore in the 'possibility of their being still alive', the Japanese government demanded their immediate return.[31] With North Korea insisting that the eight abductees were dead, it was hard to see how the gap between the two sides could be bridged.

In 2006, Kim Chol Jun was identified, with near-certainty, as a South Korean man, Kim Young Nam, who had disappeared from South Korea as a 17-year-old in 1978 – perhaps himself an abductee, though he denied it – and was briefly reunited with his South Korean mother at a North Korean reunion for separated families.[32]

Japan vented its anger over the unresolved abductee issue by freezing the dispatch of any further 'humanitarian' aid – after only about half the grain and medical supplies promised by Koizumi in May had been sent. In the dispute over the DNA analysis, the Japanese government's pronouncements were taken – at least initially – as definitive: it was assumed that Japan's technology had exposed North Korea's deception. But the Japanese findings proved to be anything but definitive. When the cremated remains provided by Kim Chol Jun had first been submitted for analysis to Japan's National Research Institute of Police Science, they were held to be degraded beyond the possibility of analysis. They were then submitted to the private Teikyo University for further analysis. But the international scientific journal *Nature*, in its 3 February 2005 issue, revealed that the professor who conducted the analysis had had no previous experience in the analysis of cremated specimens. It described his tests as inconclusive, remarking that samples such as the one he had been given to work on were very easily contaminated by contact with people, and said that he had in any case used up the samples in his analysis, so that scientific corroboration of his results would be impossible.[33] In a 1998 textbook on DNA analysis, the same analyst, Dr Yoshii Tomio, had written that the DNA extraction procedure was so delicate, error-prone, and vulnerable to legal challenge, that the principle of independent confirmation was crucial.[34] In meeting his commission from the Japanese government, he had not followed the practice that he himself had prescribed. *Nature* then published an unusual editorial:

> Japan is right to doubt North Korea's every statement. But its interpretation of the DNA tests has crossed the boundary of science's freedom from political interference. *Nature*'s interview with the scientist who carried out the tests raised the possibility

that the remains were merely contaminated, making the DNA tests inconclusive . . . The problem is not in the science but in the fact that the government is meddling in scientific matters at all. Science runs on the premise that experiments, and all the uncertainty involved in them, should be open for scrutiny. Arguments made by other Japanese scientists that the tests should have been carried out by a larger team are convincing . . .

Japan's policy seems a desperate effort to make up for what has been a diplomatic failure . . . Part of the burden for Japan's political and diplomatic failure is being shifted to a scientist for doing his job – deriving conclusions from experiments and presenting reasonable doubts about them. But the friction between North Korea and Japan will not be decided by a DNA test. Likewise, the interpretation of DNA test results cannot be decided by the government of either country. Dealing with North Korea is no fun, but it doesn't justify breaking the rules of separation between science and politics.[35]

Other experts in this highly specialized field tended to take the same, critical view as *Nature*. As Honda Katsuya – professor of forensic medicine at Tsukuba University – put it, 'all we can conclude from the tests is that two people's DNA were detected in the given material and that they did not agree with Megumi-san's. That's it. There is another huge step before we can conclude that they are not Megumi-san's bones'.[36] As for Yoshii Tomio, one week after the *Nature* editorial he was promoted to the prestigious position of head of the forensic medical department of the Tokyo metropolitan police department – making him unavailable for media comment.[37] When the suggestion was made in the Diet that this smacked of government complicity in 'hiding a witness', the minister of foreign affairs responded that it was 'extremely regrettable' for such aspersions to be cast on Japan's scientific integrity.[38]

In Pyongyang, on 31 March 2005, Song Il Ho – Deputy Director of the Asian Department of the North Korean Foreign Ministry, and a key person in negotiations between the two countries – criticized the Japanese government for a lack of sincerity. He noted that Japan had tried to distinguish between colonial rule and abduction – both of them twentieth-century phenomena, divided only by twenty-five years or so – as if one were firmly in the past while the other remained a live issue. He expressed his government's grave concern that North Korea had carried out what he described as 'exhaustive' investigation into the abductions, producing 16 witnesses for the Japanese to interview in Pyongyang in November 2004. He said that North Korea had handed over the remains of Megumi, only to be rebuffed and insulted by the Japanese. As if taking a leaf from Yoshii's textbook on DNA procedure, he suggested that the remains could be submitted to a third country institution for independent verification. Japan made no response, and there the abduction issue rested.

The national mood in Japan was one in which rage over crimes committed against it seemed to triumph over reason, injured virtue over policy. Politicians and media figures had lost the capacity to imagine how the world might look from a North Korean perspective, or to grasp the core of aggrieved justice that lay at the heart of Pyongyang's message. With negotiations frozen, the focus shifted to the issue of missiles and nuclear weapons.

Nuclear weapons

In 1994, a nuclear confrontation between the US and North Korea was only resolved, on the very brink of war, by the mission of Jimmy Carter to Pyongyang. Under the subsequent 'Agreed Framework', North Korea froze its energy-related nuclear programmes and placed its plutonium waste under international supervision. This was in return for the promised construction of two light water nuclear reactors, a supply of heavy oil until they had been constructed, and the normalization of economic and political relations.[39]

The Agreed Framework held for almost a decade. During this period, no single incident so focused Japanese attention on North Korea as the launch of the Taepodong – either a failed satellite or a missile – which soared over Japanese skies and then dropped into the Pacific Ocean late in August 1998. The thought that much of Japan might lie within North Korea's missile range helped to provoke a rethinking of security issues. Reflecting a deep fear of North Korea, Japan devoted extraordinary effort to preparing the institutional framework for an 'emergency' – the preferred euphemism for war. This had been high on the wish-list of conservative governments since the 1960s, but had always been blocked by socialist and communist opposition: the 'New Guidelines' agreement of 1997 were followed by the 1999 Regional Contingency Law, the Terror and Iraq Special Measures Laws of 2001 and 2003, the Emergency Laws of 2004, and the 'reorganization' of bases and forces carried out at US behest in 2005–06. Other new laws were explicitly designed with North Korea in mind, authorizing the interdiction of suspect shipping, the blocking of foreign exchange transactions, and the exclusion of North Korean ships from Japanese ports.

While Japan had berated North Korea from the 1990s onwards for its putative missile and nuclear programmes, it was blind to the fact that, viewed from North Korea, the US nuclear deterrent to which Japan clung as the indispensable core of its own defence was a threatening lance, rather than a shield – and that, from this perspective, Japan had been party to nuclear intimidation for more than half a century. If Japan, like the nuclear great powers, could not conceive of defence without nuclear weapons, why should North Korea do so?

The Bush administration's January 2002 'Axis of Evil' statement saw relations between the US and North Korea plummet: suspicions over the North Korean nuclear programme flared into a new crisis. When Assistant Secretary of State James Kelly returned from a visit to Pyongyang in October 2002, saying that Pyongyang had confessed to him a secret weapons-related uranium enrichment programme, the US suspended the supply of heavy oil under the Agreed Framework. In January 2003 North Korea responded by withdrawing from the Nuclear Non-Proliferation Treaty and resuming its nuclear plans. Pyongyang denied the Kelly allegations, insisting that he had misunderstood its statement of the right to such a programme as one of its possession. Despite its efforts, the US signally failed to convince other parties of its version of events. Even after a concentrated diplomatic effort by the second Bush administration, two years after the charges had first been made, both the Chinese Foreign Minister Li Zhaoxing and the director of South Korea's National Intelligence Service declared themselves unconvinced.[40]

As awareness grew of the manipulation of intelligence to justify war on Iraq, the intelligence on North Korea could not escape similar suspicion. The US journal *Foreign Affairs* published an analysis by the highly placed Washington observer Selig Harrison, who found the evidence inconclusive, based on a deliberate favouring of worst case scenarios.[41] It is too early to be sure that there was a deliberate distortion of intelligence on the uranium enrichment story, but it has become increasingly likely. North Korea may have purchased technology from Pakistan and aluminium from Russia, and tried to import other materials for an enrichment programme from Germany – in other words, it may have given serious thought to pursuing such a programme. But the dozen or so centrifuges provided by Pakistan were far too few to be of significance for weapons production. In addition, the technical difficulties in the high enrichment process were such that Pyongyang's denial that it had an active and ongoing programme was plausible. Nevertheless, the crisis escalated. North Korea responded to the US pressure – and to the abuse of Kim Jong Il as a 'tyrant' and a 'dangerous person', and of their country as an 'outpost of tyranny'[42] – with its 16 February 2005 declaration that it was a nuclear weapon state. That did not mean that the Kelly charges had been correct, because the active North Korean programme turned out to be based not on uranium enrichment but on plutonium. All observers agreed that North Korea had frozen its plutonium stocks and reactor for eight years, while subject to international inspections under the 1994 Agreed Framework.

From August 2003, a series of meetings began in Beijing in an effort to find a diplomatic solution. It became known as the 'Six-Party Talks' – involving the US, Japan, Russia, China, South Korea, and North Korea. At the centre of the Six-Party process, the American attempt to achieve regime change by the mobilization of a 'coalition for punishment'[43] confronted Seoul's approach of opening windows through which 'sunshine' might penetrate into North Korea. Where Washington adopted an essentially 'Christian' approach, seeing good and evil as polar opposites, South Korea's attitude was more 'Confucian' – rooted in a paradigm of human nature as fundamentally good, and responsive to virtue and reason. To the South Korean government Kim Jong Il was 'a man Seoul can do business with'; the Bush administration's efforts to depose him were 'fundamentalist'.[44] Their view was that the most effective approach was one of 'dialogue, not provocative rhetoric'.[45]

Despite regular assurances by Washington of the unity of the five countries sitting with North Korea around the Beijing table from 2003, disunity was characteristic. Where Washington, and sometimes Tokyo, saw Pyongyang as a source of threatened aggression, the greater threat was not so much that of an expansionist, aggressive North Korea as of the chaos that might spread should American-directed regime-change strategies be successful and the country collapse as a result.[46] Neighbouring countries feared not so much North Korea's aggression as its collapse.

After nearly two years of refusal to listen to North Korea, during which it simply repeated the demand for unilateral concessions – what it described as CVID (complete, verifiable, irreversible dismantling of nuclear weapons and facilities) – the US position weakened. This was a result not only of pressure from its negotiating partners, but also of its loss of diplomatic and moral credibility over Iraq. What had been designed in Washington as a coalition for punishment, intended to mobilize a united front of pressure on North Korea, began – under South Korean, Chinese and Russian 'reverse pressure' – to turn, on the contrary, into a coalition for engagement, which promised to become a true, multilateral, negotiating forum. In the summer and autumn of 2005, Pyongyang stated that, if only the US would treat it in a friendly manner, recognizing and respecting it, it would be ready to return to the conference table, and would not need to have 'a single nuclear weapon'.[47] The US softened its rhetoric, and ceased its abuse. The centre of gravity of the 'North Korean problem' shifted from Washington to Beijing and Seoul.

By September 2005, the elements of an agreement were clear. The major sticking point at the Beijing table was North Korea's insistence on its legal entitlement to a civil nuclear energy programme. Under the Non-Proliferation Treaty, the right of member countries to a civil nuclear programme is described as 'inalienable'. South Korea, Russia and China took the view that North Korea should enjoy it, and when even Tokyo came to the same view – while specifying certain conditions[48] – the hard-line stance of the US became untenable. Having exhausted the possibilities of delay in the hope of scuttling the deal[49] – fearful of becoming what Jack Pritchard, formerly the State Department's top North Korea expert, described as 'a minority of one . . . isolated from the mainstream of its four other allies and friends in the Six-Party Talks',[50] and facing an ultimatum from the Chinese chair of the conference to sign or else bear the blame for their breakdown[51] – the US gave way. On 19 September 2005, the parties to the Beijing conference reached a historic agreement on principles and objectives.

In a 'spirit of mutual respect and equality', North Korea would scrap 'all nuclear weapons and existing nuclear programmes', return to the Non-Proliferation Treaty, and allow international inspections. In return, the US declared that it had 'no nuclear weapons in the peninsula and no intention to attack or invade North Korea', and would respect its sovereignty and take steps towards diplomatic recognition, normalization, and economic aid and cooperation.[52] The parties expressed their 'respect' for North Korea's statement of its 'right to the peaceful uses of nuclear energy', and a clause was included in the agreement 'to discuss at an appropriate time the subject of the provision of light water reactor [*sic*] to the DPRK'. Neither missiles, nor human rights, nor the disputed uranium enrichment programme were mentioned – save for an oblique reference to the last of these, depending on the interpretation of 'existing programmes'. It was a shotgun marriage, with China – backed by South Korea and Russia – wielding the shotgun.

However vague and incomplete, the Beijing consensus of September 2005 espoused principles that conformed to international law, recognized the interests of regional countries for a de-nuclearized peninsula, and responded to North Korea's pleas for security guarantees and diplomatic and economic normalization. However, no sooner had the delegates packed their bags and left Beijing than hardliners in both Washington and Pyongyang seized the initiative to block possible reconciliation. North Korea made its commitment to end its weapons programme and return to NPT safeguards dependent on getting a light water reactor first, as a 'physical guarantee for confidence building'.[53] The US position was that a light water reactor could not even be considered until all other steps in bringing North Korea back into the NPT were complete. To underline its point, the US then summarily terminated the KEDO Agreement (at whose heart was the light water reactor project, which from 2002 had remained frozen, but not cancelled).[54] It was almost as though there had been no agreement between the parties at all.[55] Pyongyang's understanding of the 'appropriate time' for a North Korean light water reactor was 'now', while for Washington it was a prospect to be entertained in the distant future – or preferably not at all. Japan, still focusing primarily on the abductions issue, played a passive role as the crisis deepened.

Crime and human rights

The Bush administration could not be satisfied with any agreement on North Korean nuclear weapons, since many within it wanted much more: comprehensive demilitarization (especially the scrapping of North

Korea's missile programme), major political changes (in respect of human rights), and ultimately regime change – the overthrow of an enemy against which it had tried by every means to prevail since going to war with it in 1950. Policy oscillated between a pragmatism ready to follow the path of diplomatic resolution while somehow hoping for such fundamental change, and a willingness to settle for nothing less than achieving such change by force. President Bush, known for his loathing for Kim Jong Il and the North Korean regime, and for his mission to bring democracy and human rights to North Korea, tended to tip the balance in favour of the latter attitude.

From September 2005, even as the nuclear deal was being signed reluctantly in Beijing, the Bush administration changed tack. Under the direction of Vice President Dick Cheney – and in accordance with the national security provisions of the Patriot Act, designed for the struggle against terrorism – it opted to sideline and neutralize the Beijing process by widening the terms of the North Korean issue beyond nuclear matters to the issue of the nature of the regime itself.[56] Washington would squeeze North Korea hard, requiring it not just to renounce its nuclear ambitions but to 'open up its political system and afford freedom to its people'.[57] The newly appointed US ambassador to South Korea, Alexander Vershbow, denounced North Korea as a 'criminal regime' responsible for 'weapons exports to rogue states, narcotics trafficking as a state activity and counterfeiting of our money on a large scale'.[58] 'Normalization' of relations with such a regime, Washington implied, was no more likely than the normalization of relations between the US government and the mafia.

North Korea became the 'biggest threat to the United States', surpassing China and Iran.[59] It was accused of manufacturing and trading in narcotics (including heroin, opium and amphetamines – the latter via Japanese gangster groups into Japan), of money laundering, counterfeiting currency and tobacco dealing, and of various breaches of human rights, including the Japanese abductions. In many cases the allegations depended on intelligence emanating from US sources – especially those relating to the manufacture and distribution of counterfeit, so-called 'super-hundred' US dollar notes.[60] North Korea might well produce and distribute such notes if it thought it could do so with impunity – so too, no doubt, would countless organizations and many governments around the world. But the technical complexity of the note-making materials and processes made the charge extremely questionable (according to a recent study by a German specialist on the history of currency).[61] Syria and Iran had first been blamed for the 'supernotes', this specialist commented – yet the CIA was the one organization other than the US Treasury that was equipped with the sophisticated technology and materials required for their production.

When North Korea offered to cooperate in investigating the US claims, to punish anyone found responsible, and to set up an alternative, completely open North Korean account in a US bank, Washington ignored it.[62] Instead, it set out to 'strangle North Korea financially' – as *Le Monde*'s Philippe Pons put it.[63] When the US Treasury submitted a report on the matter to Congress in October 2006, it accused North Korea of producing an estimated 22 million counterfeit dollars, out of the total of 50 million that had been found.[64] It was not revealed who was responsible for the other 28 million. North Korea's sums seem particularly small beer in light of the volume of counterfeit currency circulating worldwide. For example, in evidence to a New York court in October 2006, a US Treasury official stated that in the single year from March 2004 to March 2005 the Israel Discount Bank had processed a staggering \$35.4 billion for 'originators and beneficiaries that exhibited characteristics and patterns commonly associated with money-laundering'.[65] Of course, direct state sponsorship may distinguish the North Korean case, but if so no evidence to that effect was presented.[66]

Human rights also became a major policy instrument. Following the adoption by Congress – on a unanimous vote in both Houses – of the North Korean Human Rights Act, a special US envoy for North Korean human rights took office in August 2005, and interventions along North Korea's borders and over the airwaves were stepped up. These were intended to undermine and destabilize the regime by non-military means, and thereby achieve an 'East European' outcome. In December 2005, the UN General Assembly adopted a resolution, jointly sponsored by Japan, the US and the European Union, condemning North Korea for multiple human rights abuses. Japan followed suit in June 2006, with its own North Korean human rights legislation.

Washington also took steps to ratchet up military pressure on North Korea. In June 2006 it mobilized three aircraft carrier groups, 300 aircraft and 20,000 men – including many Japan-based ships and aircraft – and in the waters around Guam conducted the largest military exercises since the Vietnam war, code-named 'Valiant Shield', with North Korea the most obvious imagined target. This was followed, from 26 June to 28 July, by a separate, large-scale naval exercise – 'Rimpac 2006' – which, ominously, brought together units from South Korea, Japan, Australia, Canada, Chile and Peru, in addition to those from the US itself. Apart from such large-scale military exercises, seven US Aegis destroyers were deployed on a regular basis at Yokosuka in Japan, equipped with hundreds of 1,300km Tomahawk missiles – enough to wipe out at a stroke most of North Korea's military and industrial installations and cities.[67]

With the Beijing process frozen, North Korea's pleas for the lifting of the financial sanctions and/or for direct talks with the US were ignored. At the same time, discussions with Japan on the abductions were at a dead end. North Korea's trade was slowly being stifled, and military intimidation stepped up. The response came in two stages – in July and October 2006. On 5 July, North Korea launched seven missiles – including Scuds, Nodongs and Taepodongs – into the seas adjacent to the Russian Far East. In response, UN Security Council Resolution 1695 – tabled and aggressively promoted by Japan – denounced North Korea for activity tending to 'jeopardize peace, stability and security in the region and beyond'.[68] Although the tests were failures – especially that of the long-distance Taepodong 2 – in Japan, as one South Korean commentator noted, it was as if a North Korean missile had hit central Tokyo.[69] Senior Japanese government figures talked of preemptive strikes against the missile sites; 92 per cent of the public favoured sanctions;[70] and a substantial majority supported prompt deployment of an anti-missile system, irrespective of its effectiveness. Three days after the North Korean missile tests, however, India launched an ICBM – and six days after the Security Council resolution the US did likewise, sending its missile over a 4,000km trajectory into the Pacific. The attention of Japan (and that of the UN) remained focused exclusively on North Korea.

Three months after the missile tests – with its pleas to the US to return to the negotiating table and ease its strangulation still ignored – North Korea conducted its first nuclear test. Japan, which happened to be chairing the Security Council at the time, again took the lead in the Security Council. Resolution 1718, adopted on 14 October, denounced North Korea again, and imposed additional financial and weapons-related sanctions.[71] Independently of the Security Council, Japan also adopted its own sanctions, suspending all trade and communication between the two countries for six months – although by then bilateral trade had already been so drastically curtailed that further sanctions might not have made a large difference.[72] If UN member countries were to implement this resolution by stopping and searching North Korean ships for weapons or supplies (or even luxury goods), anything could happen. The role of high seas interception, according to Japanese Foreign Minister Aso, could be performed by Australia and the US.[73]

During the missile and nuclear tests of 2006, the balance of diplomatic initiative that had been seized during 2005 by South Korea, China and Russia shifted back to the US and Japan. It was they who shaped the way these events were seen by the world's media; according to the resulting view, North Korea's response was unpersuasive. No country in modern history had been more friendless, reviled or ridiculed.

When the Security Council called on Pyongyang to return to the Beijing table and the September 2005 agreement, it seemed oblivious to the fact that the most unenthusiastic party to that agreement had been the US, which had signed it only with the utmost reluctance and then promptly sabotaged it. Pyongyang insisted that it wanted nothing more than implementation of the September agreement, but that it would only return when the US ceased its punitive financial sanctions (the attempt to 'strangle' it).[74] For Washington and Tokyo, however, the 'Beijing table' to which Pyongyang had to return was to be a forum not for negotiation, but for surrender, to which North Korea could come only to pledge unconditional disarmament, abandoning its long-held objectives of diplomatic and economic normalization and removal of the threat of attack. That seemed an unlikely outcome.

The best-known and most respected Korean statesman of modern times, Nobel laureate Kim Dae Jung, lamented that the UN was following the sanctions path despite the fact that this had proved ineffective against Cuba, Iraq, Afghanistan and Iran. He expressed regret that the initiative on North Korea had passed to fiercely ideological neoconservatives in the US. He predicted that the likely consequences would be deeper regional insecurity and accelerated Japanese rearmament.[75]

Despite the concentrated assault on North Korea in the areas of crime and human rights, North Korea had not launched an aggressive war (at least during the past half-century), overthrown any democratically elected government, threatened any neighbour with nuclear weapons, nor attempted to justify the practices of torture and assassination. However unwise or provocative they might have been, neither the missile launch nor the nuclear test breached any law. North Korea plainly rides roughshod over the rights of its citizens, but when, in April 2006, the US president welcomed to the White House representatives of the Japanese families of North Korean abductees, and delivered a touching homily on the fate of the young Japanese girl long separated from her mother, nobody thought to mention the plight of the citizens of many countries whom the CIA had ferried secretly around the world in recent years, delivering them to torturers in a global gulag beyond the reach of any law; and few remembered that the twentieth century's greatest crimes of abduction had been those committed by Japan, which – more than seven decades later – had still to be satisfactorily resolved.

By a paradoxical feedback process, no factor has helped sustain the Pyongyang dictatorship as much as US and Japanese hostility. It could justify itself by pointing to the threat of its two scourges of the bitter twentieth century, united in plotting its destruction in the twenty-first. Similarly, no factor helped the US to maintain its military dominance over East Asia and its bases in Japan and South Korea – and to sell its missile defence technology – so much as the 'threat' presented by North Korea. The Japanese official who, until late in 2005, headed its Foreign Ministry's North Korea desk, remarked bitterly after his resignation that it was as if the North Korean missiles of July 2006 had been launched on the orders of George W. Bush, so well did they serve US interests.[76]

As the stalemate over North Korea continued, both the US and Japan concentrated on unilateral pressure, squeezing their adversary to the point of crisis and collapse, refusing any terms of negotiation other than surrender. In following their lead, the Security Council was eerily re-enacting the disastrous UN interventions out of which the modern Korean problem had been generated in the first place: those of 1947 and 1948, which led to separate elections and the permanent division of Korea; and that of 1950, which had committed the UN, under US leadership, to catastrophic war (the only occasion on which the UN has itself prosecuted a war). In the interval between the missile launch and the nuclear test, the Brussels-based International Crisis Group sounded a rare note in the discourse on North Korea by attributing a measure of responsibility for the crisis to the Bush administration, for '[a]ttempting to squeeze North Korea into capitulation or collapse by wielding economic sanctions at the moment when negotiations were beginning to bear fruit, refusing to meet with the North outside the multilateral talks[,] and pressing human rights concerns'.[77] The only way out of the downward spiral, it suggested, was for the US to adopt a new approach. Such voices were rare in the chorus of denunciation that followed the July and October events.

Early in 2007, following the North Korean nuclear tests of October and the Republican defeat in the US mid-term congressional elections of November, the Bush administration suddenly reversed its North Korea policy.[78] An unprecedented January meeting in Berlin hammered out the basic contours of a comprehensive agreement between the two sides, which was then confirmed by the Six Party talks in Beijing on 13 February. In return for North Korea taking a series of steps towards de-nuclearization, the Beijing parties would grant it an immediate emergency shipment of oil – with a much larger shipment to follow – lift the financial sanctions and initiate steps towards removing North Korea from the list of terrorism sponsors, normalizing relations, ending the Korean War and establishing a permanent peace regime on the Korean peninsula. This 'Bush shock' was almost as dramatic and unexpected as the 'Nixon shock' reversal of China policy more than three decades earlier.

The deal, *inter alia*, required Japan to normalize its relations with North Korea. Former US Deputy Secretary of State Richard Armitage even suggested that the US might have to 'sit down with Japan and prepare for the possibility that North Korea would remain in possession of a certain number of nuclear weapons even as the [Korean] peninsula comes slowly together for some sort of unification'.[79] No more bitter pill could be imagined for Abe, who owed his rise to political power in Japan in large part to his identification with hard-line anti-North Korean sentiment and for whose government it was the abduction issue, not nuclear weapons, that constituted 'the most important problem our country faces'.[80] The North Korean abductions, framed for domestic purposes as a unique North Korean crime against Japan rather than a universal human-rights offence, carried little weight in the international arena where Japan itself was seen as responsible for the greatest mass abductions of the twentieth century, and Koreans as the greatest victims.

Abe forlornly protested that Japan would not be party to any aid to
North Korea until the abduction issue was settled, but, with the US shift,
his policy 'falls apart', as the *Asahi Shimbun* put it on 15 February.

East Asian community

The China-centred equilibrium of the pre-modern East Asian world –
shattered by a century and a half of Western (and later Japanese)
imperialism and war, the growth of nation-states, the spread of indus-
trialism and intensive economic development – seemed by the end of the
Cold War, and then of the twentieth century, to be inching towards a
new equilibrium. China's economic growth from 1987 was the miracle
of all economic miracles, and South Korea since that date provided the
model democratic transformation rooted in civil society. Across the
region, governments and public and private organizations turned their
attention to the problem of how to construct a peaceful, just and
cooperative order in East Asia – especially between the three regions
of China, Korea and Japan. The twentieth century offered one model of
East Asian regionalism – the Japanese project of the 1930s and 1940s –
but that in the twenty-first century became the counter-model, to be
avoided at all costs.

Japanese intellectuals and idealists had then flocked to the cause of the
construction of a community; but the utopian vision had been stillborn,
unable to resolve the contradiction between Japan's insistence on its non-
Asian superiority as a 'divine country centred on the emperor', and the
insistence of other Asians on equality and mutual respect.[81] The slogans of
'interracial harmony', 'harmony of the five races', and 'all the world under
one roof' were belied by the reality of a Japan-dominated empire. All
institutions bore the distinctive DNA of imperial Japan's family state, in
which Japan was superior as father or 'elder brother', and Japan's gods were
prescribed for worship by the Chinese, Korean and Mongolian peoples.

For contemporary revisionists, the 'pure' ideals, first of Manchukuo
and then of Greater East Asia, are still glorious, and are much more easily
defended than the record of the actual deeds of the imperial Japanese
forces (whether in Manchuria, elsewhere in China, or in East or
Southeast Asia). What Tojo saw as moral and imaginative failure in
Japan's encounter with Asia, they see as virtue and as a cause for pride.

In the wake of the Cold War, there has been a plethora of proposals for cooperation in East Asia – a region now accounting for 33 per cent of the world's people and 23 per cent of its trade, and likely to continue functioning as the dynamo for world economic growth for decades to come. If Goldman Sachs's estimates prove anywhere near correct, China's economy will surpass first that of Japan, and then, by mid-century, that of the US as well, with India by then also closing rapidly on the US – while Europe steadily declines in significance.[82] By 2004, around 30 per cent of Japan's trade was with the greater Chinese world (China itself, plus Taiwan and Hong Kong), as against 20 per cent with the US.[83] The combined GDP of Japan, China, South Korea, Taiwan and Hong Kong was more than $8 trillion, compared with $12 trillion for the US and $13 trillion for the EU. As intra-regional investment, trade, and technological transfer boomed, state leaders, intellectuals and representatives of civil society sought a formula to establish a stable, just, peaceful and cooperative new order. A number of factors underlined the desirability of cooperation: the financial crisis of 1997, the growing sense of shared security, environmental and energy problems, and the shared sense of the need to unite to curb the arbitrary and aggressive actions of the single superpower.

Like their forefathers, contemporary intellectuals are attracted by the idea of 'East Asia' or 'Northeast Asia' as a solution to multiple contra-dictions. The question is whether their contemporary proposals are realistic, actually addressing the contradictions, or (like those in the 1930s) fantastic – no more than elaborate verbal formulas. The first contradiction is the most superficially obvious: that between Japanese and Chinese nationalism. It is not expressed today in direct contests over territory so much as it was in the 1930s (with the exception of the contested Diaoyu/Senkaku islands and their marine surrounds), but rather in the contest for a role in steering Asia into its future, while both nations remain subject – albeit in different ways – to the same constraint: the military presence and capacity for the projection of force by the single power that does still seize and hold territory. In the 1930s, China lacked the military, political, or economic weight to challenge Japan's prescrip-tions; now it has all three, in addition to a sophisticated diplomatic establishment to pursue its agenda. Second is the contradiction between Asia and the US, or between any scheme for a *regional* identity for Asia and the US insistence on hegemony over a *global* empire. Third, and perhaps most intractable, is the classic contradiction embedded in the sense of Japanese national identity. Is Japan Asian or non-Asian? Is it an ordinary or a superior country? Is its identity based on blood and ethnicity, or on civic values? These contradictions, which in the 1930s revolved around the core geopolitical issue of Manchukuo (then contested between China and Japan), today centre on North Korea (now confronting both the US and Japan).

At the Hanoi meeting of ASEAN+3 in 1998, following a proposal from newly elected South Korean President Kim Dae Jung, an 'East Asian Vision Group' was established, chaired by former South Korean Foreign Minister Han Sung-Joo. It went on to present its report to the December 2001 Kuala Lumpur meeting. It began:

> We, the people of East Asia, aspire to create an East Asian community of peace, prosperity, and progress based on the full development of all peoples in the region. Concurrent with this vision is the goal that, in the future, the East Asian community will make a positive contribution to the rest of the world.[84]

In the agreement he signed in October 2002 with North Korea's Kim Jong Il, Prime Minister Koizumi embraced the idea of East Asian community. In the Pyongyang Declaration, the term 'Northeast Asia' appeared for the first time since 1945 in a Japanese diplomatic document. South Korean President Roh Moo-Hyun, too – in several key speeches, including his inaugural address – referred to this same ideal. In October 2004, 'Building the Common House of East Asia' was the theme of a large gathering of religious leaders from the region, held in Seoul. In late November 2004, the Japanese government presented proposals towards the realization of an 'East Asian Community' at the ASEAN+3 Summit in Vientiane; and an East Asian Summit was held in Kuala Lumpur in December 2005, bringing together the leaders of ASEAN, China, Japan, South Korea, India, Australia and New Zealand.[85]

Architects of the 'Common House', such as Wada Haruki – whose earliest design dates to 1990, and owes some inspiration to visions of a post-Cold War Europe that were sometimes referred to by that term – and his Tokyo University colleague Kang Sang-Jung, articulated the idea of a post-Cold War East Asian order in which the legacies of almost 200 years of war and confrontation would be healed and transcended by a community along something like European lines: based on a multi-cultural, multiethnic, multilingual identity, full of creative diversity, and defined by civic categories, rather than by race or nation. In Kang's vision, the problem of Korea would be resolved within this larger entity in part by granting a united Korea a central role as a permanently neutral host for some key institutions – somewhat like Luxemburg in Europe.[86]

Such proposals are more radical and idealistic than most of the schemes for an Asian commonwealth that now circulate at the behest of states and international institutions, whose 'bottom line' tends to be the neoliberal insistence on removing barriers to the free flow of capital and goods, with the ultimate goal of a single market. One lesson from Europe, however, is that a 'common market' tends to lead towards a comprehensive 'community' and 'union' – that is, to political and cultural integration. Any East Asian or Northeast Asian community must first find some way to ease and eventually overcome the tensions around leadership between Japan and China. During the five years of the Koizumi government, the Japan–China relationship drifted. As the China historian, Mori Kazuko, noted regretfully, 'Things could have been very different had Japan five years ago taken the lead in formulating a design for an East Asian community.'[87]

Chinese initiatives – its proposals in 2003 for a free trade zone with the ASEAN countries and its hosting from 2003 of the Six-Party Talks – were a matter for bureaucratic concern in Japan.[88] As Gregory Noble put it, 'China's central role in the effort to deal with the instability on the Korean peninsula . . . its increasingly active participation in the ASEAN Regional Forum and ASEAN+3 and its bold trade proposals have made it impossible for Japan simply to block or contain China'.[89] When a 'Network of East Asian Think Tanks' (NEAT) was set up in Beijing in September 2003, Japan responded by setting up its own group of scholars and think-tanks to push for the establishment of a 'Council on East Asian Community' (CEAC). The semi-governmental National In-stitute for Research Advancement (NIRA) set about drawing up a 'North East Asian Grand Design' – a twenty-year perspective for a region that would comprise Japan, the two Koreas, the three Northeast China provinces, Inner Mongolia and the North China region (Henan, Hebei, Shanxi, Shandong, Tianjin and Beijing), with Far Eastern Russia compris-ing a 'Basic Area', and the US and EU classified as related regions.[90] Its substance was undoubtedly different, but it bore remarkable similarity in purely geographical terms to the old Japanese empire in Northeast Asia.

In any move towards regional integration, the US position was bound to be problematic. What precisely is its stake? Is it a Pacific and Asian power and equal partner, and as such entitled to a voice? Or is it the global hegemon, and therefore able (even perhaps entitled) to dictate terms? The drawing of regional boundaries, and the handling of existing 'special' relationships that might or might not be contained within the community, would all prove vexing. Throughout the Cold War Japan had to 'continue to rely on US protection', and desist from any attempt to replace it with an entente with China. No surprise, then, that Richard Armitage should have given proposals for an East Asian community a clear thumbs-down.[91] The consistent thread of US Asian policy since 1945 has been firm control over Japan combined with the deterrence of any project that might lead to the emergence of any Asian or East Asian community from which the US might itself be excluded.

In 2003, the Beijing Six-Party conference table became the site for confrontation between two alternative agendas for East Asia: the US hegemonic project calling on North Korea to surrender unconditionally, and the various moves in the direction of an East or Northeast Asian community – such as those confirmed in their joint statement by Japan and North Korea in October 2002, fervently embraced by South Korea, and supported in principle by China and Russia.

North Korea played a central role in determining regional and broader relationships. Were it not for the 'North Korean threat', Japanese people would have little interest in the 'global war on terror', and would be much less likely to bow to US demands for military and financial contributions support the establishment of client regimes in Iraq or elsewhere. Fear and hatred of North Korea dictate support for the US vision, even though Japan's subordination undermines its credibility and helps isolate it from its neighbours.

To the extent that it rests on the fulcrum of North Korea, however, the US project in Asia is unstable. If the 'North Korean threat' were to be resolved, Washington strategists would have to think of some other justification for US bases in Japan and South Korea (and for the missile defence system justified by the same threat). Otherwise East Asia might move quickly in a 'European' direction, with large political, social and economic ramifications. In other words, to the extent that the US accomplishes its short-term goal (change of either policy or regime in

North Korea), it undermines its long-term goal (incorporation of the region into its empire). Paradoxically, to the extent that the US wishes to maintain its East Asian – and global – empire, it benefits from keeping Kim Jong Il in power.

While US regional and global policy offers negative priorities – *anti*-terror, *anti*-evil – to justify the promised 'New American Century' imperial regime, East Asia struggles to articulate a non-imperial vision of a future European-type East Asia of reconciliation, normalization, and economic cooperation. Koizumi's September 2002 and May 2004 visits to Pyongyang saw Japan teeter on the brink of making peace with Asia, and at last ending the 'Asia-denying' (*datsu-A*) distortion of the past century. The balance is only likely to shift decisively in favour of the 'New Asian Century' or 'Common House' regional community if and when Japan finally liquidates its colonial legacy with Korea, recasts its sense of its own identity, and renegotiates its relationship with the global superpower.

Many difficulties would have to be overcome for the Beijing deal of February 2007 to be successfully implemented, but it offered the best prospect yet, not merely of a settlement of the North Korean nuclear problem but of a new security and political order in East Asia. If it worked, the Six Party conference format would become institutionalized in due course as a body for addressing common problems of security, environment, food and energy, the precursor of a future regional community that would include North Korea and in which China would play a central role. Nothing in the Japan of Koizumi or Abe had prepared it for such a shocking eventuality

6

The Constitution and the
Fundamental Law of Education

Reopening the rulebook

As there is no game without a rulebook, so there is no social and political
order without a constitution to determine who holds what power and
under what circumstances. Modern Japan has had two constitutions.
The first, adopted in 1890, established Prussian-type parliamentary
institutions, in an emperor-centred state that allowed a limited form
of democratic participation. It continued to function through the rise of
militarism and fascism, and even for a short while after Japan's defeat in
war in 1945, but was replaced in 1946 (coming into operation in May
1947) by a new constitution substituting democratic, egalitarian, and
humanist values for authoritarian and statist ones.

Supplementing the new constitution, and also adopted and coming
into effect in 1947, was the Fundamental Law of Education, which
replaced the 1890 Imperial Rescript of Education. Both functioned as
statements of the core philosophy and values underlying the education
system in their respective eras: the Rescript was a directive from the
emperor to his subjects insisting on the priority of service to the throne
and to the state as the pre-eminent moral virtues, while the Fundamental
Law entrenched the key virtues of truth, justice, and an independent
spirit.

The sixtieth anniversaries of both the constitution and the Fundamental Law were due in 2007. The latter was revised just before the New
Year, and Prime Minister Abe made clear that he would not rest until the
former too had been revised. Alongside the constitution and Fundamental Law – best seen as transcending them and constituting the

country's fundamental charter – is the US–Japan Joint Security Treaty of 1951 (revised in 1960). In effect, Japan had two 'constitutions', complementing but also contradicting each other, and of the two, the US alliance served in practice as the higher law. As we have seen, revision of the Treaty too now proceeds apace. Comprehensive institutional revision is underway.

The 1947 constitution is in several ways distinctive among modern constitutions: it was imposed by conquering forces on their defeated former enemy; it established the key democratic principles of popular sovereignty, division of powers and basic human rights; and it has lasted unrevised for sixty years. Both its progenitors in Washington and its executors in Tokyo regretted and wanted to change it (especially Article 9, the 'peace' clause) almost from the moment the ink dried, but popular resistance has blocked them.[1] Despite its unpromising origin as the dictates of a conqueror, all attempts to revise it have so far failed.

Three points deserve special attention. First, although sovereignty was accorded to the people, the constitution was nevertheless imperial – a peculiarity, discussed elsewhere in this book, which can be aptly described as oxymoronic. Second, while the 1947 document was undoubtedly a 'constitution', and therefore fundamental law, it would be impossible to understand the Japanese polity without attention also to the Security Treaty between Japan and the US – a document that was not in existence in 1947. Third, the constitution divided the country, giving rise to the 'Okinawa problem'; subtly combining pacifism and militarism, the constitution has persisted to this day. It thus incorporated not one, but a set of related contradictions. Despite everything, it has survived unrevised longer than any other modern constitution.

Divisive

Attention has often focused on the kind of national division that was avoided, between some northern sector (most probably Hokkaido), which might have been placed under separate Soviet occupation but was not, and the rest of the country. True, the entire country was placed under US-led occupation forces, but it was divided into two distinct zones: mainland Japan as 'peace state', and Okinawa as 'war state'. Even when sovereignty was restored to the government in Tokyo in 1952, Okinawa remained under American military occupation and administration until 1972, and the division persisted in a subtle way even after its 'return' to Japan, since constitutional rights were always qualified and the prefecture was compelled to submit to US military priorities. Whether under direct military rule or nominal Japanese constitutional rule, Okinawa remained essentially a 'war state', serving as a major base for wars in Korea, Vietnam, the Persian Gulf, Afghanistan and Iraq.

Imperial

As we have seen, the occupation authorities moved quickly in post-surrender Japan to build the new state around the emperor. At a time when other countries – notably Australia – were demanding that the emperor be put on trial as a war criminal,[2] Commander-in-Chief General MacArthur's central, non-negotiable demand was that he be 'at the head of the state'.[3] That insistence was shocking, since Japan had fought its war against the US and the world in the name of that same emperor, who had also been commander-in-chief of its armed forces. It was as if the US were to have fought to overthrow Saddam Hussein in 2003, but then insisted that he remain at the helm of the Iraqi state. The haste in drawing up the new constitution was partly motivated by the fear, occasioned by information from the palace, that not only were several close associates and family members of Hirohito inclining towards abdication, but so was the emperor himself – even though he was fearful that such a transition might make it more difficult to avoid indictment.[4] Receipt of that information seems to have stirred MacArthur to a new sense of urgency.[5] Three days later, he summoned the constitution draft team and issued his instructions, giving them a one-week deadline.

The first eight articles defined the role of the emperor. He presented the document to the Diet himself, as a revision of that of his grandfather, as if – as for his Meiji predecessor – it were *his* gift to *his* people. In its opening lines, the 'We' of 'We the Japanese people', stands in an ambiguous relationship to the imperial pronoun *Chin*, the royal 'We' reserved for first-person use by the emperor. The classic study of these processes, by John Dower, describes the notion of 'imperial democracy' as an oxymoron – that is to say, an implausible blending of two opposites: emperor-centredness and popular sovereignty.[6]

With the defeated Japanese commander-in-chief being assigned, and himself welcoming, a role as chief instrument of US policy, nothing could have been further from the truth than the statement in Article 1 describing him as 'deriving his position from the will of the people'. Perhaps the sharpest formulation is that by Sakai: '. . . the postwar emperor system is an American institution created by the United States for the promotion of the policies administered by the American occupation authority'.[7]

The mythological roots and foundations of the emperor system – especially the complex myths of purity and rituals of exorcism (*harai*) – together with the structures of discrimination between inner and outer built upon them, had implications that were plainly negative for civic democracy. The emperor and his immediate family were granted immunity from the burden of taxation, and from the application of the civil and criminal law, while at the same time having no right to vote. As 'head of the state', in accordance with MacArthur's prescription, Hirohito was no longer a 'god', but neither was he a Japanese 'person', since he did not enjoy such a person's rights and duties. Despite the constitutional clauses on equality between the sexes (especially Article 24), imperial succession continued to be patriarchal, and despite Articles 19 and 20 forbidding religious activity on the part of the state, the emperor also retained a significant non-constitutional function as high priest in the Shinto religion. Despite sovereignty having passed to the people, an elaborate and archaic language of respect was reserved for reference to the imperial family, whose words were not mere words (*kotoba*), but 'utterances' (*okotoba*), as if their sovereignty had never been relinquished.

What Japanese 'nationalists' celebrated as the uniqueness and purity of Japanese culture – its organic wholeness around the emperor – was actually a careful and deliberate imposition upon Japan. The identity that had been carefully constructed for modern Japan by the rising elite in the late nineteenth century was reconstructed under US direction. As long as enough people in Japan could be persuaded to imagine that they possessed a unique, superior, non-Asian Japanese identity – in which the emperor was high priest, symbol of organic wholeness, linchpin of mono-culturalism, source of racial and cultural purity, and quintessence of 'Japaneseness' – Japan could represent no universal value, and could never threaten the US by becoming an alternative pole in the global system. Retention of the emperor carried the implicit guarantee of continuing American hegemony.

Pacifist

The necessary accompaniment of restoring an emperor-centred state system had to be an assurance to the rest of Asia, which had just been laid waste by forces acting in his name, that Japan would never again launch wars within Asia. Articles 1 to 8, concerning the emperor, therefore led to the requirement of Article 9, the declaration of state pacifism:

> Aspiring sincerely to an international peace based on justice and order, the Japanese people forever renounce war as a sovereign right of the nation and the threat or use of force as a means of settling international disputes.
>
> In order to accomplish the aim of the preceding paragraph, land, sea, and air forces, as well as other war potential, will never be maintained. The right of belligerency of the state will not be recognized.

The 1947 constitutions of Japan and Costa Rica are alone in including such a statement outlawing war and armed force. Costa Rica interpreted its commitment literally, and has no armed forces or military alliances – only a police force. Japan, by contrast, spends 1 per cent of its GDP (¥4.8 trillion – around $45 billion) on the military – roughly on a par with the nuclear powers Britain and France – has an army bigger than either of them, the second-largest navy in tonnage terms (385,000 tons),[8] and a formidable air force, larger than that of Israel. It has 200 F-15 fighters, sixteen submarines (and builds a new one each year), four Aegis destroyers (and more on order), and is building two 13,500-ton aircraft carriers (coyly de-scribed as 'helicopter carriers').

No Japanese leader has ever done what might have been thought obvious: declare with pride to the world its unique constitutional pacifism as something that should be extended to other regions, and ultimately to the world as a whole. Instead, it has been an embarrassment – even a kind of shame – and the imperative to 'normalize' the country, to overcome the 'bizarre' inhibitions of Article 9, has preoccupied government after government. Today, the government clearly feels it has drawn closer than ever before to overcoming those inhibitions, and recovering from its 'war syndrome'.

The 1947 constitutional arrangements were therefore contradictory both on the question of sovereignty (popular but imperial, Japanese but American) and on the basic posture towards the world (pacifist, but under US military hegemony – and with Okinawa completely incorporated in a war system).

Constitution in practice: 1947–1990

Given these contradictory elements, how did Article 9 function in practice? The one option never considered seriously was to implement it literally – for Japan to become a pacifist, East Asian Costa Rica. Instead, attention focused for more than half a century on how to evade and empty it. While treating the requirements of the Alliance as absolute, governments consistently treated the constitution's Article 9 as an inconvenient and troublesome shackle.

The Self-Defence Forces were established in 1954, not on the basis of any constitutional warrant but in accordance with the principle of the inherent right to self-defence – one that the constitution could not have intended to deny. Defined as the minimum necessary force 'to protect the peace and independence of Japan against direct or indirect threat',[9] they were declared legitimate, regardless of what the constitution said. The Japanese public slowly came to accept their existence, and to grant the SDF slow, grudging recognition – their use was confined to disaster relief, and the fear that they might again behave *like an army* slowly receded. Precisely because they were not an army, the SDF were slowly accepted. Thus, in the teeth of hostile public opinion and the views of constitutional experts, governments created an armed force, justified it, and slowly expanded its role. The opposition slowly yielded ground as the institution of the SDF came to be seen as a fait accompli.[10] Recognizing that formal revision of the constitution was politically impossible, governments concentrated on changing its meaning by interpretation.

Revision – requiring a two-thirds majority in both houses of the Diet and a majority in a special referendum – has long been impossible, since LDP governments have been unable to muster either. Successive governments, despite the obligation on public officials under Article 99 to 'respect and uphold' the constitution, made clear their lack of respect for or commitment to Article 9. They tried hard to persuade people to accept fundamental change, but Japanese civil society resisted, tending to embrace its constitution proudly. The LDP platform from 1955 always featured the commitment to revise the constitution, but all eighteen prime ministers from 1960 to 2001 – knowing that they had no chance of accomplishing that, and that any attempt would be political suicide – promised, on assuming office, not to attempt it. Not until Koizumi, in 2001, did any prime minister break with that tradition.

When citizen groups challenged their constitutionality in the 1950s and 1960s, lower courts declared that the SDF, the security treaty with the US, and the presence of US forces in Japan it provided for, were indeed unconstitutional. But higher courts overruled these judgments on the oblique ground that the question of constitutionality was a political one, and that the will of the legislature was supreme. The courts, in effect, decided to deny themselves their constitutional prerogatives under the division of powers. During the term of his government (2001–06), Koizumi repeatedly suggested that Article 9 was absurd and anachronistic. Yasuoka Okiharu, the senior LDP official responsible under Koizumi for coordinating party policy on the constitution, conceded that the present SDF – if a spade was to be called a spade – were in breach of the constitution, which should therefore be revised.[11] Both, by implication, recognized that present arrangements were unconstitutional. Japan is distinctive among democratic governments for having persisted in breach of its constitution for over half a century.

And yet – despite having been hollowed out by tortuous, politically driven interpretation – the constitution is not entirely without meaning. Article 9 has served to constrain governments. During the Cold War, prime ministers agreed that it would be 'absolutely impossible' for the SDF ever to function outside Japan,[12] and that '[t]he duty of the Self-Defense Forces is to protect Japan from aggression. The provisions of the constitution make overseas service impossible'.[13] There was no overseas deployment of the SDF, and no conscription; there were no military exports, and a limit was placed on the defence budget of 1 per cent of

GDP. Governments also observed the three 'non-nuclear principles', forbidding the possession, manufacture, or introduction into Japan of nuclear weapons.[14] The pacifist principle was attenuated, a process that continued in the twenty-first century, when the SDF were sent to the Indian Ocean and Iraq.

After 1990

From the end of the Cold War, the pressure grew on the constitution, and especially on Article 9. Washington wanted Japan to set aside its inhibitions and assume a more vigorous – albeit compliant and subordinate – role as military ally. Knowing that the Japanese government was agonizing over the compatibility of any troop dispatch with the constitution, Deputy Secretary of State Richard Armitage offered the gratuitous advice (already quoted in Chapter 4, above) on how Japan could best overcome the obstacle to full participation in the 'War on Terror' presented by its constitution. In July 2004 he told the head of a visiting LDP delegation that the alliance was being impeded by the constitution, and that Japan's admission as a permanent member of the Security Council would require it to revise Article 9.[15] As if to reinforce the urgency of this, Defense Secretary Colin Powell also remarked that Article 9 would have to be revised if Japan wished to be considered for a permanent seat.[16] From such senior representatives of the Bush administration, these suggestions could not be interpreted as anything but orders. The revisionist camp in Japan rushed to comply – even while insisting, at the level of rhetoric, that the constitution had to be revised to escape from the humiliation of the MacArthur imposition of fifty years earlier.

Nothing could be further from the words or spirit of Article 9 than the Bush administration's goal of having Japan become a fully fledged, Nato-style 'partner', rendering military, political and diplomatic support on a global scale: the 'Britain' of East Asia.[17] It is true that the US did not explicitly demand revision, but the repeated intimation that it was essential for Japan to cooperate in the use of force – on occasions to be determined unilaterally by the US – constituted an unmistakable intervention in Japanese political affairs, and a virtual ultimatum.

When Japanese forces embarked for Iraq, in January 2004, it was the first time in sixty years that they had been committed to a war – albeit in a subordinate and non-combat role. They were thus not only flouting the interpretation of the constitution on which Japanese governments had previously relied (the protection of Japan against direct or indirect threat), but acting with neither the legal justification of a Security Council resolution nor the moral pretext of Iraq's possession of weapons of mass destruction, as determined by intelligence later shown to be false. Koizumi spoke of the imperative of proving Japan's 'trustworthiness' to the US, as if that consideration outweighed the constitution, law, or morality. He had come close to accomplishing what previous conserva-tive leaders had only dreamed of doing: transforming the SDF into a de facto regular army.[18] It was no coincidence that he focused simulta-neously on restoring the centrality of Yasukuni as the location in which sacrificial death for the nation could be ritually celebrated, and on committing Japanese forces to a active future role under US direction in containing the 'Arc of Instability'. Future deaths, like past ones, could be celebrated.

When he decided to send the SDF to Iraq, Koizumi addressed the constitutional problem by offering a new and unique interpretation of the preamble's pledge to 'occupy an honoured place in an international society striving for the preservation of peace' – suggesting that this vague sentiment should take precedence over the specific clauses in the body of the text. It was an interpretation that left constitutional scholars aghast.[19] On the other hand, he also argued that the matter was in any case not important, since constitutional difficulties were so much 'theological quibble',[20] and what really mattered was 'common sense' – something that he, as prime minister, was uniquely qualified to offer. Koizumi's position was that

> [i]n the common-sense terms of the people, the SDF is surely 'military force' . . . if we talk in terms of principles rather than of pretence . . . the fact is that the constitution itself is out of step with international common sense.[21]

As he put it on another occasion, 'The SDF is an army . . . It should be called the National Army of Japan [*Nihon kokugun*].'[22]

Revision: the prescription of 2005

After a decade of well-orchestrated, media-led campaigning to revise the constitution, and a five-year process of Diet deliberation, in April 2005 the Diet's Constitutional Research Councils presented their reports, and in November the Liberal Democratic Party unveiled its draft revision.[23] The LDP draft had four major strands:

1) A Rewritten Preamble. Setting a framework for the detailed provisions, the Preamble would be completely rewritten. The idealistic and internationalist sentiments of the existing constitution, with its expression of the desire for 'peace for all time . . . [t]rusting in the justice and faith of the peace-loving people of the world', and its statement that 'never again shall we be visited with the horrors of war through the action of government', would be changed to a bald statement that the people of Japan shared a 'duty to support and defend the nation and society to which they belong with love, a sense of responsibility, and spirit', and a commitment to 'cooperate with other countries out of the desire to realize international peace based on justice and order'. The existing Preamble makes no reference whatever to the emperor, but the new one would declare a commitment to the 'symbolic emperor system'.

2) Revision of Article 9. The Article would be headed 'Security' instead of 'Prevention of War', and it would ratify the SDF as an 'Army' (Self-Defence Army or *Jieigun*), whose role would be (a) the defence of Japan, (b) cooperation in 'guaranteeing the peace and security of international society', and (c) maintaining public order in emergencies. An accompanying revision to Article 76 would establish special courts martial with jurisdiction over military personnel.

3) Revision of Article 20 (3). This revision would exempt acts 'within the limits of social etiquette and practice' from the prohibition on state involvement in religious activities, thereby justifying the continuation of the prime minister's controversial practice of making regular formal visits to Yasukuni Shrine.[24]

4) Revision of Article 96. This would simplify future revision by lowering the requirement of a two-thirds majority in the Diet to one-half.

The Japanese message to the world adumbrated by such changes to its basic charter could be summed up by saying: Japan would stand shoulder-to-shoulder with the US in future regional and global conflicts, including potentially Iran and Korea; Japan would continue to brush off objections from its neighbours to its religious rituals commemorating the war, and would nullify court rulings of unconstitutionality by extending state recognition to religious rituals in honour of the war dead, even at the cost of significantly worsening relations with its region; and Japan would proceed with more radical constitutional amendments in future, once the threshold for doing so had been lowered.

The draft also included a new section on the duties of citizens to the state, making the people responsible for 'public interests and public order' instead of 'the public welfare', as at present. The stress on 'duties' marks something unprecedented in modern constitutional discourse, and at last a partial return to the spirit of the constitution of 1890.

Although the rhetoric of revision made frequent reference to the establishment of a sovereign constitution – replacing the 'American' model of 1946 with a 'Japanese' one – Washington's interests and desires were reflected in the drafts of 2005 and 2006 no less than in that of 1946. In the modern history of constitutionalism, this Japanese effort is therefore unique in being undertaken at the behest, and in the interests, of a foreign government,[25] and in reinforcing the powers of the state while shrinking the rights of citizens. Taken together with the regularization of the Japanese army in the new Article 9, the revisions as a whole would have the effect of imposing patriotism as a constitutional obligation to respect and submit to the state, and also of increasing the probability of Japanese commitment to future US-led military interventions and wars.

Though such changes were very significant, they were more modest than the LDP would have liked. The draft had been softened in the interests of securing enough support from other parties to reach the necessary two-thirds vote in the Diet, and it had been sharply focused on the matters of greatest import to the US. Much of the LDP's 'identity' rhetoric – in particular that about 'the nation's spiritual dimension'[26] –

had been sacrificed; the project to have the emperor declared 'sovereign' (*genshu*) had been set aside for the time being; and references to culture, tradition, and patriotism had been minimized.

The hard-core revisionist agenda related to Articles 9 and 20: to the armed forces, and to Yasukuni. These two demands paralleled the two major impositions of MacArthur in 1946 – relating to the emperor and to Article 9 – and were equally necessitated by US, rather than Japanese, concerns. Popular sovereignty and fundamental human rights, the third principle for MacArthur, remained as subordinate a consideration in 2005 as it had been in 1946.

To try to mobilize the necessary support to get such changes through the Diet and to win a referendum, there was also a softer agenda. Early drafts waxed idealistically about Japan's destiny to help eliminate from the earth 'human calamities caused by military conflicts, natural disasters, environmental destruction, economic deprivation in particular areas and regional disorder'. Japan's armed forces would serve 'for the maintenance and promotion of peace and for humanitarian support activities'.[27] The Democratic Party's Ozawa Ichiro (former LDP secretary-general) even proposed that the Self-Defence Forces, apart from a few tactical and training units, could simply be placed directly under the control of the UN – the idea of a standing army, in his view, being as dead as the twentieth century.[28]

The closer the actual revision process became, however, the more 'realist' and American priorities swamped 'idealist' and Japanese ones. By late 2005, the 'soft' agenda comprised a few items for the protection of privacy and reputation (Article 19: 2), protection of the environment (Article 25: 2), the duty of government to explain its behaviour to the people (Article 21: 2), and even – bizarrely in light of the state of the country's finances – the duty (whose it is not made clear) 'always to take the health of the public finances into consideration' (Article 83: 2). Some of these matters – such as privacy and the environment – were more relevant to specific legislation than to constitutional provision; others – about the government explaining itself to the people – were a meaningless mishmash.

Within the LDP, both left and right wings of the party were unhappy with the October 2005 draft. From the shrunken ranks of liberals, Kato Koichi – a former party secretary-general and a sharp critic of Koizumi's 'extremely nationalistic' foreign policy – insisted that revision was premature as long as there existed 'no community consensus on the desired shape of the nation'.[29] The fiercest criticism of the draft came from the party's most passionate and committed advocate of constitutional reform – former Prime Minister Nakasone, who pronounced the Koizumi government draft 'shoddy and imprudent'. Nakasone believed that Japan was uniquely 'a *natural nation*, built on accreted history and tradition'[30] – a blood community rather than a constitutional state – and was angry that the draft adopted by the party completely neglected the nation's spiritual tradition. His belief in the organic and superior qualities of Japaneseness had led him in 1986 to remark famously that Japan was 'an intelligent society', with a much higher 'average score' than countries like the US, because, he explained, '[t]here are many blacks, Puerto Ricans and Mexicans in America. In consequence the average score over there is exceedingly low.'[31]

In the twenty-first century he insisted that Japan needed to adopt a new 'Heisei constitution', which would allow it finally to leave the 'US greenhouse' and 'normalize itself'.[32] The preamble, he insisted, should express 'the image of the nation as a whole, including the continuity of its history, culture, and tradition as well as the people'.[33] The emperor should be assigned the role of 'head of state of Japan', in an attempt to articulate the kind of ' "authority" born of Japan's cultural and historical traditions'.[34] Nakasone's own draft preamble therefore began: 'We, the Japanese people, inheritors of these beautiful Northeast Asian islands lapped by the waves of the Pacific to the East of the Asian continent, having the emperor as symbol of the unity of the people, valuing harmony . . .'[35] Since his preamble had been drawn up by the special LDP commission designed for that purpose and headed by him, he was indignant when it was rudely brushed aside.

The Nakasone agenda had clearly taken second place to the considerations judged most urgent and immediate – the one on which the US government had put the most pressure (Article 9), and the one that had caused most trouble with neighbours (Article 20). Once they had been resolved, and the process of further revision simplified, more contentious matters could be addressed. Yasuoka Okiharu, the senior LDP official responsible for coordinating party policy on the constitution, echoed Nakasone in his call for stress on what he called *wagakuni no kunigara* (literally, 'our country's distinctive character'). He expressed himself in the following terms:

> Put simply, we mean national identity . . . For example, the
> emperor is the concentrated expression of Japanese history and
> tradition. Ours is seen by the world as an outstanding culture,
> unique in our emperor system that provides a symbolic pointer for
> the expression of our people's sentiments and for their feelings of
> respectful devotion.[36]

Although Yasuoka denied it when it was put to him in these terms, it
seems clear that he was seeking to restore a sense of emperor-centred
national identity like that known in prewar and wartime Japan as *kokutai*
('national polity'). In repeating the sentiments of then Prime Minister
Mori in June 2000 that Japan was a 'land of the gods centred on the
emperor', he was reverting to the language and values of prewar and
wartime Japanese leaders. To Japan's neighbours, such talk is filled with
menace – especially since it clearly reflects the view shared by many in the
political elite.[37]

While priority had been attached to satisfying American demands, the
LDP's constitutional draft held an ominous promise of fundamental
constitutional rights, unqualified in the 1947 dispensation, that would
become conditional. Thus, Article 12 would read:

> The freedom and rights which this constitution guarantees the
> people must be maintained by the constant effort of the people.
> The people must not misuse them, and, aware that duties and
> obligations accompany freedom and rights, they have a duty to
> enjoy liberty and exercise rights so as not to infringe upon the
> public good and public order.[38]

Modern constitutional history had no precedent for such threatening
language.

The LDP's effort to regularize the armed forces, and its determination
to legitimize Yasukuni, also promised to introduce new tensions into the
Japan–US relationship, however much the revisionists were moved by
desire to please the Americans. Deprived of any constitutional ground for
resisting US pressures to send troops to one area of crisis or another, each
such US demand stood in future to become the subject of potentially
bitter political contest; and Yasukuni, whether the constitutional problem relating to it was resolved or not, commemorated those who had

died in the service of the state in past wars, including leaders of the war against the US.

The US government has so far avoided direct comment on the Yasukuni controversy, but – as one senior, dissenting LDP member (and former secretary-general of the party) has pointed out – the US cannot ignore a breach of the San Francisco treaty.[39] Before it is a problem in relations with China and South Korea, Yasukuni is therefore a problem in the US–Japan relationship. The US can scarcely continue to turn a blind eye to a Japanese revisionism that downplays or denies responsibility for the war against the US; and it is hard to imagine a US president ever accompanying a Japanese prime minister on a formal visit to pay his respects at Yasukuni.

Constitutional prospects

By 2005 the Diet had the numbers necessary to pass a revision – 83 per cent of Diet-members prior to the election of September, and even more after it.[40] The major parties and business groups, and some of the large media groups, are committed to revision. Dissent is confined to tiny opposition parties, academics, and citizens' and grassroots organizations. In opinion surveys, too, a majority now supports constitutional revision.

However, while polls conducted by major newspapers report around 60 per cent of people in favour of revision, such general sentiment does not extend to the revision of Article 9. A comprehensive study was made of the nation's newspapers, large and small, based on their editorials and on surveys conducted around constitution Day 2005. It concluded a 60:40 commitment among the public to retaining Article 9 without revision.[41] The largest paper, the *Yomiuri shimbun*, which serves as a kind of think-tank for the ruling party, after devoting intense energy for a decade and a half to the project, in 2004 expressed irritation at the stubbornness of public opinion, saying in its editorial that 'a few extremists still insist on keeping the current constitution intact' – thereby casting defenders of the constitution as extremists.[42] The following year, finding 43.6 per cent in favour of revision of Article 9 – slightly less than the 46 per cent opposing it – it concluded that there was probably insufficient political will to carry the revision process through. In March 2006, a *Mainichi Shimbun* opinion survey found a mere 17 per cent support for the LDP draft.[43] Despite the evidence of failing resolve at the heart of the revisionist campaign, however, the LDP was committed to pursuing the process to its conclusion.[44] Prime Minister Abe's New Year address for 2007 made clear that he wanted it to be a core issue for the mid-year Upper House election.

Table 6: Constitutional revision and revision of Article 9 (2005)

	Revision of Constitution		Revision of A9	
	For	Against	For	Against
Asahi	56	33	36	51
Yomiuri	61	27	44	46*

* Made up of 27.6 per cent who would either retain it as it is or else widen the interpretation, plus 18.1 per cent who insist on holding fast to a literal interpretation. A 2005 NHK survey found that 43 per cent of people had never even the Constitution, and a 2006 *Asahi Shimbun* survey found that 52 per cent knew 'almost nothing' of the Constitution.

Source: material for both tables from May 2005/2006 issues of *Asahi Shimbun* and *Yomiuri Shimbun*.

Table 7: Constitutional revision and revision of Article 9 (2006)

	Revision of Constitution		Revision of A9	
	For	Against	For	Against
Asahi	55	32	43*	42
Yomiuri	56	32	39	33

*Made up of: change paragraph 1 (9 per cent); change paragraph 2 (16 per cent); change both paragraphs (18 per cent). However, 62 per cent also said, somewhat contradictorily, that the constitution should be revised to state clearly the existence of the SDF.

The lack of political will behind the LDP's constitutional reform agenda is reflected in opinion polls on the political priorities of the Japanese majority. There is little sign of Japanese public support for the sort of future global military role being urged by the US, or for the provision of a constitutional endorsement for the practice of worship at Yasukuni. When asked, in a survey of April 2004, what they saw as the most urgent issue facing the country, 87 per cent identified pensions and welfare, and only 8 per cent constitutional revision.[45] As for what was important for the future peace and prosperity of Japan, most (51 per cent) cited the reinforcement of ties with Asian countries. Only 7 per cent identified the reinforcement of the security alliance with the US, 11 per cent the reinforcement of Japan's autonomous defence capacity, and 11 per cent the reinforcement of Japan's UN commitment.[46] More than half the people thought support for international crisis areas should be confined to medical and refugee aid. Most (just over 52 per cent) opposed the dispatch of the SDF when Koizumi committed them in 2003.[47] Only 8.7 per cent supported cooperation in the US-led coalition through weapons supply and transport (the line actually adopted by the government), while 52.3 per cent favoured medical and refugee aid.[48] Only 6 per cent believed the SDF should be able to offer logistic support to American forces.[49] In other words, popular priorities were almost precisely the inverse of those pursued by government.

In Washington, Canberra and London, high-level manipulation of Japan's constitution was taken as realism, and as evidence of positive engagement with the region and the world. By opening the path to Japanese participation in 'international' coalitions, with or without UN sanction, Japan would be assuring itself a prominent role in the future 'War on Terror' and other wars; and the price for the gratitude it would earn from the US for 'stepping up to the plate' would be a widening gulf between Japan and its neighbours.

While many Western commentators think a newly assertive Japan will soon opt for revision of Article 9, and thus for a 'normal' military posture and collective security capacity, Chinese and Korean analysts, on the other hand, tend to see Japan as poised on the brink of 1930s-style militarism. Both may be underestimating the popular strength of commitment to Article 9, and the difficulty of persuading the majority of people to accept radical institutional change – as well as overestimating the ability of the US and Japanese governments to impose their will. Things might yet move in a different direction: US pressure on Japan may provoke a counter-reaction that threatens the alliance. The rumblings in Okinawa and elsewhere about the proposed reorganization of US forces in Japan, and the assimilation of the SDF to their purposes, suggest a widespread frustration and anger.

Constitutionalist alternatives

The elections of September 2005 had the effect of reducing parliamentary opposition to constitutional revision to the handful of Communist and Social Democratic Party members, plus a very few mavericks on the government benches. That did not necessarily mean that the LDP bill would secure the necessary two-thirds majority, however, since the sentiment for revision was not matched by agreement on exactly what revisions should be made – and also because, outside the Diet, popular coalitions were mobilizing to oppose revision.

A 'Citizens' constitutional Forum', involving a number of constitutional scholars, drew up a provisional draft constitution in April 2005. It featured retention of the symbolic emperor, but relegated it to a single clause (Article 6), while clarifying popular sovereignty by substituting the word 'citizens' (*shimin*) for 'Japanese people' (*kokumin*). References to the duties of the people (under Chapter 3, in 31 clauses in the section entitled 'Rights and Duties of the People') were deleted, and new rights were added, including rights for foreign residents. Article 9 was retained without amendment.[50] Their approach could thus be described as 'moderate reformist'.

Another significant attempt to reconcile Article 9 with Japan's commitment to its own defence and to regional and global security was the 'Proposal for a Basic Law on Peace',[51] first articulated in 1993 and 1994, and then reformulated in 2005 by a prominent group of academics.[52] The joint US–Japan security relationship, they argued, was in the process of transformation from its present scope – Japan-centred, confined to a perspective defined by the Far East and Cold War – to become an ill-defined, flexible relationship to deal with any 'regional contingency', under the 'New Guidelines' of the 1990s. Following 9/11, this would entail the deployments of the SDF to the Indian Ocean and Iraq, as part of their assimilation within the US-led global, permanent war on 'terror'. In this scheme, China was projected as a hypothetical enemy – a term not applied to the Soviet Union even at the height of the Cold War. These academics argued that, although the SDF looked like an army – which they defined as an armed state force primarily dedicated to the extermination of enemies – and although the prime minister said it was tantamount to one, the various constraints upon it in fact gave it a quite different character.

They therefore proposed that the existing SDF be shrunk, abolishing any conventional attack force elements, and then split and reorganized into (a) a territorial defence unit, (b) a disaster relief unit (for dispatch both domestically and overseas), and (c) an international emergency force under UN command. They argued that the danger of foreign invasion was slight, while the possibility of a large earthquake, nuclear power plant accident, volcano eruption, flood, tidal wave, outbreak of infectious disease, disaster induced by climate change, food crisis, or energy crisis, was real, and that a large standing army offered little protection in any of these events. The SDF role in Cambodia, the Golan Heights, Rwanda and East Timor had gained acceptance within Japan, as well as international gratitude; but the SDF was not trained to deal with such events. To deal with such eventualities in the future – and to address problems such as piracy, drugs, weapons, human trafficking, and so on – they argued that specialist training and skills were required.

Early in 2006, the opposition Social Democratic Party adopted a policy that drew on these recommendations, holding that, while the existence of the Self-Defence Forces was not in itself unconstitutional, they were now in a 'clearly unconstitutional state' because of their activities in the Middle East and the Indian Ocean, and that they should be downsized and reorganized into separate units for border security, disaster relief, and international cooperation.[53]

Meanwhile, at the grassroots level, a remarkable attempt to stem the political and bureaucratic tide of constitutional change was underway, paralleling the citizens' initiatives against the Vietnam War undertaken by the *Beheiren* (Citizens' League for Peace in Vietnam) in the 1960s and 1970s. A group of citizen-intellectuals came together in June 2004 to organize what they called an 'Article 9 Association'. Their initial appeal included the statement that

> [t]he United States' attack on Iraq and the morass of the occupation that followed makes it clearer to us day by day that the resolution of conflict through force is unrealistic . . . That is why, in such places as Europe and Southeast Asia, efforts are being strengthened to create regional frameworks that can help to resolve conflicts through diplomacy and dialogue.

Today, as we question our path in the twenty-first century

based on the lessons of the twentieth, the importance of grounding diplomacy on Article 9 emerges with renewed clarity.

. . .

Based on Article 9, Japan needs to develop ties of friendship and cooperation with the peoples of Asia and other regions, and change a diplomatic stance that only prioritizes a military alliance with the United States. Japan must play an active role in the tide of world history by exercising its autonomy and acting in a pragmatic manner. It is precisely because of Article 9 that Japan can engage its partner nations in peaceful diplomacy while respecting their various positions . . .

Within the span of two years, 5,000 such Article 9 Associations had spread across the country.[54] Like the grassroots organizations that had proved so successful in blocking the adoption of revisionist history textbooks in schools, these expressions of local initiative pointed to the continuing strength of democratic and constitution-alist forces.

The Fundamental Law of Education

The Fundamental Law of Education was adopted in 1947, just over one month before the constitution came into operation. Japan's 'Fundamental Laws' occupy a special constitutional position in the framework of state institutions and principles, setting out the philosophy, para-meters and guidelines covering particular fields. Thus there are Fundamental Laws of Land, Environment, Science and Technology, Food Safety, Small and Medium Enterprises, and so on. The ethos of the education Fundamental Law was clearly the same democratic and humanist one as that of the constitution. Unlike the constitution, however, it had been drawn up entirely by Japanese officials, in Japanese.

The 1947 Fundamental Law of Education began:

Having established the constitution of Japan, we have shown our resolution to contribute to the world and welfare of humanity by building a democratic and cultural state. The realization of this idea shall depend fundamentally on the power of education.

We shall esteem individual dignity and endeavour to bring up the people who love truth and peace, while education aimed at the creation of culture, general and rich in individuality, shall be spread far and wide.

The aim of education was defined in the following terms:

Education shall aim at the full development of personality, striving for the rearing of the people, sound in mind and body, who shall love truth and justice, esteem individual value, respect labour and have a deep sense of responsibility, and be imbued with the independent spirit, as builders of peaceful state and society.

Conservatives have long resented such universalist, humanist sentiments. They look back instead with nostalgia to the Imperial Rescript on Education of 1890, from which prewar and wartime education took its spirit. That sacred text, committed to memory in schools and recited on ceremonial occasions, served as a central pillar in the construction of the emperor-centred – and later emperor-worshipping – society and state. In it, the emperor commended his subjects for their 'loyalty and filial piety', and called on them to be ready at any moment to sacrifice their lives when bidden to do so in his name.

Our Imperial Ancestors have founded Our Empire on a basis broad and everlasting and have deeply and firmly implanted virtue; Our subjects ever united in loyalty and filial piety have from generation to generation illustrated the beauty thereof. This is the glory of the fundamental character of Our Empire, and herein also lies the source of Our education.

Ye, Our subjects, be filial to your parents, affectionate to your brothers and sisters; as husbands and wives be harmonious, as friends true; bear yourselves in modesty and moderation; extend your benevolence to all; pursue learning and cultivate arts, and thereby develop intellectual faculties and perfect moral powers; furthermore advance public good and promote common interests; always respect the constitution and observe the laws; *should emergency arise, offer yourselves courageously to the State; and thus guard and maintain the prosperity of Our Imperial Throne* coeval with heaven and earth [italics added].

From the 1950s to the 1990s, successive prime ministers – including Kishi, Tanaka, Nakasone, and Mori – all expressed admiration and praise for the Rescript. In the 1990s, bullying, collapse of classes, suicide, violence and juvenile crime became subjects of national concern, feeding a growing sense of national crisis, institutional fatigue, and loss of direction. An astonishing 45 per cent of Japanese high school students said that they did no study at all outside their classrooms (the figure being one-third of that in the US, and just under one-sixth of that in China), and over 70 per cent reported feelings of worthlessness.[55] In 1998, the UN Committee on the Rights of the Child issued a report heavily critical of the fact that Japanese children were exposed to 'developmental disorders due to stress of a highly competitive educational system', and to widespread corporal punishment and bullying in schools.[56] Bureaucrats and conservative thinkers interpreted the crisis of education as evidence of the loss of national pride and identity. Under the postwar US model, they came to believe that individual rights had been overemphasized and social and national purpose neglected. In the 1990s, they launched a national media campaign urging enforcement of the principles of public-spiritedness, morality (*dotokushin*) and love of country. Students would also be compelled to undertake community work experience. They urged the adoption of textbooks designed to inculcate a sense of 'national pride' and a 'correct' understanding of history. Revision of the Fundamental Law of Education became the central proposal in their platform.

Former Prime Minister Nakasone has for decades been at the forefront of the movement to revise the Fundamental Law. As he put it, 'The Fundamental Law is like distilled water. It doesn't have the taste of Japanese water. There is too much American or British-style individualism . . . nothing about collective order, discipline, self-sacrifice or responsibility'.[57] When asked what he meant by the 'Japanese tradition and culture' that was somehow being neglected, and that should be given emphasis in education, Nakasone replied that he meant 'the emperor system, plus *wabi, sabi,* and *mono no aware*' (almost untranslatable expressions meaning, roughly, a sensitivity to the solitary, the ancient, and the impermanence of things).[58] Liberals, on the one hand, tended to see the problem in terms of a standardization of education through excessive egalitarianism and neglect of talent, producing a failure to cultivate the competitive spirit necessary for globalized Japanese capitalism. For them, reform was to be pursued by shrinking the state role, increasing competition, cultivating links with industry, fostering individual talents and competitiveness, and adapting corporate business models to the schools – in short, precisely the 'American or British-style individualism' that Nakasone deplored. It was hard to see how the two agendas could be reconciled, but the revision movement strove to square precisely this circle.

Bureaucratic thinking was influenced too by the knowledge of the dire state of the national finances, and by the inevitability of budgetary cuts affecting welfare and education. Having squandered the people's wealth and borrowed massively from future generations over the past two decades, governments were now compelled to impose tight constraints on future spending. If the projected budget cut in the decade to 2015 is to be anything like the 32 per cent recommended by the Fiscal System Council in its 2006 advice to the finance minister,[59] the neoliberal agenda would be hard to resist.

For Nakasone, Japan at the beginning of the twenty-first century was facing 'its biggest crisis not only of the fifty postwar years, but also of its more than 100 years of post-Meiji Restoration history . . . Postwar education has destroyed the nation . . . above all with its emphasis on rights'.[60] Abe Shinzo, then chief cabinet secretary, offered revision of the Fundamental Law of Education as his prescription for the immorality of the times, exemplified by 'children killing their parents, parents abandoning their children, and the climate of money-worship'.[61] A prominent opposition party parliamentarian, Nishimura Shingo, addressed the inaugural meeting of the Association for Revision of the Fundamental Law of Education with the statement that the purpose of revision was 'to produce Japanese ready to die for their country'.[62] For him, the purpose was not strictly speaking educational so much as that of turning the clock back to the era when the country was taught to long for glorious death, united around the emperor.

The thinking of men such as Nakasone, Nishimura, and Abe is contested from within as well as beyond conservative ranks. One of Japan's best-known scholars of philosophy and religion, and himself a prominent conservative, Umehara Takeshi, comments on the values of the Rescript that

[n]owadays some people argue that the Fundamental Law of Education . . . should be revised, because it does not spell out respect for Japanese tradition, and after that the constitution too should be revised. It is unclear how these individuals perceive tradition, but it seems that they see the Imperial Rescript on Education . . . as something rooted in Japanese tradition, and believe that the Japanese will become fine, moral people if moral education rooted in the spirit of this Rescript is implemented. But is it really the case that the Imperial Rescript on Education is rooted in Japanese tradition?[63]

For Umehara, the Rescript, with its injunction to 'die for the emperor', had been responsible for immeasurable suffering in a reckless and irresponsible war, and – far from being the crystallization of some deep Japanese value – was actually a deliberate assault on Japanese religion and tradition. Killing off both the Buddha and the Kami (Shinto deities), '[i]n the space created by the absence of both Buddha and Kami [the Meiji state leaders] set the emperor as the new divinity'.

Let me repeat. The Imperial Rescript on Education is not some-thing rooted in Japanese tradition. Is it not rather the case that revival of the Imperial Rescript on Education would allow poli-ticians, who have neither knowledge nor virtue and who have no love whatever for traditional culture but care only for their self-interest, make the people do their will by representing it as the order of the emperor?

Like the constitution, the Fundamental Law had been subjected to decades of 'hollowing out' under successive conservative administrations and increasingly assertive bureaucrats. Its plain words were twisted to serve other ends. As Norma Field notes, the LDP was 'consistently opposed to the principles embodied in these documents'.[64] Already, in the late 1950s, the Ministry of Education wrested control of the nation's schools back from the locally elected boards and re-imposed what it called 'moral education' (using a different term – *dotoku kyoiku* – from the prewar *shushin*, with its strongly emperor-centred and militarist connotations). The level of bureaucratic intervention in the daily routines of the classroom also steadily increased, through complex directives covering all aspects of schooling – not least the keeping of confidential personal reports on each middle school student (*naishinsho*), and 'lifestyle guidance' (*seikatsu shido*) on appearance, clothing, and private life.[65] From 2002, students were required to maintain a personal notebook, *Kokoro no Noto* ('Notebook on the Heart') recording their efforts to achieve self-discipline, concern for others, respect for the law and for superiors, and love of country. Their thoughts were then subject to scrutiny and accompanying psychological guidance from their teachers, who in turn were under ministerial direction.[66]

Intervention in the details of the curriculum and supervision over texts for the teaching of history and social science were slowly stepped up from the 1980s. Known technically as 'screening', the Japanese Ministry of Education insisted it did not amount to censorship, although the pattern of official interventions – especially in history and social science – made that claim implausible. Especially from 1982, when a furor erupted over the substitution of a word meaning 'advance' (*shinshutsu*) for 'invasion' (*shinryaku*) to refer to Japan's 1930s expansion into China, neighbouring countries have also been acutely sensitive to the way matters of war responsibility – including 'comfort women', the Nanjing Massacre, and the biological and chemical warfare units centring on Unit 731 in Harbin – were addressed. For two decades and more, bitter 'culture wars' have raged over these issues both within Japan itself and between officials representing Japan and other regional countries. During the early 1990s, when LDP hegemony was temporarily ruptured, state responsibility for the 'comfort women' system was admitted, and a resolution of apology for colonialism and aggression passed the Diet.[67] Textbooks began to cover hitherto untouched questions of Japan's modern history, including the 'comfort women' system, the Nanjing Massacre, Unit 731, aggression and war crimes, and the truth about the Battle of Okinawa. A national consensus of contrition seemed to be emerging.

In reaction, however, a diehard movement of nationalist resistance grew, directed at implementing a 'correct' history, centred on Japan's pure and proud traditions, justifying the war of the 1930s and 1940s as one for the liberation of East Asia, and denying or belittling the atrocities and crimes committed. Officials steadily exercised their prerogatives in 'suggesting' revisions, and authors and publishers slowly adjusted their texts in order to conform. Education Minister Nakayama Nariaki expressed his satisfaction at the outcome: 'It is really good that there are now fewer references to comfort women and forced labour.'[68]

In the 2006 screening process, particular care was exercised to water down references to atrocities by the armed forces of Imperial Japan; territorial disputes with neighbour countries (Korea, China, Russia); the meaning of Article 9 of the constitution; the constitutionality and legality of the dispatch of the SDF to Iraq and of the prime-ministerial visits to Yasukuni shrine; and to questions of nuclear energy and gender.[69] Passive formulations were to be preferred – to women *being abducted* and turned into sex slaves – rather than active ones in which the Imperial Japanese Army did the abducting and enslaving; discussions of Nanjing were required to avoid the word 'massacre' and insist on the uncertainty over the number of victims; Dokdo (Takeshima island) had to be described as unambiguously Japanese territory, despite having long been under South Korean control; the 'humanitarian' mission of the troops dispatched to Iraq had to be mentioned in any discussion of Japan's role in the Iraq War; the prime minister's visits to Yasukuni should not be described as 'official' – and so on.

But while bureaucratic interventions in the screening process steadily whittled down and shaped the content of the curriculum, the attempts by protagonists of a 'pure' Japanese history to produce and promote their own texts for classroom use bore little fruit. Although branches of the organization were set up even at the local level through the country, and a text on Japanese history was submitted and approved in 2001, not one of the country's 542 public middle schools adopted it. When a revised text was submitted and approved in 2005, a fierce struggle erupted at grassroots level throughout the country. A few schools – even public ones – did adopt the text, but the figure nation-wide reached less than 1 per cent, far from the 10 per cent target. It amounted to defeat and humiliation for the Association for New History Textbooks (*Tsukur-ukai*). The organization was reported to be suffering frustration and doubt over the deepening diplomatic isolation to which its campaign had contributed, and several key members defected.[70]

Traditionalists attached special importance to the symbols and rituals of national identity, especially to the flag and anthem, *Hinomaru* and *Kimigayo*. These were far from trivial matters, since to Japan's neighbours the *Hinomaru* and *Kimigayo* were symbols of imperialism, war and aggression, much as are the Swastika and *Deutschland über Alles* in Europe. Many Japanese had at best mixed feelings about steps to compel their reinstatement. From 1985, at the direction of then Prime Minister Nakasone, the *Hinomaru* flag and *Kimigayo* anthem began to be accorded pride of place in school opening and graduation ceremonies, but the pattern of compliance was irregular. In some prefectures observance of the flag and anthem rituals was as low as 10 per cent. Hiroshima and Okinawa – the places that had suffered most from the war and had the strongest attachment to the principles of peace and democracy – showed greatest resistance, and not a single Okinawan school included the flag and anthem in its ceremonies.[71] Bureaucratic pressure was therefore stepped up – notably by a formal directive from the Ministry of Education in 1998. In February 1999, the principal of Sera High School in Hiroshima committed suicide, unable to cope with the contradictory pressures from the Ministry of Education – which had begun to impose sanctions (including pay cuts) in the effort to achieve compliance – and from teachers, students, and parents, who resisted. In the graduation ceremony held at his school in the following spring, the entire graduating class of the school sat in silent protest through the performance of the *Kimigayo*.[72] The bureaucratic response was to step up the pressure even further – this time with special legislation, adopted in 1999, to declare *Hinomaru* and *Kimigayo* the national flag and anthem. Prime Minister Obuchi promised at the time of introducing the law that there would be no compulsion.[73] By 2000, national observance was reported to have jumped to 100 per cent.[74]

Despite the assurances of non-compulsion and the reported 100 per cent observance, however, in 2003 the Tokyo metropolitan government issued an explicit directive that the flag and anthem rituals be carried out at school opening and graduation ceremonies, and thereafter the numbers of recalcitrant teachers grew steadily. Governor Ishihara Shintaro's nominee on the Board of Education, Toriumi Iwao, former president of the Marubeni Corporation, insisted that there could be no relenting. 'Unless we thoroughly extirpate [those opposed to the flag and anthem rituals], the root of evil will persist, especially since this cancer has been left to fester for fifty years. We have to uproot it so that no trace remains, otherwise it will replicate.'[75] Inspectors were dispatched around the schools to videotape the proceedings of school ceremonies, reporting teachers whose mouths did not open during the singing, recording the levels of vocal output (low, medium, full-throated).[76] In some schools chairs were removed, so that teachers opposed to the routine would have no place to sit. In Kitakyushu, the local department of education further specified that all staff and students must not only stand for the anthem but must sing 'sincerely' (*tadashiku kokoro o komete*) – precisely the formula used in the 1930s to specify the way students under the Meiji constitution had had to sing the very same anthem as part of their state Shinto, emperor-worshipping education.[77] Such centralizing and intrusive 'reforms' were difficult to reconcile with the guarantees of freedom of thought and conscience in Articles 19 and 20 of the constitution, or with Article 14 (1) of the UN Convention on the Rights of the Child – 'State parties shall respect the right of the child to freedom of thought, conscience, and religion.' Ironically, the emperor himself intervened in an attempt to put a brake on this clampdown, admonishing a Tokyo education department official who had told him at a reception late in 2004 that he was making sure that all schools complied with the new directive: 'It would be better', Akihito responded, 'if it were not done compulsorily.'[78]

By 2006, hundreds of Tokyo teachers were facing disciplinary measures. They were asked to reflect on their 'misdeeds' and pledge not to repeat them, and they faced pay cuts and temporary suspensions. It was a contemporary equivalent of the prewar and wartime ritual of 'recantation' (*tenko*) and submission to the will of the state. One teacher described it as 'torture of conscience'.[79] Repeat offenders were summoned to appear before a panel for 'study', which involved being told repeatedly that they must obey the orders of their superiors and stand and sing when ordered to do so.[80] Many teachers submitted, but hundreds – eventually 401 – sued the metropolitan government under the constitution's Article 19 (on freedom of thought and conscience) against forced participation in such rituals. In September 2006, a Tokyo district court issued a dramatic, landmark judgment. It held that the government directive was in breach of the constitution, insisting that teachers had no obligation to stand and sing, and noting that the flag and anthem had indeed been 'the spiritual backbone that supported imperialism and militarism until the end of World War II'.[81] The judgment had great constitutional and political significance, not least because it directly contradicted a core part of the neo-nationalist agenda only days after one of its most committed supporters had become prime minister.

The justice minister described it as an 'unbelievable' outcome and governor Ishihara was quick to announce that he would appeal.

For neo-nationalists, the major effect of the judicial reversal was to highlight the importance of revision of the Fundamental Law. Conservative administrations had attempted from time to time to revise it, and from 2000 had devoted considerable energies to mobilizing the necessary political support. The *Motomerukai*, or Association for a New Fundamental Law of Education (*Atarashii kyoiku kihonho o motomeru kai*), was established in that year, headed by Iwate University President Nishizawa Jun'ichi. Unlike the constitution, the Fundamental Law could be revised by legislation, without the complication of a referendum. The *Motomerukai* shared a common purpose with the movements to revise the constitution, initiated by the *Yomiuri shimbun* at the beginning of the 1990s. The *Tsukurukai* (Association for New History Textbooks) was launched in 1996 to demand revision of history textbooks in line with a 'proud' Japanese identity.[82] All stressed morality, patriotism, tradition, national virtue and pride; and all enjoyed close links with the LDP and had strong media and corporate backing.[83]

Under the Koizumi government, LDP and government leaders took the occasion of reports of shocking events, especially violent schoolroom or school-related crimes, to call for revision, suggesting that 'unthinkable things' were occurring in the society because of the flaws in the Fundamental Law – especially its failure to promote public-spiritedness and the will to serve the public.[84] Children had to be taught, as Cabinet Secretary Abe put it, 'the importance of life and the splendour of Japan, our country'. Philosopher Takahashi Tetsuya, a prominent figure in the movement to conserve the Fundamental Law unrevised, objected that the 'importance of life' under the old regime of the Imperial Rescript had always been qualified by insistence on readiness to lay it down for the country when required:[85] one life – the emperor's – overshadowed all others.

Former Prime Minister Mori was one of the keenest of the advocates of educational reform. In March 2000 he had adopted educational reform as a 'top-priority agenda' and appointed an advisory panel, the National Commission on Educational Reform. Mori spoke of the 'cleansing' from Japanese education of influences from the 1947 law.[86] In 2001, the Ministry of Education, Culture, Sports, Science, and Technology (MEXT) adopted its 'Education Reform Plan for the

Twenty-First Century' (2001), a design for 'the rebirth of Japan' that stressed creativity and individuality combined with nationalism, tradition, and morality: freedom with control. Class sizes and hours would be reduced, students streamed according to ability, cultural and sports programmes expanded, headmasters given more power, links to the corporate sector introduced, and schools made more competitive.[87] As the public education sector was slimmed down, the role of the private sector would naturally expand, and the planners were clear that the gap between elite and run-of-the-mill students would, and should, widen. For the former, freedom, flexibility and creativity would be the watchwords, and accelerated progress the norm, while for the latter moral and patriotic principles would be given priority, with community service and moral education made compulsory. In the words of Miura Shumon, a prominent *Motomerukai* member and adviser to the Ministry of Education: 'all we can do for the absolute no-hopers is to have them brought up simple and sincere'.[88] An opinion survey sponsored by the Cabinet Office in 2006 indicated that over 80 per cent of people supported the principle that students should be taught to love their country[89] – so the advantage was with Miura and other 'reformers'.

Following the formal recommendation of revision by the minister's advisory body, the Central Education Council, in March 2003,[90] a new Fundamental Law was drawn up. Objections among minority parties to the provisions for cultivating 'love of country' were overcome by the adoption of a convoluted formula about requiring students to cultivate 'an attitude that respects tradition and culture, loves the nation and homeland that have fostered them, while respecting other countries and contributing to international peace and development'.[91] Supported by all major parties – including the chief opposition, the Democratic Party of Japan – the new law was adopted in December 2006. It struck out the phrase 'respecting the value of the individual' as an educational goal from Article 1, and listed in Article 2 twenty provisions or 'goals' concerning morality – initiative, self-control, public-spiritedness, and so on, as well as love of nation and homeland. Morality, as in the prewar period, was to become a matter for the state rather than the individual, but 'within parameters set by the state'.[92] 'Love of country' would become a core moral virtue – something that even militarist governments in the past had never required by legislation – and the provision of the 1947 law forbidding the exercise of 'undue authority' over education, declaring that education had to serve 'all citizens', was replaced by a clause subjecting it to 'this and other laws'. By law, education was henceforth obliged to inculcate patriotism, and the bureaucratic and political control necessary to ensure this would be bound to intensify. 'In other words', as Miyake Shoko put it, 'the new law enables the educational authorities to be completely in control without having to heed criticism from teachers, parents, or civic movements'.[93]

Hardly anyone had thought Fundamental Law revision should be a top priority for the Abe government, or anticipated that it would help to resolve the many problems within education.[94] A majority of the country's primary and middle school principals (66 per cent) opposed the bill.[95] The Diet that passed it had been elected on the single issue of postal reform – and Fundamental Law revision scarcely figured on the list of matters that were thought most urgent, the most prominent of which had been pensions, welfare, and jobs.[96] The government tacitly recognized this by organizing a series of 'town meetings', supposedly to make them better able to reflect public opinion. The meetings were later found to have been bureaucratically 'fixed' in advance, with people chosen and paid to ask specific questions in a bid to drum up support for the reforms.[97] In other words, the state manipulated opinion to ensure that its citizens would be required to love it. The official promulgation of patriotism was integral to Prime Minister Abe's vision of a 'beautiful country'. But compulsory patriotism is a cause repugnant even – or perhaps especially – to those who think of themselves as patriots, to whom the idea of compulsory love is both absurd and offensive. To the radical nationalist Mishima Yukio, love of country was a term 'smelling of something made by government' – it was a phrase that sent shivers down his spine.[98]

Bureaucrats administering the new law are likely to be just as assiduous in policing the requirements of patriotism and morality as they have proved with the rituals of the anthem and flag, ostracizing dissenters as delinquents – or worse, placing them in a category akin to the prewar *hikokumin* ('non-Japanese' – in effect, traitors). The practice adopted by local education authorities in Fukuoka in 2002 according to which love of country was assessed and graded (A, B, or C) could now be expected to spread nation-wide.[99] Prime Minister Koizumi himself remarked in an exchange in the Diet that he could not see the need for grading students on their levels of patriotism, but his off-the-cuff comment was no more likely to be heeded in practice than was the emperor's protest against compulsory observance of the flag and anthem rituals.[100]

The revisionist agenda blended neo-nationalism with neoliberalism. As patriotic discipline and 'public-spiritedness' produce 'simple and sincere' masses, the private sector will play a larger role in a 'streamed' system to produce the technocratic and managerial elite. Ezaki Reona, the prominent educationalist – 1973 Physics Nobel Prize winner, and later head of the National Council for Educational Reform – looked forward to the time when students of modest abilities could be offered a level of education 'appropriate to their DNA'.[101] He appeared to favour a society founded on the principle of genetic privilege and discrimination. If so, his thinking had more in common with Nazi eugenics than with the principles of the 1947 Fundamental Law. As for those with disabilities – despite the UN Treaty on the Rights of the Child (1994) and the accompanying Salamanca Declaration affirming the principle of 'inclusive' education of children with disabilities as 'the most effective means of combating discriminatory attitudes, creating welcoming communities, building an inclusive society and achieving education for all' – the insistence on education in accordance with ability was bound to mean separation and exclusion.[102]

Under Koizumi, the 1947 package – in respect of both the constitution and the Fundamental Law of Education – was opened to debate, and to the possibility of revision. Under Abe the Education Law was actually revised, and revision of the constitution within his term of office was declared to be part of the 'grand historical task' to which he was committed. The Education Law was sometimes seen as the outer moat defending the constitution. With that barrier removed, Abe was probably confident of success, as he promised to 'shuck off' (*dakkyaku*) other remnants of Japan's postwar legacy. But the debate had so far been confined to the elite, and heavily promoted by special interest groups within politics, business and the media. Citizens in general were only slowly asserting their views, and the outcome was far from certain.

The argument that the constitution needed to be revised because of the existence of the Self-Defence Forces depended on an implicit recognition that the Japanese state had been acting unconstitutionally for half a century (as LDP spokesman Yasuoka recognized). The argument that the Fundamental Law had to be revised because schools were in crisis likewise ignored the possibility that such a formulation might be putting the cart before the horse – that the problem might rest in non-implementation of the Fundamental Law, rather than in the Law itself. The gap between the words of the constitution and Fundamental Law and actual practice existed because political, bureaucratic, judicial and media elites had for five decades been complicit in ignoring or stretching the two documents.

The US view that the constitution must be revised has become an increasingly pressing matter. It might be too embarrassing to include it on the annual list of 'Reform Requests', but the statements by senior US officials – which always add apologetically that, naturally, it is a matter for the Japanese themselves to decide – left no doubt that Japan would have to revise its constitution and 'regularize' its military forces in order to function in its assigned role as the 'Great Britain' of East Asia. While ridding the constitution of the awkward sentiments of Article 9, attention also needed to be paid to the psychological conditioning necessary to fight future wars. For that, inhibitions rooted in the residual guilt complex deriving from the Second World War would have to be tackled, and compulsory patriotism was a necessary part of that process.

Sixty years on, MacArthur's command that the emperor should be at the centre of the Japanese state has been so deeply internalized that there is no public reference to the fact that the most vociferous proponents of 'Japanese' tradition are those most faithful to the US order. Those who most vehemently protest against the constitution as MacArthur's 'imposition' confine their discussion to Article 9, ignoring Articles 1 to 8 on the imperial institution. That institution continues to operate as something sacred or magical – beyond rational discussion, protected by powerful, if rarely articulated, taboos, and on occasion by intimidation or even terror. Only in muted terms do academics occasionally suggest that republicanism might be worthy of debate.[103] One such proposal calls for revising the constitution by substituting for the existing clauses on the emperor (Articles 1–8) a simple Article 1 declaring that 'the sovereign authority in the Japanese nation resides with the people', so that the emperor and his family could hand over their existing constitutional functions to the prime minister and retreat to Kyoto to 'live freely as normal citizens with human rights'.[104] In similar vein, an opposition politician recently proposed that Japan spin the emperor off as 'something like a religion', or privatize the institution.[105]

The seventeenth-century sense of 'pure Japaneseness', on which all subsequent notions of the concept rest, saw it as something unadulterated by foreign influences, which then meant Chinese influences. Today, purists who resent US influence as similarly polluting of true Japaneseness may be a minority, but the potential for sentiment to be mobilized around such ideas is undeniable. The tighter the US embrace, the more likely it is to provoke resistance.

7

Okinawa: Disposal and Resistance

Far from Tokyo, Okinawa comprises a scattered group of sub-tropical islands in the South China Sea. Its main island is about the size of Los Angeles, or of about half of Australia's Capital Territory. It is closer to Taiwan and to China's Fujian Province than to metropolitan Japan, and is populated by a mere 1.3 million people. The last of the territories to be incorporated within the modern Japanese state (in 1879), it still maintains a distinct cultural identity, and a pride in its memory of the kingdom of Ryukyu (*Liuchiu*) – the name under which it flourished for half a millennium as an independent kingdom. Ryukyu ships plied routes along the China coast and down as far as Siam. The kingdom, distinguished by its policy of reliance on peaceful diplomacy rather than on maintaining an army, was an 'Article 9' state long before the ideal was expressed in Japan's 1947 constitution; told of this peculiar kingdom when in exile, Napoleon is said to have expressed astonishment. Even when its sovereignty became only notional, following an invasion by the Japanese territory of Satsuma in 1609, it maintained a semblance of independence and continued to participate in the China-centred order regulated by ritual tribute. Its nominal independence was not extinguished until 1879, when the kingdom was abolished and Okinawa was incorporated into the Japanese state as the last and least of its prefectures.

Okinawans refer to the way in which this was done as a *shobun*, or 'disposal', and apply the same term to each of the following major occasions when Okinawa and Okinawans have been 'disposed of' in deals in which their interests were disregarded, and over which they had no control. *Shobun* punctuated the modern Okinawan experience, and the intervals between them have shrunk as the toll of the centralized modernizing state and its wars has risen. Within the modernizing

Japanese state, Okinawa's status was ambiguous. It was peripheral not only geographically, but in relation to the emperor-centred polity. It continued to be essentially 'an attachment' and therefore 'expendable, under duress, if thereby the interests of the home islands can be served advantageously'.[1]

Okinawa's subordinate status was demonstrated sharply by its experience of the Second World War, which came to the area in 1945 as an utter and overwhelming catastrophe in which it was used – even sacrificed – in an attempt by Japan to fend off any attack on the mainland. It was then severed from the rest of the country as an offering to the US, precisely as George Kerr wrote: so that metropolitan Japan be 'served advantageously'. In the rain of steel and napalm that poured onto Okinawa in that spring of 1945, one-third of the population died, and the memory of the mass suicides (strictly speaking 'compulsory mass suicides' – committed under orders of the Japanese military commanders), and of the execution of hundreds of innocent Okinawans – sometimes for the crime of speaking Okinawan dialect – is forever etched on the collective memory.[2] An occupation that was generally experienced elsewhere in Japan as benign and 'soft', in Okinawa was harsh and oppressive. The islands were turned under direct military administration into a US military colony, 'Keystone of the Pacific', by the Treaty of San Francisco in 1951. Okinawa was formally excised from the national territory to remain under US military occupation – a 'grotesque appendage to the US nuclear strategy in Asia',[3] while sovereignty over the rest of the country was restored to the government of Japan. Okinawa's disposal under the 1951 Treaty is considered its second *shobun*.

Okinawans recall bitterly the involvement of the Japanese emperor, Hirohito, in setting the scene for this *shobun*, in two respects. It was the refusal of Hirohito to consider defeat when his close adviser pointed to its inevitability in March 1945 that had led to the Battle of Okinawa in the first place.[4] It was his explicit suggestion, in a September 1947 letter to General MacArthur, that Okinawa be leased to the US on a 'twenty-five, or fifty-year, or even longer' basis, to facilitate US opposition to communism, that helped to crystallize the US decision to opt for a separate peace with Japan, and the retention of Okinawa as a long-term military colony.[5] This intervention was at odds not only with the role of constitutional emperor that he had embraced only half a year earlier; it was one that set the stage for the division of Japan into a 'peace state' mainland and 'war state' Okinawa, enveloping both in the Cold War system. Under direct US military jurisdiction until 1972, Okinawa's *raison d'être*, for both Washington and Tokyo, was as a centre for the cultivation of 'war potential', and for preparation for 'the threat or use of force' – forbidden under Article 9 of the Japanese constitution.

When the islands were eventually returned to Japan, they were returned with their bases intact.[6] Indeed, while mainland bases had been cut to one-quarter of their former strength, as the economic miracle got into gear, the Okinawan burden was doubled after the 'reversion', so that 75 per cent of all US bases came to be concentrated there.[7] The constitutional pledges of pacifism (Article 9) and of local self-government (Articles 92–95), which had so attracted Okinawans, proved empty. Though Okinawans had demanded, and the national government had promised, a return 'without nuclear weapons, and on a par with the rest of Japan', under the deal between Prime Minister Sato Eisaku and the US government the American bases were preserved and expanded, and its nuclear privileges retained. The reversion was Okinawa's third *shobun*. The island and its people were again disposed of without being consulted, and with no regard for their interests or aspirations. Small wonder that the official ceremonies to celebrate the 'return' were dwarfed by angry gatherings protesting against its terms.[8]

In a bizarre twist, Sato (who happens to have been the great-uncle of Abe Shinzo, prime minister from 2006) was awarded the 1974 Nobel Peace Prize for his efforts to achieve a nuclear-free Japan, and for bringing Japan into the Non-Proliferation Treaty. The Nobel Committee was then ignorant of the secret understandings accompanying the formal agreement for Okinawa's return, under which Japan would turn a blind eye to American infringements of the 'Three Non-Nuclear Principles'.[9] But when, years later, the history of the Nobel Peace Prize came to be written, this decision was seen as the Committee's 'greatest mistake'.[10]

The reversion agreement was a matter for satisfaction in Washington, because it not only assured the free use in future of the American bases, but committed the Japanese government to support the US war in Vietnam (and, by implication, future wars) as 'essential' or 'very important' to Japan's own security. Japan would also pay substantial subsidies to support such wars.[11] It was a significant step towards the eventual US objective of a full military partnership between the two countries.

The various documents through which the reversion was negotiated between the two governments provide a window into the US–Japan relationship at a time when it was being transformed by US failure in Vietnam, the enfeeblement of the dollar, and the economic rise of Japan. According to the official account of its government, Japan paid the sum of $320 million to cover the cost of government utilities and buildings on Okinawa that were being transferred to it, and for the removal of nuclear weapons. But recent study of the documents – especially those accessible in US archives – shows that the negotiations had been profoundly duplicitous, and that their core components had been conducted in absolute secrecy. The Japanese government was particularly insistent that as much as possible should remain confidential, lest any hint of the truth leak to the Japanese people: that Japan was buying its territory at a hugely inflated price, and in addition offering gratuitous support for the global military position of the US.

The complex nature of the deal makes it impossible to determine the precise amount of Japan's payment, but the Okinawan scholar Gabe Masaaki estimates it to have been not $320 million, but around $685 million.[12] It included an agreement to deposit $112 million – on a twenty-five-year interest-free basis – in the US Federal Reserve in New York, under the heading of 'Currency Conversion' (as the islands' currency changed from the dollar to the yen). This was the first of many Japanese efforts to prop up the dollar, and the dollar-based world financial system; a further $250 million was to be paid over five years for maintenance of the bases, and for the defence of Okinawa. Both were essentially tribute payments – expressions of Japanese fealty – and had little directly to do with Okinawan reversion. To appreciate the scale of this total 'reversion' sum, it suffices to note that Japan was paying the US about twice what it had paid to South Korea seven years earlier, to compensate an entire country for forty years of colonialism. Moreover, where Koreans had been paid mostly in kind (in Japanese goods, for example) the US took its payment, or at least the large part of it, in cash.[13] To make matters worse, hardly anything in Okinawa was in fact 'returned': the proportion of Okinawan land occupied by bases shrank only marginally – from 14.8 per cent to 12.3 per cent; and some of what was returned went to the Japanese Self-Defence Forces rather than to landowners. Since Japan promised to do what it could to support the dollar and the US position in Asia – including of course its war in Vietnam – the US could contemplate its slight loss of acreage with equanimity.

Once the precedent of payments for ongoing maintenance of US bases had been set, there was no looking back. When the initial five-year support period under the reversion agreement expired in 1978, the system of Japanese subsidy was regularized. The 'sympathy' budget (*omoiyari yosan*) – or what in English became known as 'host nation support' – continued, and over a little more than three decades the Pentagon squeezed just under ¥2 trillion from a willing Japanese milch cow.[14] The annual amount rose from just over ¥6 billion in 1978 to ¥233 billion (roughly $2 billion) in 2006.[15] It is hard to think of a precedent for a 'host' country making voluntary payments of such sums to subsidize an occupying army – although similar subsidies were apparently levied during the Cold War on East Germany to cover the costs of occupying Soviet forces, and during the 1930s on the government of the puppet state of Manchukuo to cover the costs of Japanese occupying armies. In other words, the 'return' of 1972 was actually a purchase, and Japan has continued ever since to pay huge amounts in the form of the 'sympathy budget' (in effect a reverse rental fee, by which the Japanese landlord pays its American tenant).

Early in 2006, Yoshino Bunroku, who four decades earlier had been head of the Foreign Ministry's North America Bureau, revealed some of the hitherto hidden portions of the 1972 reversion deal (in which he had been centrally involved).[16] In particular, he confirmed the secret payment of $4 million for compensation to Okinawan landowners for the cleaning up of land being vacated by US forces. In itself, it was a relatively minor part of the overall deal, but it was an item that, under Article 4 of the reversion agreement, the US government was obliged to pay. From what we now know, the security, nuclear, and economic relationship with the US as a whole was characterized by the same deception and manipulation exposed by Yoshino, and it has continued to this day. When a *Mainichi Shimbun* journalist, Nishiyama Takichi, learned of the secret $4 million deal and published the story, the government retaliated by launching a savage personal attack on him, exposing an affair between him and the female official from the Ministry of Foreign Affairs who had furnished him with the leaked cables. Nishiyama was arrested, convicted for breaches of the public service law, and fired from his job. In March 2006, following the Yoshino revelations, he launched a suit against the government for having destroyed his reputation more than thirty years earlier.[17]

The eighty-seven-year-old Yoshino's efforts to clear his conscience, and to let the public know the shameful truth of the reversion, were dismissed by then Chief Cabinet Secretary Abe Shinzo.[18] The Japanese state stuck to its position. Much was at stake – and the shameful truth of the reversion remains unacknowledged by Japan's parliament, and unappreciated by the Japanese people in general. Yoshino noted bitterly that in the 1970s the Japanese government had no way of knowing how any of the money would be spent, and that is surely still the case today.

Twenty-five years later, Okinawans assumed that the need for their interests to be subordinated to Cold War imperatives would cease with the disappearance of the Soviet and Chinese 'threats', that the bases would be removed, and peace-orientation substituted for war-orientation. Nothing changed, however. Washington came to a different conclusion – that the US would have to maintain a force of 100,000 soldiers indefinitely in East Asia (Japan and the Koreas) – and Tokyo endorsed it.

Since the reversion agreement did indeed lead to a reduction of US forces elsewhere in Japan, while concentrating them in Okinawa, it escaped serious political scrutiny. In Okinawa, however, anger and frustration over its inequity increased. When a twelve-year-old Okinawan girl was abducted and raped by three US soldiers in 1995, the island exploded. The US position in Okinawa, and to an extent East Asia as a whole, seemed threatened, and something had to be done. The Clinton administration promised in the April 1996 SACO (Special Action Committee on Facilities and Districts in Okinawa) Agreement that, within five to seven years, it would return to Japan the Futenma Marine Air Station – a huge, sprawling base that sits in the middle of Ginowan township, and which played a major role over half a century in US wars in Korea, Vietnam and Iraq. Warplanes continue today to circle menacingly around the town's schools, hospitals and residences – a military helicopter even crashed onto a nearby university building in August 2004. Clinton's promise had a catch, however. Futenma, crowded and obsolescent as it had become, would have to be replaced. Those replacement facilities would also have to be located in Okinawa, and

Japan would have to foot the bill. In December, Henoko, a tiny fishing hamlet (population: 1,458) in the administrative unit of Nago City (population: 54,000), in the north of Okinawa's main island, was designated as the site for construction of the replacement base. This would represent not so much a 'return' as a reshuffle, and it soon became clear that the move would be combined with a significant upgrading. The SACO 'Futenma Return' agreement became Okinawa's fourth *shobun*.

Ota Masahide – scholar, survivor of the Battle of Okinawa, and the island's best-known historian – was elected governor of Okinawa in 1990 on a platform of progressive demilitarization. Following the 1995 rape case, when he had withheld his signature to documents authorizing the continued occupation of Okinawan lands by the US military, Tokyo took the extraordinary step of arraigning him before the courts for 'neglect of duty' – ultimately securing a peremptory two-sentence judgment from the Supreme Court ordering him to sign the compulsory land use orders, to which Ota reluctantly submitted. Tokyo also went to the length of passing a 'Special Measures Law' in April 1997, stripping the governor of the power to authorize (or refuse) the leasing of private land to US forces.[19] Such legislation – though it flew in the face of the constitutional provision forbidding any 'special law, applicable only to one local public entity' unless the consent had been secured of 'the majority of the voters of the local public entity concerned' (Article 95)[20] – was endorsed by around 90 per cent of members in the Lower House and 80 per cent of those in the Upper House.

No local government in modern Japan had ever challenged the Japanese state in the way Okinawa had done under Ota; nor had any sought, as he had, to assert their rights under the constitution – especially its clauses on pacifism and local self-government. And none had been so decisively rebuffed as had Ota by the national legislature and judiciary.

Resistance, phase one: the 'heliport' plan

The SACO Agreement inaugurated a new phase in Okinawan history: ten years of epic struggle between the central government in Tokyo, which tried by every means to break the will of Okinawans,[21] and a coalition of local fishermen, farmers, teachers, shopkeepers, small businesspeople and elected representatives of local governments, who lacked almost everything but belief in the justice of their cause. With the governor cowed, at least temporarily, into submission, the initiative passed to Japan's civil society. Local citizens' groups took the initiative – especially in Nago City, where the people of its small east-coast hamlets, living in or near the site designated for the Futenma replacement airport at Henoko, were especially important. To those at the centre of power in the Japanese state, these people must have looked a little like Asterix and Obelix (from the Goscinny and Uderzo comic-strip set in ancient Gaul) would have done to the rulers of the Roman empire: a maddening nuisance, rather than a serious threat. Yet these Okinawan Asterixes held the mighty Japanese state at bay for more than a decade.

The initial Futenma replacement plan was for something described as a 'heliport'. Though the word was suggestive of an area something like of a city rooftop, the plan was in fact for something that would take up several city blocks, rivalling Osaka's Kansai airport. It would comprise an offshore, floating base, resting on steel poles encased in the seabed, with a runway 1,500 metres long and 600 metres wide.[22] Assuming that any opposition could be either bought off or bullied, Tokyo resorted to grand financial inducements and political pressures. But when the people of Nago City conducted a plebiscite in 1997, the response to the plan was a 'no'. The outcome was unambiguous, but pressure from Tokyo remained implacable. In the most bizarre of outcomes, the mayor promptly flew to Tokyo, pledged his *support* for the construction, and then resigned.[23]

Two months later, however, in February 1998, Governor Ota endorsed the plebiscite, overruled Nago City's administration, and declared that there would be no heliport. Relations between his administration and Tokyo plummeted, and Prime Minister Hashimoto refused to see him again. No governor in a system as centralized as Japan's could hope to survive if deprived of channels of communication with the national government, and the Tokyo 'cold shoulder' was a key factor in causing Ota's electoral defeat the following December.[24] With the 'Ota rebellion' crushed and the customary dependent relationship between Tokyo and Naha restored, the first phase of the 10-year war ended. The outcome was a moral victory for the forces opposed to the plan, combined with an ambiguous and short-lived victory for the state in securing the nominal local assent it required.

Resistance, phase two: on the reef

Tokyo showered blessings upon the new governor, Inamine Keiichi, a local Okinawan businessman. He was given a ¥10 billion special Okinawan Development Fund (twice the sum available to his predecessor, Ota). The Okinawa Programme (suspended altogether for the last ten months of Ota's term of office) was resumed, and a special ¥100 million 'Northern Districts Development Fund' was set up, to be concentrated on the local districts in the vicinity of the planned new base. Various additional 'special subsidies' were also doled out on 'social and economic revitalization' projects.[25]

The financial 'sweeteners' to Nago City were immense: its dependence on base-related subsidies reached about 20 per cent. Large sums of money were poured into projects in Nago. The 2000 G7 'Kyushu-Okinawa Summit' was held in the city, at a cost of $1.3 billion dollars,[26] and a new ¥2,000 note was issued featuring the gate of Okinawa's Shuri castle. Tokyo even sought to reconstitute Okinawan identity so that it would 'grow out of' its pacifism and opposition to the island's military role by learning to understand and take pride in maintaining the peace and security of East Asia.[27] That campaign, known as the 'Okinawa Initiative', seemed to bear little fruit. But the straitened circumstances of the islands, with their high unemployment and structural dependence on Tokyo and the bases, meant that the economic incentives had an effect. Conservative candidates were elected to office in one local governing body after another during this period of intense economic pressure.

The dilemma of all Okinawan local governments is their structural dependence on the bases. Since reversion from US to Japanese administrative control in 1972, ¥8 trillion (roughly $70 billion) has been spent, 90 per cent of it on public infrastructure, supposedly to bring Okinawa to mainland levels of development, and to compensate it for its hosting the lion's share of military base facilities in Japan. Such public works were until recently wholly subsidized, and remain 90 per cent subsidized today. But although the subsidy system succeeded in raising Okinawan social capital to mainland levels, income levels remained the lowest in Japan, at 70 per cent of the national average, and unemployment the highest in the country, at 7 per cent. The funds that continued to flow in seemed unable to close the gap in living standards between Okinawa and mainland Japan.

Under the plan agreed between the national government and the Okinawan administration during 1999, Governor Inamine Keiichi assented to the construction of the offshore base, but only on three conditions: it would be used as both a civil and military airport, US military use would be restricted to 15 years, and there would be appropriate assurances that the construction and use of the airport would not result in environmental damage. The agreement was for a grander structure than had originally been conceived, with a runway now grown to 2,500 metres in length. It would take over a decade to complete, at prodigious expense (¥330 billion just for the reclamation of land, and a likely total cost estimated at around ¥1 trillion), and would straddle the relatively unspoiled coral. Futenma would only be returned when the new facilities were in place, and the Japanese taxpayer would meet all costs.

Though the 1996 Agreement had stipulated Futenma's return 'within five to seven years', it was 2002 before the two governments had signed off even on a basic plan for construction. Environmental assessment and preliminary test drilling in the seas adjacent to Henoko were expected to take three years, and construction a further ten or more. The Futenma return was thus pushed back until 2015, at the earliest. Defense Secretary Donald Rumsfeld and the Pentagon found Japanese dilatoriness increasingly irksome.

The Henoko sea was known to be home to the internationally protected dugong, and the shores to a colony of sea turtles, while the reef included some of the island's few remaining live, relatively healthy, coral colonies. Any serious environmental assessment should therefore have been enough to kill the plan. But Tokyo assumed that the survey would be perfunctory, and would come up with a scheme to 'protect' the dugongs and turtles and to plant more coral. But it might not in fact prove so easy to deal with environmental considerations. The local and international movements to protect the dugong, and the region's ecology generally, gathered force, and Greenpeace took up its cause. In September 2003 a suit was launched in the US Federal District Court of San Francisco against Secretary Rumsfeld and the US Department of Defense, seeking a halt to the project.[28]

It was local residents' and opposition groups, however, that thwarted the government's plans once again. Just after sunrise on 19 April 2004, government survey vessels appeared off Henoko to begin engineering works. This, as Okinawan architect and citizen-activist Makishi Yoshi-kazu pointed out, was illegal, because it was in breach of the review and public notification procedures prescribed by Article 31 of the Environ-mental Assessment Law.[29] A sit-in protest was launched at the site around makeshift, tented headquarters, where Okinawan elders – some of them in their 80s or 90s – mingled with fishermen and townspeople from around the island. Meanwhile an offshore 'blockade' was con-ducted by fishing boats, canoes, and even hardy swimmers. As the sit-in and blockade continued without pause, all that the state's survey team could manage to accomplish was to count the dugongs (there seemed to be between 30 and 50 of the marine mammals regularly grazing the sea-grasses of the bay – many more than anticipated) and erect four lighting beacons, which had to be dismantled with each typhoon.[30]

In October 2005, faced with the continuing opposition blockade at Henoko, Prime Minister Koizumi acknowledged that the government had been 'unable to implement the [initial] relocation [plan] because of a lot of opposition'.[31] In other words, the political risk involved in arresting and detaining the protesters was judged to be too great. Suddenly, and dramatically, the Henoko offshore plan was dropped – the second Henoko plan thus going the way of the 1996 heliport. The October outcome was an admission of defeat by those nominally possessing almost absolute power, and a tribute to the determination and persistence of the local coalition, the 'Association to Defend Life'. Okinawa – strictly speaking, the fishing village of Henoko – had defeated the Japanese state.

Resistance, phase three: the Camp Schwab option

The state would, however, concede no such defeat. High-level inter-governmental talks led to a two-part agreement, consisting of a general statement of principles in October 2005, and a detailed 'roadmap' at the end of the following April. Futenma was a key issue in both documents. As with the (pseudo-)reversion of 1972, the crucial point was the service of US military designs. Okinawans were like the citizens of North Korea – subject to a 'military first' (*songun*) policy – and the Japanese government continued to pay huge sums for a 'reversion' that would simply concentrate and upgrade US military facilities. While 8,000 US marines would be withdrawn, the military burden would scarcely be reduced, because Japanese forces were expected to replace the Americans under the 'joint operations posture' and 'interoperability' principles agreed between the two governments in 2005 and 2006.

The site for the base that would replace Futenma was shifted to Camp Schwab, a US facility on Cape Henoko in close proximity to the abandoned offshore site. Some of the existing camp facilities there would be demolished, and a 'V'-shaped runway of 1,800 metres constructed across the Cape, stretching northeast on land reclaimed from Oura Bay and southwest onto the reef. A 'Combat Aircraft Loading Area' (CALA) – consisting of a pier and storage facilities – would be added; and since Oura Bay is around 20 metres deep, US nuclear aircraft carriers could be comfortably accommodated.[32] The 1996 heliport had thus transmuted into a vast military complex, with two runways instead of one.

Despite the appearance of a newly devised plan intended to facilitate the return of Futenma and satisfy the longing of the Okinawan people for a release from their military burden, the idea of concentration of US military functions was in fact rooted in the US military's pursuit of rationalization and reinforcement, and dated back to 1966, during the height of the Vietnam War. In both the SACO agreement of 1996 and the US–Japan agreements of 2005 and 2006, plans for an offshore airport, 'loading area' (ammunition store) and naval port facilities in the Henoko area, drawn up thirty years earlier, were thus simply being dusted off.[33] Hitherto scattered US military functions and services would be gathered and reinforced in a single, giant northern Okinawa military complex, as part of the global reorganization of US forces. Most importantly, the construction would take place within the confines of the existing US base on Camp Schwab, with the intention of thwarting opposition (to whom the site would be off limits). The deal was described with satisfaction by US Defense Secretary Rumsfeld and Japanese Foreign Minister Aso as marking an end to the long-running debate over Futenma. It was widely assumed that the two governments would have their way, and that Okinawa's role as a joint military base for the future projection of regional and global force would be consolidated. However, it soon became clear that that outcome was far from assured.

The reaction in Okinawa was one of universal outrage. Governments in Tokyo had formerly always promised consultation, had at least gone through the motions of honouring local sentiment, and promised that no deal would go against Okinawan wishes. It was possible, as Nago Assemblyman Miyagi Yasuhiro put it, to 'refer to a logic of agreements, laws, environmental assessment principles, and argue point by point'.[34] This new agreement, however, was reached over the heads of Okinawans, and without any consultation. The governor – a conservative and supposedly a reliable ally for the LDP authorities in Tokyo – described the plan as 'totally unacceptable', and said that 'everyone in the prefecture and in Nago City opposes it'.[35] Around the island, it was denounced by local government authorities – the mayors and local governments of Ginowan and Nago prominent among them. During 2004, and until October 2005, prefectural opposition to the Futenma transfer to Henoko – or indeed to any place in Okinawa – had been running at around 80 per cent. After the announcement of this agreement, it jumped at the end of October to 85 per cent.[36]

In January 2006, when a mayoral election was held in Nago City, all three candidates opposed the construction of the base. Once victorious, however, Shimabukuro Yoshikazu wasted little time afterwards in reversing his position (like his predecessor in the aftermath of the 1996 Nago plebiscite). But when he did so, 68 per cent of his electorate opposed him, according to an *Okinawa Times* survey,[37] while the prefecture-wide opposition to the construction plan stood at 71 per cent.[38] Unmoved, the Koizumi government simply insisted that it would make the utmost effort to explain its position sincerely, and seek Okinawan cooperation – as if somehow that would make the imposition acceptable.

The government of Japan had rarely, if ever, faced anything like this resistance from an entire prefecture. The respected Okinawan scholar, Hiyane Teruo, described the islands as being in a state similar to that of the island-wide struggles of resistance that marked the seizure at bayonet-point of agricultural lands for base construction during the 1950s.[39] As Governor Inamine wavered – looking and sounding at times remarkably like his predecessor, Ota Masahide – the government was reported to have been considering dealing with him as it had with Ota: by passing a 'Special Measures Law Concerning US Bases' to bring him in line. Specifically, this would involve stripping him of his constitutional authority over the open seas, and 'simplifying' environmental assessment procedures in such a way that the reclamation of the waters adjacent to Cape Henoko could proceed with or without his approval.[40] Already the prefecture is deprived of control over 20 per cent of its main island's land and 40 per cent of its air-space (for US military purposes) – so a law stripping it of sea rights too would be a bitter pill, tantamount (as Hiyane Teruo put it) to a denial of the history and culture of Okinawa.[41]

The familiar panoply of 'economic incentives' was employed in an effort to buy off or divide the opposition. Defence Agency chief, Nukaga Fukushiro, hinted at the vast economic benefits that Okinawa's business groups (Inamine's support base) could expect to start flowing once they had submitted: 'Japan paid through taxes about ¥1 trillion at the time of the Gulf War and about ¥500 billion to help the reconstruction of Iraq. This time, taxes will be used to lessen the burden on the people of Okinawa.'[42] Mayor Shimabukuro caved in first, setting aside his campaign promises. Governor Inamine was more equivocal. From initial outright rejection, he began to talk of the Agreement as 'reducing Okinawa's base hosting functions', so that 'as such I evaluate it highly',[43] and to suggest that 'the acceptance of the plan would be possible on condition the Japanese and US governments reach an agreement on a package of measures to reduce Okinawa's burden in hosting the bases'.[44] The prospect of ¥1 trillion, or even half that, sounded irresistible in relatively backward Okinawa; but Inamine could not simply reverse his own political pledge and ignore the way Tokyo had treated him. He thus continued to decline the overtures to participate in a council to oversee implementation of the plan, and to denounce the national government's general approach as 'extremely regrettable'.[45]

In May 2006 the base relocation plans were finalized. A target date of 2014 was set for the construction of Futenma replacement facility, and for the transfer of 8,000 Marines to Guam. A 'roadmap' was adopted for the relocation of US facilities. By then, however, ten years had passed since the return of Futenma had been promised, during which time military flights had been substantially increased.[46] Reversion in 2014 was as remote as ever.

Prime Minister Koizumi's October 2005 promise that the base would be built, despite almost universal opposition in Okinawa, contrasted sharply with the position of Prime Minister Hashimoto, who in 1998 had promised that 'the heliport will not be built without local consent'.[47] The hardening of attitude in Tokyo was paralleled in Okinawa. Governor Inamine – installed by Tokyo only six years earlier to replace the recalcitrant Ota, and long believed to be a crucial ally in the process of persuading Okinawans to accept the base – appeared after October 2005 to match his predecessor in fury and bitterness at the national government. From top to bottom, Okinawan society appeared to reject the imposition of the base as unjust, unreasonable and unconstitutional.

Former Governor Ota, by then a member of the Upper House in the national parliament, commented that special laws designed to strip the powers of a prefectural governor would have aroused uproar if directed at one of the major metropolitan prefectures, but had passed without notice when directed against Okinawa. Former Deputy Governor Yoshimoto Masaki said, 'it is as if there were no constitution'.[48] Okinawa, excluded from the constitutional order for twenty-five years from 1947, under direct US military rule – and then offered a watered-down version of it, in which US military prerogatives were entrenched and pacifist and regional autonomy clauses emptied of substance – would, it seemed, now be stripped of further rights and harnessed even more decisively to the requirements of a revamped military alliance, as a permanent, joint US–Japanese military colony.

Much of 2006 was taken up with manoeuvring, as both sides adjusted to the implications of the US realignment of forces. Although Japan's Defence Agency chief ate 'goat soup' (the Japanese equivalent of humble pie) in his efforts to impress his sincerity upon the key figures in Okinawan local governments, he made little impression on Governor Inamine, who persisted in withholding prefectural participation in the council that Tokyo had set up to supervise the construction plan. He continued to promote alternative views long dismissed by Tokyo.[49]

In November new gubernatorial elections were held. Itokazu Keiko, a 59-year-old woman supported by a coalition of opposition political parties, trade unions, and civic and environmental groups, opposed the conservative camp's 67-year-old Nakaima Hirokazu, former chairman of the Okinawa Electric Power Co. Itokazu was an anti-base activist who had been elected to the Upper House in Tokyo in 2004, and based her candidacy on unequivocal rejection of any Okinawan base construction. Even Nakaima, backed by the national government and the LDP, likewise did his best to distance himself from the Washington–Tokyo formula. He called for the new base to be built somewhere outside Okinawa, but dropped what Tokyo considered a hint at his flexibility and readiness to negotiate. He made every effort to shift the focus of the election away from the base and onto economic issues, recognizing that opinion in the prefecture was so negative towards the officially endorsed plan (consistently around 70 per cent in the polls) that it would be political suicide for any candidate to favour it. Instead, he insisted that the election was about jobs and the economy, and promised to reduce Okinawa's unemployment level from nearly twice the national average (7.6 per cent) to the average (4.3 per cent). He thereby replayed the 1998 Inamine campaign, which had made precisely the same promise. Inamine had promised lift Okinawa out of recession, negotiating better deals with Tokyo on behalf of the prefecture through his conservative connections. But after eight years he had failed to dent the unemployment level. Meanwhile, the prefecture's economic growth rate had fallen slightly under his stewardship (from 1.7 per cent to 1.6 per cent), the ratio of prefectural to mainland income had scarcely changed (70.8 per cent, from 70.6 per cent), and levels of debt had risen, with more than half of Okinawa's towns and villages being reduced to critical – or even bankrupt – conditions.[50] Despite the conspicuous failure that had characterized Inamine's eight years, Nakaima achieved the remarkable feat of persuading electors to opt for another four on broadly the same terms. He won the election by 347,000 to 310,000 votes.

Many who voted for Nakaima did not see any contradiction between that act and their opposition to the base construction plan. In fact, exit polls on election day found that a majority of his supporters were against the base plan: only 22 per cent of Okinawans supported it, according to *Yomiuri Shimbun* on 20 November. Although in Tokyo the election result was acclaimed as indicating that a deal on the construction of the base could at last be done, such a conclusion was far from obvious. Having come to office in 1998 with the backing of the ruling coalition in Tokyo because they believed he could deliver on the base, Inamine had merely stalled, raised impossible conditions, and blocked it through two consecutive terms of office. There was no particular reason for thinking that Nakaima would prove different.

When Tokyo turned to implementing another component of the US–Japan defence agreements of 2005–06, by allowing Patriot-3 anti-missile defences to be installed around US bases in Okinawa in October 2006, local mayors declared themselves almost unanimously opposed.[51] They saw the deployment as designed to reinforce the military function of the bases, making Okinawa even more of a military target than it already was – in breach of the national government's promise to reduce the burden of the bases on them. They bitterly resented the fact that Tokyo had once again acted without consulting them. The mayor of Okinawa City angrily remarked that it was as if Okinawa remained under military occupation, sixty-one years after the war had ended.[52]

Okinawan alternatives

In the decade from 1996, the Japanese state had twice had to abandon its Okinawan airport construction plans in the face of local opposition. Tokyo officials talked of patience, persuasion, and sincerity – but their patience and persuasive powers were sorely limited, while their 'sincerity' only thinly disguised a combination of browbeating and bribery, with the implicit threat of force as last resort. The assumption in Tokyo that – providing the pressure was steadily raised – Okinawa could be bought off, fed contempt in Tokyo and humiliation in Okinawa.

The plan is clear: to pour so much money into Okinawa – especially the impoverished north, where the base was to be constructed – as to overwhelm resistance. If not winning actual support, it is hoped that this strategy might win grudging consent to the construction of a major new military complex. While, throughout the rest of Japan, straitened fiscal circumstances and corruption scandals have discredited local development based on public works, in Okinawa the policies that underpin it are to be stepped up so that up to 95 per cent of public works projects will be funded in future from the national treasury.[53] The experience of development in Japan, and in Okinawa since its reversion to Japan in 1972, is that such largesse is illusory: debt continues to mount anyway. For Okinawa, however, that is the point: as debt mounts, dependence on Tokyo rises, sapping the capacity of local governments to resist Tokyo's will and protect the interests of local people and the environment. Despite all the monies poured into Nago City during the Inamine years to 'offset' the burden of the construction of the base, the degree of dependence on bond issues (just over 18 per cent) scarcely changed. Financially, Okinawa was in no position to resist Tokyo's blandishments.

While the Koizumi government and the LDP spoke of establishing new rights and advancing regional autonomy under a new constitution, in Okinawa (and indeed other parts of the country) they moved to curtail the autonomy of local government, to shuck off restraints on the possession and use of force, and to demand that citizens prioritize their duties to the state over their rights from it, at the same time as loving it (through compulsory patriotism). The constitution that Koizumi, Abe, and others wanted to scrap and rewrite embodied ideals for which Okinawans had been struggling for a generation. The contest between the two conflicting visions – between Okinawan defenders of the constitution and its Tokyo attackers – had never been sharper.

The pressure on local communities stemming from Tokyo's determination to foist the base on hostile local communities has been unrelenting. Urashima Etsuko, the chronicler-historian of the Northern Okinawa movement, writes:

> The base problem has been a cause of unbroken anguish for us, setting parents and children, brothers and sisters, relatives and neighbours, at each other's throats. The base problem, and the 'money' that goes with it, have torn to shreds human relations based on cooperation and mutual help, relationships that used to be so rich even though we were poor, or rather, because we were so poor.
>
> Public facilities such as civic halls and schools and the like were refurbished one after the other and Defense Agency funds, salted with wads of ten thousand yen notes, forced people's mouths, especially those of community leaders, shut . . . clinics that had been sought in vain for years were built in no time at all with Defence Agency funds.[54]

The structure of dependence humiliates the recipients even as it degrades the benefactors. Okinawan citizens and scholars began to argue that, only by insisting on its constitutional rights – by turning to maximum advantage the Tokyo government's tentative, and so far insubstantial, talk of increased regional autonomy, and ultimately pursuing the principle of self-government – could Okinawa begin to stand on its own feet. They talk mostly of 'autonomy' and 'self-government', rather than 'independence'; but if they are right, there could be no other path for Okinawa than to end its dependence on government through the bases, and to build a quite new kind of relationship.[55] They suggested that Okinawa should seek to become a 'super-prefecture', with enhanced self-governing rights. They pointed out that the plans currently under consideration by the national government would have the effect of pushing 'autonomy' on the prefectures in any case. Better, therefore, to go one better, and for Okinawa to try to seize the initiative, aiming at a higher level of self-government – a special administrative status as an 'autonomous prefecture',[56] giving Okinawa the status of a Japanese 'Hong Kong'.

An alternative, though less likely, outcome is that, despairing of accommodation within the Japanese state (and the US–Japanese condominium), Okinawa might attempt again to flourish as an independent (and demilitarized) centre of culture and trade. With its population of 1.3 million, high levels of education and culture, and pivotal geopolitical location, if it chose to become an independent state it would be larger than more than forty current UN states. That aspiration is occasionally expressed in the radical formulation: 'Japan is not the fatherland of Okinawans.'[57] Such projects, needless to say, are utterly at odds with the designation by Tokyo and Washington of Okinawa's central role in the projection of regional and global force in the interests of their superpower alliance. Okinawa's prize-winning novelist Medoruma Shun wrote recently that Okinawa's problems would only be resolved when its people stood up, overcoming their fear of being cut loose by Japan and the US, and themselves took active steps to remove the Japanese and US heel from their necks.[58]

Since 1945, Okinawa has been the quintessential child of the US–Japan relationship, where the nature of both, and of their relationship, is best revealed. Now, as the rest of Japan faces the implications of US pressure to become a fully-fledged ally, the 'Great Britain of the Far East', and as forces associated with the LDP seek to advance this prospect, Okinawa presents a possible, even likely image of the future for mainland Japan – a condition in which Japan's 'war state' and 'peace state', sundered since 1945, are rejoined. Okinawa would thereby lead the country along a path of militarized dependence on the US and alienation from Asia.

As both Washington and Tokyo did their best to build their relationship along the lines of that between Washington and London, Okinawa came to resemble nowhere so much as Diego Garcia – the Indian Ocean coral island in the Chagos Archipelago, whose population of several thousand people the British government had summarily evicted in the 1960s so that it could be turned into an American military base (convenient subsequently for the launch of bombing raids on Iraq).[59] Like the British government, the Japanese government had no compunction about lying to its own people (most recently denying the 1972 'deal' to which Mr Yoshino had given his witness), while serving Washington obediently. As in Diego Garcia, many Okinawan citizens (about 250,000)[60] were in fact rounded up and evicted from their lands during the 1950s – often at bayonet point – while many others became exiles in Bolivia, Argentina, Peru or Brazil. There were simply too many Okinawans, however, for the US to have attempted the Diego Garcia solution – complete, compulsory evacuation. The problem facing the Japanese government today is whether further efforts at persuasion and bribery can work, or whether it will ultimately prove necessary to resort to force in disciplining the troublesome Okinawan people.

In Okinawa, more than anywhere else in Japan, the precarious and one-sided nature of the supposedly mature and unparalleled US–Japanese relationship is palpable. Military priorities, rather than constitutional principle, hold sway. In his eagerness to please his Washington friend, Koizumi promised Bush something that he almost certainly could not deliver: a solution to the long-running dispute over relocating the Futenma base. Okinawa's conservative governor, Inamine, referred to the discontent in the prefecture as magma continually threatening to erupt.[61] Tokyo under Koizumi – and, from late 2006, under Abe – gambled that the magma could continue to be contained, as in the past, by platitudes, promises, financial inducements, appeals to the 'national interest' – and in the end by an insistence on the prerogatives of state power.

Okinawans continue to confront their fifth *shobun*. With the confidence born of a decade of successful resistance, and the memory of the terrible cost of an earlier generation's submission to the 'national', military-first agendas imposed by Tokyo, they might yet – despite their fatigue – begin to write an Okinawa-centred history.

8

Japan as a Nuclear State

For sixty years the world has faced no greater threat than nuclear weapons. Japan, as a nuclear victim country, with its 'three non-nuclear principles' and its 'Peace constitution', has had unique credentials to play a positive role in helping the world find a solution, but its record has been consistently pro-nuclear – that is to say, in favour of nuclear energy, nuclear reprocessing, and, as detailed below, nuclear weapons.

Weapons

So far as defence policy is concerned, Japan is unequivocal: at the core of its defence strategy are nuclear weapons – American rather than Japanese, but nonetheless weapons of mass destruction. The nuclear basis of defence policy has been spelled out in many government statements, from the National Defence Programme Outline (1976) and 'Guidelines for US–Japan Defence Cooperation' (1997) to the 2005–06 agreements on transformation and realignment (see Chapter 4).[1]

So supportive has Japan been of American nuclear militarism that in 1969 it entered secret clauses into its agreement with the US, so that the 'principles' could be bypassed and a blind eye turned by the Japanese towards American vessels carrying nuclear weapons docking in or passing through Japan – an arrangement that lasted until 1992.[2] Thereafter, nuclear weapons continued to form the kernel of US security policy, but there was no longer any need to stock them in Japan or Korea, since they could be launched at any potential target – such as North Korea – from submarines, long-range bombers, or missiles. In 2002, the US articulated the doctrine of pre-emptive nuclear attack, under Conplan 8022. Conplan 8022-02, completed in 2003, spelled out the specific direction of pre-emption against Iran and North Korea.[3] By embracing an alliance with the US, Japan also embraces nuclear weapons and pre-emption.

Japan's position in denouncing the nuclear programme of North Korea rests on the distinction between its 'own' – i.e. American – nuclear weapons, which are 'defensive' and therefore virtuous, and North Korea's, which constitute a 'threat', and must be eliminated. Logically, if Japan's security can only be assured by nuclear weapons, the same should apply to North Korea, whose case for needing a deterrent must in any case be stronger than Japan's. Mohammed ElBaradei, director-general of the International Atomic Energy Agency (IAEA), criticizes as 'unworkable' precisely such an attempt to separate the 'morally acceptable' case of reliance on nuclear weapons for security (as in the case of the US and Japan) and the 'morally reprehensible' case of other countries seeking to develop such weapons (Iran and North Korea).[4]

Discussions of Japan's 'non-nuclear' status note that formal opposition to possession of nuclear weapons has never been very robust. Prime Minister Kishi, in 1957, is known to have favoured nuclear weapons. In 1961, Prime Minister Ikeda told US Secretary of State Dean Rusk that there were proponents of nuclear weapons in his cabinet; and his successor, Sato Eisaku, told Ambassador Reischauer in December 1964 (two months after the first Chinese nuclear test) that 'it stands to reason that, if others have nuclear weapons, we should have them too'. US anxiety led to the specific agreement the following year on Japan's inclusion within the US 'umbrella'.[5] Prime Ministers Ohira (in 1979) and Nakasone (in 1984) both subsequently stated that acquiring nuclear weapons would not be prohibited by Japan's Peace constitution – provided they were used for defence, not offence.[6] In the late 1990s, and with North Korea clearly in mind, the chief of the Defence Agency, Norota Hosei, announced that in certain circumstances Japan enjoyed the right of 'pre-emptive attack'.[7] In other words, if the government chose it could invoke the principle of *self-defence* to launch a pre-emptive attack on facilities related to North Korean missile or nuclear facilities.

The Defence Agency's parliamentary vice minister, Nishimura Shingo, then carried this line of argument even further by putting the case for Japan to arm itself with nuclear weapons.[8] More recently, balloons have occasionally been floated on the topic of Japan developing its own nuclear weapons. Abe Shinzo – then deputy chief cabinet secretary –

remarked in May 2002 that the constitution would not block Japan's possession of nuclear weapons, provided they were small.[9] North Korea's declaration that it was a nuclear power in 2005, and its 2006 launch of missiles into the Japan Sea and then its October nuclear test, further stirred these calls. Should the North Korean crisis continue to defy diplomatic resolution, and North Korea's position as a nuclear-armed country be confirmed, such pressures would become almost irresistible.

The moral and political coherence of Japan's Cold War nuclear policy depended both on reliance on the US 'umbrella' and on support for non-proliferation and nuclear disarmament under the Non-Proliferation Treaty (NPT). But as the US – and indeed other nuclear club powers (Britain, Russia, France and China) – made clear their determination to ignore the obligation they had entered into under Article 6 of the 1970 Non-Proliferation Treaty, and reaffirmed in 2000 as an 'unequivocal undertaking', for 'the elimination of their nuclear arsenals', the policy became completely meaningless. As the dominant Western powers turned a blind eye to the secret accumulation of a huge nuclear arsenal by a favoured state (Israel) that refuses to join the NPT, so they tend to treat Japan as a special case, extending it nuclear privileges for reprocessing partly because of its nuclear victim status and partly because they are well aware that it exists in a special, protected relationship with the US.

Over time, like the nuclear powers themselves, once having embraced the weapons, Japan paid increasingly less attention to the supposed imperative of getting rid of them. Its cooperation in the projection of nuclear intimidation against North Korea contributed to proliferation, and brought closer the time when it might decide to possess its own weapons. Should it make such a decision, Japan already possesses a prototype intercontinental ballistic missile, in the form of its H2A rocket capable of lifting a five-tonne payload into space. It also possesses huge stores of plutonium and high levels of scientific and technical nuclear expertise.[10] No country could match Japan as a potential member of the nuclear weapons club.

In May 2005, when the NPT Review Conference collapsed, responsibility was equally shared by the established nuclear powers, whose hypocrisy discredited the system. Those outside the club sought to justify themselves according to the superpower principle: without nuclear weapons there is no security. In Jimmy Carter's words:

The United States is the major culprit in the erosion of the NPT. While claiming to be protecting the world from proliferation threats in Iraq, Libya, Iran and North Korea . . . they also have abandoned past pledges and now threaten first use of nuclear weapons against non-nuclear states.[11]

Needless to say, countries such as Japan, which choose to base their national policy on 'shelter' beneath the US umbrella, associate themselves with that umbrella's threatening, as well as its defensive, function. It is a system within which Japan has become steadily more integrated, despite an almost total absence of public debate. Japan's leaders appear to embrace their resulting nuclear status without qualm.

While Japan seems to have no concerns about the nature of the 'umbrella' under which it shelters, the US has been plainspoken on its determination not to rule out first use of its nuclear force. The Pentagon's 'Global Strike Plan', drawn up in response to a January 2003 classified directive from the president, integrated nuclear weapons with 'conventional' war-fighting capacity, and made clear the reservation of the right of pre-emption.[12] What that might mean for Korea (and for the region) beggars the imagination. According to a 2005 study by the South Korean government, the use of US nuclear weapons in a 'surgical' strike against North Korea's nuclear facilities would, in the worst-case, make the whole of Korea uninhabitable for a decade. If things worked out somewhat better, it would only kill 80 per cent of those living within a 10–15km radius in the first two months, and would spread radiation over a mere 1,400km, thereby engulfing Seoul.[13]

The same US that in March 2003 had launched a devastating war on Iraq based on a groundless charge that that country was engaged in nuclear weapons production maintains its own arsenal of around 7,500 warheads – most of them 'strategic', making them far more powerful than the bombs that destroyed Hiroshima and Nagasaki. In 2006 the US adopted a replacement schedule to produce 250 new 'reliable replacement warheads' per year; it is making great efforts to develop a new generation of 'low yield' small nuclear warheads, known as 'Robust Nuclear Earth Penetrators' or 'bunker busters', specially tailored to attack Iranian or North Korean underground complexes; it deploys shells tipped with depleted uranium, which spread deadly radioactive pollution likely to persist for centuries; it has withdrawn from the Anti-Ballistic

Missile (ABM) Treaty and declared its intent not to ratify the Comprehensive Test Ban Treaty (CTBT); and it promises to extend its nuclear hegemony over the earth into space. Nuclear analyst Ted Daley outlines some of the highlights of US plans:

> . . . new ICBMs – our long-range, land-based nuclear missiles that can incinerate entire cities, anywhere in the world, within the hour – coming on line in 2020 . . . new nuclear submarines and new submarine-launched ballistic missiles in 2030 . . . a new intercontinental strategic bomber in 2040.[14]

Robert McNamara, who used to run the American system, in March 2005 described US nuclear war planning as 'illegal and immoral'.[15]

Even though cooperation on civil nuclear energy with a non-signatory (especially a nuclear weapons state) contravenes the very essence of the NPT, in 2005 the US also lifted a thirty-year ban on the sale of civilian nuclear technology to India, describing it as 'a responsible state with advanced nuclear technology'. In early 2007, Japan declared that it too would recognize India as a nuclear power, ignoring its non-adherence to the NPT.[16] Iran and North Korea, on the other hand, were roundly denounced for their insistence on a right guaranteed to them by Article 4 of the NPT.

Like the US's, Japan's non-proliferation policy is contradictory – it turns a blind eye to US-favoured countries that ignore or break the rules, such as Israel and India, while taking a hard line on countries not favoured by the US, such as Iran and North Korea. It is also passive in the area of disarmament – specifically downplaying the obligations of the US and other superpowers; and because its own defence policy rests on nuclear weapons, it is unenthusiastic about the idea of a Northeast Asian Nuclear Weapons-Free Zone.[17]

As we have already seen, the idea of Japan becoming the 'Great Britain of the Far East' has been prominent in both US and Japanese thinking over the past decade. The nuclear implications of this aspiration have mostly escaped attention. Britain has long seen its power and prestige as inextricably tied to its possession of nuclear weapons. Tony Blair's government made clear in 2006 its intention – at huge expense and in defiance of its obligations under the NPT – to replace its Trident nuclear submarine flotilla, which meant in effect a commitment to retaining nuclear weapons for the foreseeable future.[18] Not only has Britain 'persistently deployed tactical nuclear weapons around the world for more than forty years', as Paul Rogers notes, but 'it is prepared to use nuclear weapons first, and . . . it has thoroughly embraced the idea of nuclear war fighting'.[19] The Japan of Koizumi and Abe sets great store on the paraphernalia of 'great power' status, and has thoroughly embraced this dimension of its chosen model.

Energy

The Japan of 'non-nuclear principles' is also in the process of becoming a nuclear superpower – the sole 'non-nuclear' state that is committed to possessing both enrichment and reprocessing facilities, as well as to developing a fast-breeder reactor. Japan's Atomic Energy Commission drew up its first plans as early as 1956, and the reprocessing and fast-breeder programmes were already incorporated into its 1967 Long-Term Nuclear Programme. The dream of energy self-sufficiency has fired the imagination of successive governments, and of generations of national bureaucrats who have channelled trillions of yen into nuclear research and development programmes. The lion's share of national energy research and development (64 per cent) goes on a regular basis to the nuclear sector, and additional vast sums – already well in excess of ¥2 trillion – have been appropriated to construct and run major centres such as the Rokkasho nuclear complex.[20]

Nuclear power currently makes a modest and declining contribution to world energy needs – from 17 per cent in 1993 it had declined to 16 per cent by 2003. Just to maintain existing nuclear generation capacity globally, it would be necessary to commission about 80 new reactors over the next ten years (one every six weeks), and a further 200 over the decade that followed.[21] Of that sort of commitment, there is at present virtually no sign. The United Kingdom, for example, has more than 40 reactors; but closures were set to cut that to just one by the mid-2020s; and the US, though it has 100 reactors, was also expected to decommission many of them during the 2020s.[22]

At present, there are 440 reactors operating worldwide, with 28 more under construction, and a further 30 promised by 2030 in China.[23] The head of the French government's nuclear energy division, speaking to the April 2006 Congress of the Japan Nuclear Industry Association at

Yokohama, estimated that, in order to raise global reliance on nuclear power from its present level of 6 per cent to 20 per cent by mid-century, it would be necessary to construct between 1,500 and 2,000 *new* reactors globally.[24] Even such a mammoth undertaking – trebling current nuclear capacity – would still make only a modest contribution to solving global energy problems.

Japan nevertheless seems intent on playing a leading role in pioneering a hitherto unprecedented level of nuclear commitment. Central to the Japanese vision of a nuclear future is the village of Rokkasho, in Aomori prefecture. Rokkasho encapsulates perhaps more than anywhere Japan's transition over the past century from an agricultural and fishing tradition, through a traumatic burst of construction state excesses, to the full embrace of the nuclear state. Initially, a remote provincial community – a vast stretch of land, at over 5,000 hectares, and still at that time relatively untouched by industrialization – was set aside in 1971 under the Comprehensive National Development Plan, as one of eleven gigantic development sites. It was designated to host a petrochemical complex, petroleum refining, electricity generation and non-ferrous metal smelting on a scale exceeding anything then known in Japan. In due course, the oil shocks and consequent industrial restructuring saw the fading of the dream of an industrial complex, and instead large-scale oil storage facilities were set up on part of the site from 1979. From 1985, nuclear enrichment, reprocessing and waste facilities were established on one-third of the original site. Local government officials had no enthusiasm for the nuclear course, but the deeper they sank into financial dependence, the more difficult they found it to oppose plans generated in Tokyo. An accumulated debt of ¥240 billion was written off with an infusion of taxpayer money in 2000. Until 2005, hopes were high that the International Thermonuclear Experimental Reactor (ITER) might be built there, but that hope itself collapsed, when the project was allocated to France.[25] The likely outcome in the early twenty-first century was one that nobody in the village had dreamed of in 1971: that of becoming a centre of the global nuclear industry.

Despite the Koizumi government's mantra of privatization and deregulation, huge sums continue to be poured into nuclear projects that would never have got started – much less been sustained – by market forces alone. Public and political attention focused on the privatization of the Post Office, but much greater issues were at stake for Japan's future in decisions and commitments being made by bureaucrats far removed from public scrutiny or debate. While Japan has cosseted the nuclear industry and given it trillions of yen, its renewable energy sector (excluding large-scale hydropower) constitutes a miserable 0.3 per cent of its energy generation – planned to rise over the next ten years to 1.35, but then to *decline* slightly by 2030. By contrast, China plans to double its natural energy output (also excluding large-scale hydropower) to 10 per cent by 2010, and the EU has a target of 20 per cent by 2020.[26] In short, Japan stands out as a country following a course radically at odds with that of the rest of the international community. It continues to be driven bureaucratically, rather than by market forces – let alone democratic consensus.

The nuclear state: waste, fast-breeding, and the magic cycle

Whereas Three Mile Island in 1979 and Chernobyl in 1986 led to nuclear energy projects in other advanced industrial countries being frozen or drastically cut back, and reactors being mothballed and closed down, Japan increased the number of its reactors from 32 in 1987 – the year after Chernobyl – to 55 in 2006, which produced 29 per cent of its electric power. Two more reactors were under construction, and ten were at various planning stages.[27] By 2006, the objective set out in the Ministry of Economics, Trade, and Industry (METI)'s 'New National Energy Policy' was to turn Japan into a 'nuclear state' (*genshiryoku rikkoku*): the proportion of nuclear-generated electricity was to rise steadily to 'between 30 to 40 per cent' by 2030 (compared with 80 per cent in France in 2006, making it the world's most intensive producer, and consumer, of nuclear energy).[28] Other reports suggested a goal of 60 per cent by 2050.[29] In August 2006, METI's Advisory Committee on Energy Policy produced its draft 'Report on Nuclear Energy Policy: Nuclear Power Nation Plan'.[30] Its 'Hiroshima Syndrome' would be put behind it, and inhibitions about safety, radiation, waste disposal and cost cast to the wind, as Japan – once a nuclear victim – set out to become a nuclear super-state.

The scale of Japan's current nuclear energy commitment is not particularly exceptional, but among non-nuclear weapon states it alone pursues development of the full nuclear cycle, in which plutonium would be used as fuel after the reprocessing of spent reactor waste. It is this bid for plutonium superpower status that distinguishes Japan. It already has stocks of plutonium amounting to more than 45 tonnes[31] – almost one-fifth of the 230-tonne global stock of civil plutonium,[32] and the equivalent of 5,000 Nagasaki-type warheads; it has thus become 'the world's largest holder of weapons-usable plutonium',[33] and its stockpile continues to grow steadily. Barnaby and Burnie estimated in 2005 that, on current trends, Japan's stockpile would reach 145 tonnes by 2020 – more than the plutonium in the US nuclear arsenal.[34] Japan therefore ignored the February 2005 appeal from the director-general of the IAEA for a five-year freeze on all enrichment and reprocessing activities, arguing that such a moratorium was applicable only to 'new' projects, not those such as Japan's, which had been underway for decades.[35]

When, or if, Japan begins a full programme of commercial reprocessing at Rokkasho (planned for 2007), it will be undertaking with impunity what ElBaradei sees as a highly dangerous activity that should be placed under international supervision and strictly limited, steadily adding to Japan's plutonium stocks (another 30 tonnes by 2012).[36] Moreover, it will be doing this with the positive blessing of the US, while Iran and North Korea are told that they must absolutely be stopped from doing the same – and, indeed, while countries like South Korea are also blocked from following Japan down the enrichment and recycling path. If Iran and North Korea are a threat to global non-proliferation, then so is Japan. Japan's 45 tonnes of plutonium may be usefully compared with the 10–15kg of fissile material that North Korea was accused of illicitly diverting in the 1994 crisis, or the 0.7 grams that South Korea produced in the early 1980s, and for which it was severely rebuked by the IAEA.[37]

The Federation of Electric Power Companies puts the cost of the Rokkasho facility over the projected forty-year term of its use at ¥19 trillion.[38] That would certainly make it Japan's – if not the world's – most expensive facility in modern history. Experts point out that it would cost very much less to bury the waste unprocessed (provided, that is, there was somewhere to bury them . . .), and fear that the actual cost might climb to several times the official estimate.[39] When – or if – Rokkasho's reprocessing unit begins operation in July 2007, it will be capable of reprocessing 800 tonnes of spent fuel per year, yielding each year about eight further tonnes (1,000 warheads' worth) of pure, weapons-grade plutonium.[40] But even such a plant, though it would be the only one in Asia, would make little more than a small dent in

Japan's accumulated and accumulating wastes – estimated at approximately 12,600 tonnes in 2006[41] – let alone in the 40,000 tonnes of toxic nuclear spent fuel wastes so far accumulated throughout Asia.[42]

What will Japan then do with its plutonium mountain? To address the general perception that it is the most dangerous substance known to mankind, in the 1990s it took two steps. First, it issued an assurance that it would not hold more than was necessary for commercial use. From the beginning, however, that pledge was empty. The stockpile has grown steadily because of the many delays to the plans, due largely to the many accidents (including some causing fatalities)[43] and cover-ups,[44] and continual budget over-runs that have galvanized public opposition to proposed projects.[45] Even if Rokkasho were to function for forty years without delays and technical problems, processing without any hitches 800 tonnes of spent fuel per year, spent fuel volumes would continue to grow. Japan's nuclear reactors are currently discharging 900 tonnes of waste each year – more than can be reprocessed. This figure is set to reach between 1,200 and 1,400 tonnes discharged each year by 2015, as more reactors are commissioned, so that waste would continue to accumulate steadily – mostly remaining stored at reactor sites or proposed regional interim storage sites.[46] This waste would be added to the current global stockpile of separated plutonium, standing at approximately 250 tonnes,[47] with the gap widening further as more reactors are built.[48] The second assurance the Japanese government gave was that there was no need to worry about plutonium. The Japanese Power Reactor and Nuclear Fuel Corporation issued an informational video featuring a character – Mr Pluto – who declared that plutonium was safe enough to drink (which he duly demonstrated), and that there was little risk of it being turned into bombs.[49] When the US Energy Secretary, among others, protested at the video's inaccuracies, it was withdrawn – but the advertising campaign continued.

Until 1995, the plan had been to operate fast-breeder reactors, which 'breed' very pure, 'super-grade' plutonium (in other words, they produce more than they start with). Such programmes make little economic sense, since they cost four to five times as much as conventional power plants, and most projects around the world – including those in the US and UK – have been abandoned on grounds of either safety or cost.[50] The Japanese Citizens' Nuclear Information Centre judges that they are 'completely incompatible with non-proliferation'.[51] Japanese plans were thrown into disarray by the shutting down of the Monju prototype fast-breeder reactor (at Tsuruga, in Fukui prefecture on the Japan Sea coast) after a sodium leak and fire in December 1995. Evidence was subsequently uncovered of negligence and cover-up, and the project was suspended for almost ten years. After years of protest, opponents of the project won a court victory upholding their stance that the design of the reactor was flawed. In May 2005, however, the Supreme Court overturned that ruling and upheld the government's decision to proceed. By then, it had already cost ¥600 billion, but had yet to light a single lightbulb. Under current government plans, the fast breeder was to be commercialized by 2050 – a remarkable seventy years behind its original schedule.[52] Kondo Shunsuke, head of the Atomic Energy Commission, insisted that it would nevertheless form 'an important part of Japan's overall nuclear energy strategy for the twenty-first century'.[53] Not only was Monju itself to be resuscitated, but a second reactor was also to be built to replace it by around 2030, at a cost of 'about ¥1 trillion'.[54] The bureaucratic dream of energy security for the twenty-first century seemed to operate on a higher plane of logic than that of economics.

Whatever the outcome of the fast-breeder project, the government also adopted a plan to burn recycled plutonium in conventional light-water reactors in the form of a plutonium-uranium oxide (MOX) fuel.[55] This process is also several times more expensive than the use of low-enriched uranium fuel, and involves much higher risk. Efforts in the late 1990s to start plutonium MOX use had failed. On current plans, Japan's utilities would begin to load plutonium fuel from around 2007–08; but on past performance it is likely to take longer, and the gap between the production of plutonium (from both European-based stocks belonging to Japan and that coming out of Rokkasho) and the ability to load it into reactors will widen further.[56]

The bottom line is that waste continues to accumulate. Low-level waste – basically comprising contaminated clothing, tools, filters, and so on – are held in over 1 million 200-litre drums, both at nationwide reactor sites and at Rokkasho's repository, whose projected eventual capacity is for three million drums.[57] Forty vast repositories are planned, each 6 metres high and 24 metres square, and containing 10,000 drums, destined eventually to be covered in soil, with something like a mountain built over them. They must then be closely guarded for at least 300 years, slowly spreading – like giant, poisonous mushrooms or the mausolea of ancient Japanese aristocrats – across the Rokkasho site. Meanwhile, fluids containing low levels of radiation are piped several kilometres out into the Pacific Ocean for discharge. The standards for effluent control at reactor sites around the country are being drastically raised in order to make regular discharges possible.[58]

High-level toxic waste – in other words, spent fuel – has since 1992 been shipped regularly across vast stretches of ocean to reprocessing plants at Sellafield, in the north of England, and la Hague, Normandy, in France. Each shipment contains the equivalent of about seventeen atomic bombs' worth of plutonium, despite the protests of countries en route and the risks of piracy or accident.[59] Once processed, the liquid high-level waste is vitrified and put into canisters, each measuring 1.3 metres by 0.43 metres, which are returned to the Rokkasho site. There they are to be stored initially for 30 to 50 years, while their surface temperature slowly declines from around 500°C to 200°C, at which point it is planned to bury them in 300-metre-deep underground caverns, where their radiation will continue to decay over millennia. There are already enough canisters to fill more than half of their first giant storehouse.

As Japan's reactors reach their 'use by' date, they must be decommissioned and dismantled, and the sites cleaned. No one yet knows the exact cost, but the British authorities calculated early in 2006 a figure of £70 billion ($170 billion) for dealing with twenty of their civil nuclear sites.[60] Whatever the short-term financial inducements on offer from Tokyo, local communities are steadfastly opposed to hosting such facilities, and governors balk at the thought of their prefectures being turned into nuclear waste dumps for literally millennia. In 2002 the Fukushima prefectural governor withdrew his consent – granted four years earlier – for the construction of one such plant, and a review conducted by the prefecture reported that

> [t]he way [the nuclear bureaucrats] go about things is that, from the viewpoint of the state, there can be no change once a policy is settled, regardless of what the people or local authorities may think. But at the same time they quite readily make changes to the plan when it suits themselves, paying scant heed to the people or local authorities.[61]

But the determination of the state and nuclear energy industry to press ahead with all possible nuclear developments, and the imperative of doing *something* with the plutonium mountain, constitute powerful – perhaps irresistible – forces.

Due to the inadequacy of international nuclear standards, the proliferation hazards associated with reprocessing are greater than is widely believed. The best estimates are that, within such a vast system of uranium and plutonium processing and transport, a 1 per cent loss of fissile material – or 'about a nuclear weapon's worth each month' – would be impossible to detect.[62] This feeds further uncertainty on the part of Japan's neighbours – especially South Korea and China.

Nuclear partnership

In the United Nations, Japan declines to associate itself with the 'New Agenda Coalition' (NAC), which came into existence following the nuclear tests by India and Pakistan in 1998. The NAC seeks to exert more urgent pressure for disarmament and non-proliferation. Japan sees it as too 'confrontational' – in other words, too directly challenging of the nuclear privileges of the US and the other nuclear powers. It was reported that in 2003, in the context of delicate negotiations over the North Korean nuclear issue, Japan had prevailed upon the US not to issue any security guarantee such as North Korea was seeking that might rule out the option of nuclear retaliation.[63] For Japan to join the NAC, against US wishes, might also have been to weaken the US-provided 'umbrella'.

While Japan's government and bureaucracy single-mindedly pursue their chosen nuclear superpower path, its embrace with the US tightens as its distance from Asia grows. In February 2006, Washington included Japan on a shortlist of countries to be included in a projected Global Nuclear Energy Partnership (GNEP) – a kind of nuclear energy 'coalition of the willing' that would include the US, Great Britain, France, Russia, China and Japan (the existing nuclear club members plus Japan). It would be designed to sidestep the existing international framework of the 1970 NPT, and establish a new nuclear cartel to control the production, processing, storage, sale, and subsequent disposal of uranium. The project would develop a so-called proliferation-resistant recycling and reactor technology, maintain monopoly control over it, and then offer facilities to the rest of the world on a lease basis.[64]

Whereas Japanese governments have long been negatively disposed towards regional attempts to forge a Northeast Asian nuclear-free zone, it jumped at this American invitation to join a global nuclear superpower club, seeing it as offering an international framework for maintaining its existing activities. Australia, too – initially caught unawares by the proposal – soon became enthusiastic. Prime Minister Howard eagerly sought American advice on a visit to Washington three months later,[65] secured the blessings he sought, and issued a call for a national debate on nuclear energy. Australia could expect to play a key role in such a project – mining, manufacturing, selling and monitoring uranium for the duration of its cycle – since it is the 'Saudi Arabia' of global uranium deposits (although it has so far chosen to remain a source of raw uranium, not processing it itself).[66] The prime minister – along with the defence, industry and environment ministers – has said that Australia should 'consider' the option of a nuclear energy industry.[67] The global orientation of US power – evident in its construction of special relationships with the UK, Australia and Japan – would here take on a nuclear dimension.

Yet the problems are many. The major process advocated in the projected programme (advanced burner reactor or ABR technology) exists only as a theoretical proposition. The principle is the same as for the fast breeder reactor, but without the use of a breeder blanket (where the super-grade plutonium is produced). However, the application of a blanket is simple compared to the technical challenge of designing a fast reactor that would operate reliably. Thus the GNEP, if realized, would be likely to worsen the problem of nuclear proliferation.[68] Commercial-scale demonstration of the new, American-proposed technology could not be expected for twenty or twenty-five years.[69] The costs are expected to be enormous, and it is not at all clear who would bear them – although the US energy secretary has indicated that a fund of between $20 billion and $40 billion will be needed, and implied that a major contribution would be expected from Japan.[70] This requisitioning may in time come to dwarf even the levies imposed on Tokyo to fund the Gulf and Iraq wars, to prop up the dollar in international financial markets, and to feed the missile defence industry. The waste would still accumulate, and the notion that the countries supplying the technology would also be responsible for accepting and dealing with it seems inherently implausible; at any rate, Japan has been quick to exclude itself from any such obligation.[71] Not least among the problems of such a regime would be the fact that the resentments of those countries excluded from the nuclear club under the NPT regime towards its members would be bound to continue and deepen.

Above all, the Partnership would be based on positive promotion of nuclear power as the core source of future global energy, and would require that public investment by the core countries flow to the most costly and dangerous option, rather than to true renewables. There are in any case serious doubts that the world has enough uranium to follow the nuclear course, even if safety and other issues could be resolved. Uranium supplies peaked in 1981, and the existing mines can supply only half the existing demand – the rest being made up from dismantled nuclear weapon stockpiles, a source likely to be exhausted by 2013. Mines currently being developed might fill half the current gap, but unless new sources are discovered and developed (a process that takes a minimum of fifteen years), even existing plants will be forced to close.[72] John Busby calculates that '[p]rimary production would have to be increased 167-fold to match the anticipated global energy needs exclusively from nuclear power in 2020', and, even if nuclear power generation could be doubled – an unlikely proposition – it would be enough to meet only 5 per cent of world energy consumption.[73] Advocates of fast-breeder reactors refer to this uranium shortfall to justify the development of new designs of reactors, despite their failure over past decades. The agenda of massive expansion – whether of the still-to-be-developed Partnership technologies or of the existing light-water reactors – is simply fantastic.

The Japan of 300 years ago was a more-or-less sustainable, zero-emissions and zero-waste society. Under current Japanese government plans, 300 years from now (and indeed for 10,000 years into the future), provided all goes well, the country's northern and eastern regions will be dominated by a vast, poisonous and threatening complex, over which generation after generation – virtually forever – a heavy, militarized guard will have to be maintained. Whether Rokkasho is to become the representative model of twenty-first-century civilization (its legacy to future centuries and millennia) will be determined by the ongoing contest between Japan's nuclear bureaucracy and its civil society. The nuclear bureaucrats pursue the chimera of limitless clean energy, global leadership, a solution to global warming, and the maintenance of nuclear defences (whether American or Japanese). Japan's civil society, by contrast, is committed to the abolition of nuclear weapons, the phasing out of nuclear projects and the adoption of renewable, non-nuclear energy technologies, within a framework of democratic decision-making and social, ecological and economic sustainability. Much depends on the outcome of this contest.

9

The Schizophrenic State?

The Koizumi legacy

The edifice of the postwar Japanese state was erected over a series of unresolved contradictions. Imperial militarism and fascism gave way to popular sovereignty and pacifism, but still many continued to look back nostalgically to the 'good old days' when Japan had headed the struggle for the liberation of Asia. There could be no logical way to integrate the emperor system with popular sovereignty; the peace system (Article 9) with the war system (the security treaty and the Cold War); democratic education and human rights with the requirements of a global capitalist class, neo-nationalist bureaucrats and politicians. Japan's postwar 'imperial democracy' may have been an oxymoron, as Dower put it, but it nevertheless endured for sixty years. Now it faces unprecedented challenge.

National sovereignty was restored to Japan in 1952 under the San Francisco Treaty, but an ambiguous, semi-dependent orientation towards the US remained, and subsequently became entrenched. Sovereignty was vested in the people, but under a 'symbolic emperor'. The world's most democratic constitution was put in place, but in practice was subordinate to the security treaty with the US. The contradictions were contained easily enough during the Cold War decades, as the nation was mobilized in pursuit of economic goals, but became increasingly vexed once it ended.

Koizumi – populist, magician, entertainer – brilliantly expressed a fragile, early twenty-first-century national mood that fused currents of profound economic anxiety, servility towards the US, concern about the rise of China, contempt towards North Korea, and national assertiveness. His performance made up in emotional force what it lacked in intellectual consistency. His policy blend of neo-nationalism – itself a combination of dependence and assertiveness – and neoliberalism satisfied the electorate and the US government, but without resolving any of the structural contradictions.

In his last months in office, Koizumi travelled widely, Japan's equivalent of Air Force One ferrying him to the US, Israel, Palestine, Jordan, Russia (for the St Petersburg G-8 Summit), Mongolia (to commemorate Genghis Khan's foundation of the Mongolian state), Uzbekistan, Kazakhstan, and Finland. His extravagant itinerary was nonetheless restricted, in the sense that the countries with which relations had plummeted during his term of office – China, Korea (North and South), and Russia – were excluded, since there was no prospect of resolving any problems with them. His most important visit – his last as prime minister to the US – was a disappointment, since he had to set out knowing that the privilege of an address to a joint sitting of the two Houses of Congress had been denied him, despite his faithful service on so many fronts, because of his stubborn commitment to Yasukuni. Instead of Congress, he and the president journeyed together to a different shrine: Graceland, in Memphis, Tennessee,[1] where he performed his Elvis act, which included 'Love me tender' and 'I want you, I need you'. It was reported as a piece of vaudeville, but it is better understood as his true political statement – a message from the heart of love and submission to the US president that neatly summed up his five years of service.

He received his warmest reception on his politically least significant visit – to Finland, where his hosts were surprised and delighted by his familiarity with the music of Sibelius. Elsewhere, his typical message was the one he had delivered from the back of a camel in Petra, Jordan, where, clowning for the camera immediately after visits to Israel and Palestine and on the very day that Israel launched its bombing attack on Beirut, he had punned that 'riding a camel is a cinch' (*rakuda rakuda*). He had little or nothing to say on other major issues, from the critical state of Japan's relations with its neighbours to global warming and climate change, from the spiral of violence in Iraq to the deteriorating situation in the Middle East as a whole.

It was as if, performing his final strut upon the international and national stage, he had no lines to speak. He quietly abandoned the one significant diplomatic initiative he had launched during his office – to normalize relations with North Korea – after it had been sabotaged by his then subordinate, Abe Shinzo (see Chapter 4). Although he also briefly tried, following his second Pyongyang visit in 2004, to persuade George W. Bush to meet Kim Jong Il, he soon gave up on that too, remarking in St Petersburg, 'I understand that the North Koreans are hoping for bilateral talks with the United States',[2] but making no serious effort to press the point. Abe Shinzo, long before he took over the prime-ministership, had in effect seized the reins of North Korea policy.

Koizumi could leave office, however, with the satisfaction of having done all that he had been asked by Washington: he had put Japanese boots on the ground in Iraq; paid billions for the anti-terror cause; sent in his government's orders for missile defence systems; incorporated Japan's Self-Defence Forces into US strategic planning; constructed or promised new bases; reopened the Japanese market to US beef; privatized the Post Office; enacted various measures to further liberalize Japan's markets; and brought revision of the constitution to the top of the agenda for his successor. No prime minister had done more. Whether all of this had earned him respect in Washington was another matter. Noting the contempt with which President Bush treated British Prime Minister Tony Blair in the brief unguarded exchange between them captured by the media at St Petersburg,[3] one suspects that there might be some truth to the story that Bush also spoke to his cronies of 'Sergeant Koizumi',[4] or joked with them about Japan being 'just some ATM machine'.[5]

However, where Blair – despite the crumbling of his political support base in Britain – was at least listened to on regional and global matters, and seems to have believed in the cause he was committing Britain to, Koizumi was ignored, and – because of the threat from North Korea – seemed to believe only that whatever was necessary to keep America on side had to be done. Japan was indeed 'like an American state', as the present (2007) minister of defence had put it in 2003.[6] And yet no prime minister had been so popular for so long as Koizumi. After taking over from Mori Yoshiro, when Mori's support rating was below 10 per cent, Koizumi began at around 80 per cent, following his dramatic promise to destroy his own party if necessary in order to reform Japan. Thereafter, his figures fluctuated somewhat, though never plumbing anything like the depths of his Iraq war associates Bush and Blair; and as he entered his final month in office, in September 2006, his government still enjoyed 47 per cent popular support, and his overall five-year average stood at 50 per cent. His opposite numbers in Washington and London could only look on with envy at such figures.[7]

Looking back over Koizumi's five and a half years, and at the unbridled enthusiasm with which he responded to the American embrace, one is struck by his naiveté, and his apparent obliviousness to the immense changes underway in the US and what it stood for. He seemed to see only an idealized homeland of freedom, democracy, and economic vitality, when in fact – and especially under George W. Bush – America was beset by multiple crises, and faced catastrophic failure in the Middle East. Koizumi surely did not think of it in such terms, but the unconditional commitment he promised was a de facto commitment to the policies of pre-emptive war; nuclear intimidation; defiance of international laws and treaties; sidelining of the UN; and defiance of the rules and customs of war, including the Geneva Conventions. Where all previous Japanese prime ministers had based Japanese foreign policy on the twin principles of support for the UN and cooperation with the US, under Koizumi, for the first time the two diverged, and he chose the latter. Such was Koizumi's charisma, however, that he carried a largely unwitting public with him, cooperating willingly as Washington piled demand upon demand.

Along with many Japanese who think of themselves as 'nationalist', Koizumi was critical of the Japanese constitution because of its American roots, but paid no attention to other aspects of the imposition. Neither he nor any other 'nationalist' queried why it should be that MacArthur's key demand had been the installation of the emperor at the centre of the state. While vigorously declaring Japan's 'national' interests, they tended to support uncritically the military and strategic subordination of the country, much deepened on Koizumi's watch by the revamped defence and 'emergency' arrangements.

During the Koizumi years, North Korea provided the means for the effective resolution of the contradiction between national assertiveness and passivity within the American embrace. The majority who supported Koizumi seemed to have no problem with the reorganization of US forces. They supported – albeit passively – Tokyo's efforts to persuade, buy off, or deter those (like most in Okinawa) who opposed it, because of their even greater concerns about the threat from North Korea. Hostility to China had also welled up significantly under Koizumi; but the memory of the catastrophe of the twentieth century's fifteen-year war with China could not easily be erased, and the sense of growing interdependence with China was strong, especially among Japan's economic elite.

'Nationalists' in Tokyo's political leadership and bureaucracy undoubtedly hoped for Japan to become a 'great power' with a permanent seat on the UN Security Council, and with the capacity to project political power in the global arena commensurate with the country's economic weight. But that ambition was always cast within the frame of the alleged need for Japan to be defended by the US in case of emergency. The Japanese term for emergency, *yuji*, means literally 'something happening', and for many decades now that 'something' has always been war on the Korean peninsula.

Abe's 'beautiful country'

Like Koizumi, Abe Shinzo was the choice of the US government to become prime minister, and was trusted to complete the process Koizumi had so loyally pursued of turning Japan into the 'Great Britain of East Asia'. Taking office as Koizumi's chosen heir, and pledged to continue his policies, he was nevertheless a very different politician. Where Koizumi had come to power promising to smash the LDP, Abe succeeded him as the quintessential LDP man – with the bluest of political blue blood, as the grandson of one prime minister, great-nephew of another, and son of a foreign minister. He was a party loyalist, not a destroyer. His political hero and model was his grandfather, Kishi Nobusuke – a key figure in Japan's prewar China policy, a member of Tojo's cabinet when war had been declared on the US, and for two years an A-class war criminal in Sugamo prison. He had then been rehabilitated and, as prime minister from 1957, was an influential architect of the US–Japanese alliance.

Abe's political career before taking office as prime minister had been marked by historical revisionism and denial: the negation of Japan's war responsibility; the belief that Japan in the 1930s and 1940s had fought a glorious and legitimate struggle for national defence and for the liberation of Asia; a commitment to the Shinto view of Japan articulated in 2000 by Prime Minister Mori; a nostalgia for imperial fascism; and hostility to the institutions and principles of postwar democracy. He appeared to see himself as destined to fulfil the mission of his beloved grandfather. Either the office of prime minister would transform him, or he would transform the country in line with that vision. Close friend and ally of Washington though he was taken to be, he nevertheless referred to Japan's war of the 1930s and 1940s as a 'so-called aggressive war', and to the convicted A-class war criminals as innocent of any crime under Japanese law. In that he doubted Japan's war guilt and believed it was something for 'experts' to settle, he resembled the Iranian president, Mahmoud Ahmadinejad, who expressed doubts about the Holocaust and proposed calling on 'experts' to settle whether it happened or not.[8] Ahmadinejad's doubts made him a pariah, but Abe's had little if any effect on his international standing.

Abe's problem would be how to move beyond the postwar order, as he had promised, while at the same time serving US interests: how to deal with the constitution and the Fundamental Law, which needed revision because they were 'American', without also challenging the American-imposed security arrangements and emperor-centred national identity. Both he and the US government agreed on the need to revise the Japanese constitution – but where the Americans thought in terms of doing so in order to free Japanese forces to be able to fight shoulder-to-shoulder with their American counterparts in future wars, Abe seemed to be thinking more in terms of Japan as a great power, able to project force where and when necessary in defence of its interests, whether congruent or not with those of the US. Like Koizumi, he talked of remaking the postwar system. His Japan would possess regular armed forces and an unambiguous right to collective defence. Education would be revamped so that children were taught 'love of family, region, and country'.[9] Whether Washington would find that palatable in the long term was not so clear.

On the very eve of Abe's assumption of office, a special hearing of Washington's House International Relations Committee denounced wartime Japan's coercion of women across Asia into sexual slavery as 'one of the greatest crimes of human trafficking'. Senior Republicans and Democrats condemned Prime Minister Koizumi's Yasukuni visits, senior

Californian Democrat Tom Lantos describing them as 'the most egregious example of Japan's historical amnesia'. The message was clear:
'This practice must end'.[10] It was a signal that Abe might not relish, but
could ill afford to ignore. He had been a central figure among those who
doubted that any such 'great crime' as the exploitation of 'comfort
women' had ever occurred. But on taking office, faced with persistent
questioning, Abe soon reversed his position, saying that his government
would not attempt to change the established position, which had been
expressed in the Murayama and Kono apologies over the issues of
colonialism, aggression, and 'comfort women'. It was a welcome reversal,
however grudging.

On Yasukuni, too, Abe was in a cleft stick: he could not maintain
his previous stance without causing a diplomatic storm; but neither
could he drastically shift ground without eliciting fierce protest among
his supporters at home. The subterfuge solution – his secret Yasukuni
visit in the spring of 2006 before launching his bid for the party
presidency – was a card that could be played only once. For the long
term, constitutional revision or the establishment of a national shrine
might be his preferred solution, but his short-term dilemma looked
insoluble. Ever since, as deputy chief cabinet secretary late in 2002,
Abe had blocked Prime Minister Koizumi's initiatives for normalization, his greatest source of public support had been his 'tough'
stance on North Korea. Being at the forefront of Japan's hardliners on
North Korea, he was at one with neo-conservatives in Washington in
favouring North Korean regime change. It was a position that came
with considerable risk, and the Bush policy reversal of 2007 left him
exposed and vulnerable.

In 2002, Abe had insisted that Japan should ignore the undertaking
with Pyongyang over the abductees, and simply wait for Pyongyang to
yield, as it would be forced to do by its economic plight. Events showed
him to have seriously misread the situation, and Koizumi had to make a
second visit to Pyongyang in May 2004, essentially to apologize and
reopen negotiations. As the North Korean crisis worsened in 2006, Abe
was again at the forefront of international pressure. When he had been
chief cabinet secretary, in the summer of 2006, he had played a key role
in securing UN Security Council Resolution 1695 denouncing North
Korea's threats to peace after the July 2006 missile launches, then
describing it triumphantly as 'Japan's first Security Council initiative

in 60 years, since the Security Council was founded'.[11] Shortly afterwards, as prime minister, he joined in helping to coordinate a severe and
punitive international response to North Korea's nuclear test – Security
Council Resolution 1718 of 14 October 2006 – focused on tightening
the screws still further. His 'toughness' helped to consolidate his support
base in Japan, and was appreciated in Washington; but it opened a gap
between Japan and its Asian neighbours, who were anxious not to push
Pyongyang into a corner. They were intent on a comprehensive resolution of North Korea's abnormal situation – not just of the nuclear and
abductee issues. It should have been enough to recall Japan's behaviour
in 1941 to doubt the likely success of sanctions, condemnation, and
isolation in bringing about peaceful change.

In the areas of economic and social policy, although Abe pledged to
continue Koizumi's 'reform' line, he had been a late convert to
neoliberalism and showed early signs that he might soft-pedal privatization and deregulation, returning to more inclusive, interventionist,
traditional LDP ways.[12] When he decided, late in 2006, to readmit
to the party eleven of the postal rebels against whom Koizumi, only
months earlier, had sent 'assassins', confidence in his commitment to
reform was shaken even among the party faithful. That, and a series of
scandals, saw support for his government plummet – from 63 per cent
in October to 53 per cent in November, and 47 per cent by December.[13] The party had not exactly been destroyed by Koizumi, but it had
certainly been weakened; and unless the slide in support for it could be
reversed, Abe faced potential disaster in the Upper House elections
scheduled for July 2007. His hostility to the 'American-imposed'
constitution and Fundamental Law of Education – combined with a
commitment to neoliberal, US economic nostrums and the deepening
of Japan's military and strategic assimilation to the US – was inherently
unstable. As Kato Koichi put it, it was like driving a car with both the
heater and cooler on at the same time.[14]

Lacking Koizumi's theatricality and charisma, Abe nevertheless
inherited from him a massive parliamentary majority, and made good
early use of it, in December 2006, to pass his revised Fundamental
Law of Education and to upgrade the Defence Agency to a Ministry.
Reference in Article 1 of the 1947 education law, on 'respecting the
value of the individual', was struck out and replaced with the
prescription of a set of moral virtues, including love of country, that

the schools would henceforth be required to instil in children. Morality, as Miyake Shoko put it, would henceforth function 'within the parameters set by the state'.[15] As 2007 began, Abe declared his determination to press on with revising the constitution too, with the goal of ensuring that the country's basic charter should also set public, state goals (loyalty preeminent among them) above 'selfish' considerations of individual rights.

Abe's core agenda – encapsulated in his best-selling manifesto, *Utsukushii kuni e* ('Towards a beautiful country') – was moral and ideological, with a strong sentimental and romantic strain.[16] A national movement to clarify just what was 'beautiful', and to identify Japan's '100 quintessential elements', was to be launched in 2007.[17] This project had the potential to provide criteria for defining the Japan that people would be required to love. Like much of Abe's agenda, this had strong echoes of his grandfather's era, when the 'Movement for Clarifying the National Polity' defined Japan's beauty in a set of principles known as 'The Fundamentals of National Polity', which the Ministry of Education then took pains to incorporate at the core of the school curriculum. Dissenters were then driven out as 'un-Japanese', while Abe's grandfather and his colleagues consolidated imperial fascism.[18] One former student of early 1940s Japan recalled the 'beautiful country, Japan' of his school reader, which his generation had been obliged to love even as it spread chaos and mayhem across Asia.[19] For much of the Abe agenda, the closest parallels were to be found on the far right of European politics.

As 2007 dawned, Abe's call for a state-enforced patriotism was endorsed by the head of the country's main business organization, Keidanren – Mitarai Fujio. According to Mitarai's 'vision', nothing was more urgent in order to turn Japan into a 'country of hope' than for the schools to instil patriotism in children.[20] Ironically, the term 'country of hope' had in 2000 provided the title of a best-selling novel by Murakami Ryu (*Kibo no kuni no exusodasu* – 'Flight to a Land of Hope'). Murakami's 'land of hope', however, was a refuge to which people fled, escaping the 'fascism of love and illusion' (the title of one of his earlier novels). His was therefore a hope diametrically at odds with that shared by Abe and Mitarai.

The perennial 'Japan problem'

As economic links between the countries of East Asia grow ever more complex, and as the public figures of the region seek the formula for a social and political community, the 'Japan problem' becomes more intractable. In Japan, modernity was for long synonymous with escape from – or denial of – Asia (*datsu-A*), predicated on combining Japanese uniqueness and non-Asianness with Westernization. Prime Minister Abe's 'beautiful country' is merely the latest incarnation of the unique and superior Japan canard. By insisting that postwar Japanese identity preserve its prewar core and be reconstituted around the emperor, the US psychological warfare unit understood that a non-Asian Japan would remain tied to the US. Like the best of such stratagems, it was not seen as an imposition, instead being acclaimed in Japan as an insight drawn from the depths of the Japanese mind. Generations of Japanese saw Benedict's essay as uniquely insightful, and reproduced uncritically the emperor-centred Japanese identity on which US wartime intelligence had insisted. In the process, they replicated notions of Japanese superiority and non-Asian-ness, and the structures of discrimination and prejudice rooted in them.

As long as enough people in Japan could be persuaded to imagine that they possessed a unique, superior, non-Asian Japanese identity, there would be no risk of the emergence of any Asian community or commonwealth – much less of one resting on the foundation of a partnership between Japan and China. As the US State Department foresaw many decades ago, it is therefore much to the US's benefit to insist that the emperor be at the head of the state. The neo-nationalist attempt – led by Abe, Mitarai and others – to set a course for Japan into a solipsistic sea of unique and emperor-centred Japaneseness functions to isolate Japan from its neighbours and to ensure its continuing dependence on the US.

If Habermas is right that all European, and many other, states are in the process of becoming 'countries of immigration and multi-cultural societies',[21] and if Edward Said is right that all cultures are 'involved in one another, none is single and pure, all are hybrid, heterogeneous, extraordinarily differentiated, and unmonolithic', then Japan is an example of what Said describes as 'defensive, reactive, and even paranoid nationalism . . . where children as well as older students are taught to venerate and celebrate the uniqueness of their tradi-tion'.[22] By definition, a unique and distinctive Japan possesses no universal value, and such thinking constitutes a major obstacle to Japan's performance of a positive, cooperative role in the region and the world.

The link between militarization, service to the US, and patriotic and nationalist ideology has been plain at successive stages of Japan's postwar political evolution. During the occupation, it was the emperor himself who displayed the greatest enthusiasm for the US bases, while carefully setting about reconstructing his own centrality to the state. During the period immediately after the Korean War – when the US was preparing for the Third World War and wanted massive Japanese rearmament – the 1954 Ikeda-Robertson Agreement stated that it was

> most important to encourage an atmosphere in Japan in which the Japanese people would want to increase responsibility for their own defense, for which the Japanese government bore the primary responsibility of encouraging a climate in which a spontaneous spirit of patriotism and self-defense would grow.[23]

Prime Minister Kishi in the late 1950s, and Nakasone in the 1980s, exemplified this fusion of nationalism, militarization, and enthusiasm to serve the US. Nakasone's January 1983 offering of Japan as the US's 'unsinkable aircraft carrier', even as he attempted to revive the Yasukuni cult, prefigured what Koizumi and Abe would attempt two decades later.

Japan's attempts to relate to its neighbours, to come to terms with its twentieth-century history, and to cooperate in the construction of an Asian commonwealth, have all been affected by this deep-seated identity problem. So too has Japanese society itself. The special representative of the UN Commission on Human Rights, Doudou Diene, concluded in 2005 that Japan was a country in which discrimination was 'deep and profound', and that Japan's society was 'spiritually and intellectually closed'. He added a year later that the current mutation of that racism was anti-terrorism – discrimination against foreigners and minorities in a climate of nationalism and xenophobia.[24] The special, 'emperor-centred', non-Asian Japanese identity could only be constructed by exclusion of those who did not belong: it required and reproduced discrimination.

The 'Japan problem' in late twentieth- and early twenty-first-century Asia tended to be seen as one of what Japan *did* – especially its aggression against and control over Asia in the early to mid-twentieth century. It may be, however, that the deeper problem, still unresolved, is how Japan imagines itself: in other words, what it *is*. As East Asia (or Northeast Asia) moves inexorably towards some sort of community, it will be difficult to accommodate a Japan that has not addressed this problem.

As 2007 dawned, talk of love, beauty and hope filled the air in Tokyo. It was not that Japanese people were suddenly smitten with the romantic sentiments of an unseasonably early spring, but rather that their leaders were demanding these things of them – insisting that they love their country. This perhaps provides the country's closest parallel with neighbouring North Korea, whose citizens were also required to love their 'Dear Leader'. The critic Sataka Makoto described it as the phenomenon of the 'stalker state'.[25] Those in Japan with long memories recall the time in the first half of the twentieth century when citizens were compelled to love their state, and told that its deeds were incomparably beautiful. It did not end well.

Perhaps the most striking feature of the vision articulated by Koizumi, Abe, and Mitarai is their neglect of any concern for the shared fate of humanity. While the earth inches towards catastrophe, they concentrate on outdated notions of the state, boast of their closeness to the centres of global power, scheme to win a seat at the 'top table' of the UN, and promise an ever-rising GDP. Their orientation towards Japanese power and leadership, their stress on its unique and unsullied 'beauty', seem profoundly narcissistic; their concept of state power is rooted in the nineteenth century; and their ideals – not those of freedom and equality, but those of discipline, order, and the authority embodied in rituals associated with the flag and anthem, and unquestioning service to state and corporation – are almost Prussian. Their prescriptions may be boiled down to a combination of neo-nationalism and neoliberalism. There is no trace in their thinking of the moral or intellectual concerns of the British government's 'Stern Report' of late 2006 on the crisis of humanity, our common civilization, and our planet.[26]

Stern suggests that a 'tipping point' is imminent in relation to global warming. And it does not require a reading of his 700-page report to realize that, indeed, while the violence of terror and war spreads, the polar ice continues to melt; the seas rise; the earth warms; fisheries collapse; coral dies; forests shrink; deserts spread; water tables sink; the earth is buffeted by increasing storms, droughts and floods; and the fifth great extinction of species proceeds. The quest for a sustainable mode of industrial civilization – symbiotic with the natural world rather than exploitative of it – is a matter of life and death. Tinkering with the system no longer suffices. What is called for is nothing less than a rethinking of the deep paradigms of capitalism and modernity.

In an earlier book, I wrote of the founder of National Panasonic, Matsushita Konosuke, who in the 1970s conceived the idea of a 200-year project to expand the Japanese territory by mobilizing the people to level mountains and fill in the sea in order to construct a new, fifth, Japanese island. This was a madcap idea if ever there was one – yet his purpose was plainly serious: to find a goal to focus and draw out the energies of the people, and to generate the sense of national purpose that had formerly come from war without stirring renewed conflict with neighbouring countries.[27] What is needed today, however, is not grand Sisyphean schemes – much less more Japanese territory – but the grandest of all imaginable schemes: the rescue of our planet. This task will require political and social leaders who can transcend the pettiness of present-day politics, articulate the crisis, and design ways to tap the imagination, intelligence, and generosity of the Japanese people. A kind of mobilization, certainly – but not of soldiers and weapons (the kind of 'international contribution' of which the Japanese government tends always to think first, both because it is in line with traditional ideas of state power and because it is what Japan's importunate US ally demands), but of talent and wisdom, mobilized in accordance with the high ideals of the constitution.

The three young Japanese who were briefly held captive in Iraq in 2003 – and were then excoriated by their government and mass media for not having a sufficient sense of responsibility (especially compared to Japan's soldiers, who were lauded ceaselessly) – may be seen as pointing a finger in such a direction. The sentiments of the residents of Samawah in Iraq, who complained when Japan sent them its soldiers instead of a Sony or Mitsubishi 'army', are almost certainly widespread. Instead of perpetuating a Japan that concentrates on ways to 'normalize' its armed forces and to become a nuclear power – sitting on mountains of plutonium and striving to serve a distant master by becoming an offshore US, a client state, East Asian Britain, or *zokkoku* – politicians are called for who can chart a fresh way forward, reconceptualizing Japan's identity so as to transcend both the fantasies of Japanese essentialism and the impositions of American hegemonism, and redefining its Asian-ness without negating its friendly ties to the US.

Notes

1   Forever Twelve Years Old?

1   US Senate, 82nd Congress, 1st Session, Committees on Armed Services and Foreign Policy, *Military Situation in the Far East* (Washington, 1951), pp. 310–11.

2   Edwin O. Reischauer, 'Memorandum on Policy Towards Japan', 14 September 1942, document introduced and discussed in Fujitani Takashi, 'The Reischauer Memo: Mr Moto, Hirohito, and Japanese–American soldiers', *Critical Asian Studies*, 2000, vol. 33 no. 3.

3   Kato Tetsuro, '1942 nen rokugatsu Beikoku 'Nihon puran' to shocho tennosei', *Sekai*, December 2004, pp. 132–43.

4   *Asahi Shimbun*, 19 February 2003.

5   In 2006, Kyuma created some confusion by expressing doubt, later withdrawn, as to whether the Japanese government had indeed supported the war in Iraq, suggesting it might have been just a personal commitment made by Koizumi for a war that he himself had not supported. When he went on then to state, 'Self Defense Forces were not sent to Iraq to support the war or to support the Americans', he left the waters thoroughly muddied. ('Kyuma retracts comment on Iraq', *Japan Times*, 9 December 2006.)

6   *Asahi Shimbun*, 21 September 2004.

7   Sakakibara Eisuke, 'Japanese nationalism: Conservatives have derailed', *Japan Times*, 2 May 2004.

8   Minoru Morita, 'An 'outsider' speaks out', interviewed by Eric Prideaux, *Japan Times*, 3 September 2006.

9   See Gavan McCormack, *The Emptiness of Japanese Affluence* (New York: M.E. Sharpe, 2001, second edition).

10   Koizumi speech on the fiftieth anniversary of the foundation of the Liberal Democratic Party, 22 November 2005, http://www.jimin.jp/jimin/jimin/toutaikai/toutaikai72/05/01.html. Accessed 16 December 2005.

11   John W. Dower, *Embracing Defeat: Japan in the Wake of World War II* (New York: W. W. Norton, 1999).

2 The Dependent Superstate

1 'Toa minzoku no honto no kyoryoku o ushinatta koto', quoted in Terashima Jitsuro, 'Shidosha no ishi kettei sekinin', *Sekai*, December 2004, pp. 33–5, at p. 33.

2 *Kokutai* in prewar Japan, literally translated as 'national polity', referred to the supposedly unique and superior Japanese way centred on the emperor.

3 Toyoshita Narahiko, 'Showa tenno-Makkasa kaiken o kensho suru', *Ronza*, two parts: part 1, November 2002, pp. 56–69; part 2, December 2002, pp. 122–35, at p. 134.

4 Herbert P. Bix, *Hirohito and the Making of Modern Japan* (New York: Harper Collins, 2000), p. 640; Toyoshita, 'Showa tenno', p. 128.

5 John Dower, 'Tennosei minshushugi no tanjo', *Sekai*, September 1999, pp. 221–32, in English as 'A message from the Showa Emperor', *Bulletin of Concerned Asian Scholars*, vol. 31, no. 4 (1999).

6 Bix, *Hirohito and the Making of Modern Japan* (New York: Harper, 2001) pp. 626–7; Toyoshita, 'Showa tenno', pp. 122–35.

7 My translation of the emperor's famous remark on 31 October 1975: '. . . so iu kotoba no aya ni tsuite wa, watakushi wa so iu bungaku homen wa amari kenkyu mo shite inai no de, yoku wakarimasen'.

8 Ruth Benedict, *The Chrysanthemum and the Sword: Patterns of Japanese Culture* (Boston: Houghton Mifflin, 1946). For recent thoughts on Benedict and her significance, see Sonia Ryang, 'Chrysanthemum's Strange Life: Ruth Benedict in Postwar Japan', *Asian Anthropology* 1 (2002); *Japan and National Anthropology: A Critique* (London: RoutledgeCurzon/Asian Studies Association of Australia East Asia Series, 2004); and Michiba Chikanobu, *Senryo to heiwa*, Tokyo, Seidosha, 2005.

9 1.4 million, according to Michiba, *Senryo to heiwa*, p. 50; 2.3 million is the highest estimate quoted in Ryang, *Japan and National Anthropology*, pp. 29, 49.

10 Michiba, *Senryo to heiwa*, passim.

11 Samuel Huntington, *The Clash of Civilizations and the Remaking of World Order* (New York: Simon & Schuster, 1996).

12 See Chapter 6.

13 Strictly speaking, even Marine Day, the third Monday in July, may be added to this list, since it began in 1941 as a commemoration of the Meiji emperor's safe return by sea from a visit to northern regions of the country in 1876.

14 The Hinomaru and Kimigayo were the anthem and flag of prewar militarist Japan. Their adoption as national symbols in 1999 ruffled the feathers of neighbouring Asian countries, and angered those in Japan who sought a clean break with the militarist past.

15 'Yasukuni sampai – Kokkai giin no kai ga teigen, Koizumi shusho o ato-oshi e', *Mainichi shimbun* (9 August 2006).

16 'Shinto seiji renmei koryo kaisetsusho', July 1987, http://www.torigai.net/

activity/2000/link/kamikunidoc.html. The homepage of the organization is: http://www.sinseiren.org/. See also Tawara Yoshifumi, 'Kiken na "nakayoshi naikaku" ko shite dekiagatta', *Shukan kinyobi*, 13 October 2006, pp. 12–13. Accessed 16 December 2006.

17 For my earlier analysis, see 'Introduction' to second revised edition, *The Emptiness of Japanese Affluence*, pp. xi–xxxi; 'The Japanese movement to "correct" history', in Laura Hein and Mark Selden, eds, *Censoring History: Citizenship and Memory in Japan, Germany, and the United States* (New York: M. E. Sharpe, 2000), pp. 53–73; and 'New tunes for an old song: Nationalism and identity in post-Cold War Japan', in *Nations under Siege: Globalization and Nationalism in Asia* ed. Roy Starrs (London: Palgrave, 2002), pp. 137–68.

18 Tawara Yoshifumi, 'Tenmo shikan o kyokasho to kodomo oshitsukeru "atarashii rekishi kyokasho o tsukuru kai" no sakudo', *Shukan kinyobi* 25 June 1999, pp. 29–31, at p. 31.

19 Utsumi Aiko, Takahashi Tetsuya, and So Kyungsik, eds, *Ishihara tochiji 'Sankokujin' hatsugen no nani ga mondai no ka* (Tokyo: Kage shobo, 2000).

20 Tawara Yoshifumi, 'Kiken na "nakayoshi naikaku"', pp. 12–13.

21 On the latter, see Gavan McCormack, 'War and Japan's Memory Wars: the Media and the Globalization of Consciousness', *Japan Focus* (13 February 2005).

22 T. Fujitani, *Splendid Monarchy: Power and Pageantry in Modern Japan* (Berkeley, Los Angeles, and London: University of California Press, 1996).

23 One estimate is that 'two out of every three temples that existed during the Edo period were burned to the ground as a result of the suppression of Buddhism'. Tamamuro Fumio, 'On the suppression of Buddhism', Helen Hardacre and Adam L. Kern, eds, *New Directions in the Study of Meiji Japan* (Leiden, New York, and Koln: Brill, 1997), pp. 499–505, at p. 505.

24 Carol Gluck, *Japan's Modern Myths: Ideology in the Meiji Period* (Princeton, NJ: Princeton University Press, 1985).

25 Abe Shinzo, *Utsukushii Kuni e*, (Tokyo: Bungei shunju shinsho, 2006).

26 See Wada Haruki, 'Abe Shinzo shi no rekishi ninshiki o tou', *Sekai*, October 2006, pp. 57–65.

27 Takahashi Tetsuya, *Yasukuni mondai*, (Tokyo: Chikuma shinsho, 2005). See also his 'The national politics of the Yasukuni Shrine' (translated by Philip Seaton), in Naoko Shimazu, ed., *Nationalisms in Japan* (London and New York: Routledge, 2006), pp. 155–80.

28 Tanaka Nobumasa, 'Seiji no Yasukuni', *Shukan Kinyobi*, 10 August 2001, pp. 30–3.

29 'Fiery protests at Koizumi homage', *The Australian*, 15 August 2001.

30 'Korean spirits captive to Japan war amnesia', *The Australian*, 18 July 2001.

31 Quoted in 'Horokobiru Koizumi seiji', *Asahi Shimbun*, 17 July 2004.

32 As of 2006, there had been nine court rulings – six from district and three from high courts. The Fukuoka District Court and Osaka High Court

issued clear rulings of unconstitutionality, while the Tokyo High Court ruled to the opposite effect, on the ground that the prime ministerial visit could not be regarded as an 'official' act by the prime minister. 'Koizumi an official at Yasukuni', *Japan Times*, 27 November 2004; 'Shrine visits "unconstitutional"', *Asahi Shimbun*, 1 October 2005.

33 Kaho Shimizu, 'Top court upholds shrine trip, dodges constitutionality', *Japan Times*, 24 June 2006.

34 See the articles by Tanaka Nobumasa, translated at *Japan Focus*, 2003–5.

35 'Watanabe Tsuneo-shi ga Asahi to "Kyoto" sengen', *Ronza*, February 2006.

36 Hiroko Nakata, 'Bid to address Congress has Yasukuni proviso', *Japan Times*, 17 May 2006.

37 'Business lobby seeks end to Yasukuni visits', *Daily Yomiuri*, 10 May 2006.

38 'Yasukuni no A-kyu senpan goshi – Showa tenno no fukaikan', *Asahi Shimbun*, 20 July 2006 (evening edition).

39 *Asahi Shimbun*, 25 July 2006.

40 'Koizumi goes ahead with shrine visit', *Asahi Shimbun*, 16 August 2006.

41 For a lucid discussion of the event and its significance, see Tanaka Nobumasa and Takahashi Tetsuya, 'Yasukuni mondai no honshitsu', *Shukan Kinyobi*, 11 August 2006, pp. 10–16.

42 *Nihon Keizai Shimbun*, 22 August 2006.

43 Foreign Minister Aso Taro was prominent among those who called for the shrine to disband voluntarily as a religious institution, and be transformed into a government-controlled public entity.

44 Utsumi Aiko, 'Yasukuni Shrine imposes silence on bereaved families' (translated by Richard H. Minear), *Japan Focus*, 7 September 2006.

45 Editorial, *New York Times*, 13 February 2006.

46 Hirotaka Kasai, 'Maruyama Masao's Japan', in Naoki Sakai, Brett de Bary and Iyotani Toshio, eds, *Deconstructing Japan* (Ithaca, NY: Cornell East Asia series, no. 124, 2006), pp. 185–208, at p. 201.

47 Words used by former LDP Secretary-General Kato Koichi; see the interview with Kato cited below.

48 David McNeill, 'Murakami Ichiro and ultra-nationalist intimidation in Japan', *Japan Focus*, January 2004, http://japanfocus.org/products/details/1750.

49 Ibid.

50 'Japan: No justice for murdered *Asahi Shimbun* reporter', CPJ News Alert 2002, (New York: Committee to Protect Journalists) http://www.cpj.org/news/2002/Japan02may02na.html. Accessed 6 October 2004.

51 The 'society of spectacle' is a reference to Guy Debord's *La Société du Spectacle* (1977 and subsequent translations), which argues that late capitalism reduces people to passive spectators who can only see the show but have no power to act. Debord was a founding member of the Situationist International, an influential anarchist group. On the case of 'Mr K', including photographs of

his artwork, see Shinya Watanabe, 'Anti-war graffiti and the Dudgement [*sic*] in Japan – La Spectacle (12/5/2004)', (New York: SpikyArt.com) http://www.spikyart.org/graffitijudge.com. Accessed 21 December 2006.

52 *Mainichi Daily News*, 23 August 2003.
53 Kasuya Koichiro, 'Kikanshi haifu de 32 nen buri kokukoho tekiyo no yuzai hanketsu', *Shukan Kinyobi*, 7 July 2006, p. 5.
54 'Education policy on trial', editorial, *Japan Times*, 7 June 2006.
55 Ibid.
56 Quoted in David McNeill, 'Enemies of the State: Free Speech and Japan's Courts', *Japan Focus*, 8 February 2006.
57 For details, Glenn D. Hook and Gavan McCormack, *Japan's Contested constitution* (London and New York: Routledge, 2001).
58 Kamata Satoshi, 'Hyogen no jiyu o yuzuranai Tokyo kosai no hijoshiki', *Shukan Kinyobi*, 3 March 2006, pp. 22–5.
59 'Trespassing acquittal', editorial, *Asahi Shimbun*, 29 August 2006.
60 Kamata Satoshi, 'Nukiuchi shobun no kage ni seijika no kainyu ka', *Shukan Kinyobi*, 12 May 2006, pp. 36–9.
61 The Tokyo education authorities refused to specify her offence, on grounds of privacy.
62 Narusawa Muneo, 'NHK toron bangumi sankasha ni inshitsu na iyagarase', *Shukan Kinyobi*, 7 July 2006, p. 5.
63 Shin Sugo, ' "Ganbare" tte watakushi ni iu anata jishin wa, doko ni iru nda', Keisen joshi daigakuin kokusai shinpojiumu jikko iinkai, ed., *Chotto yabai nja nai? Nashonarizumu*, (Tokyo: Kaiho Shuppansha, 2006), pp. 61–79.
64 Quoted in *Tokyo Shimbun*, 25 August 2006.
65 Gavan McCormack, 'War and Japan's memory wars: the media and the globalization of consciousness', *Japan Focus*, 13 February 2005.
66 McNeill, 'Murakami Ichiro and Ultra-Nationalist Intimidation in Japan'.
67 'Free speech targeted', *Asahi Shimbun*, 24 July 2006; 'Alarm at fire-bomb attack against financial paper', *Reporters Without Borders*, Japan, 21 July 2006, at http://www.rsf.org/print.php3?id_article=18334. Accessed 3 August 2006.
68 'Rightist linked to attack on Kato's home', *Asahi Shimbun*, 17 August 2006.
69 Author's notes on a talk given by Kato in Tokyo, 7 April 2004. See also 'Kato moto kanjicho jikka hoka', *Tokyo Shimbun*, 25 August 2006.
70 Kakumi Kobayashi, 'Following arson attack, Kato warns of "dangerous" nationalism emerging', *Asahi Shimbun*, 20 August 2006.
71 'Kato Koichi shi ni kinkyu intabyu – tero no haikei to nashonarizumu no arikata', *Ohmynews*, 30 August 2006 at http://www.ohmynews.co.jp/News.aspx?news_id=000000000308. Accessed 30 August 2006.
72 'Shusho, boryoku de no genron fusatsu o hinan', *Asahi Shimbun*, 28 August 2006.
73 'Kato moto kanjicho jikka hoka – tonai bokyaku modo', *Tokyo Shimbun*, 25 August 2006.

3 Dismantling the 'Japanese' Model

1 For fuller discussion, see Chapter 1 of my *The Emptiness of Japanese Affluence*, and 'Breaking Japan's iron triangle', *New Left Review* 13, January–February 2002.

2 Jetro, 'Japan's $3+ trillion postal privatization to have significant impact on financial markets', Newsletter, New York, 22 December 2004. http://www.jetro.go.jp/usa/newyork/focusnewsletter/focus37.htm. Accessed 24 December 2004.

3 McCormack, 'Breaking Japan's iron triangle', p. 14.

4 'Interview/Masaharu Gotoda: Pork-barrel politics has poisoned the well', *Asahi Shimbun/International Herald Tribune*, 5 September 2002.

5 Uchihashi Katsuto, 'Nihon keizai, dai tenkan no toki', *Sekai*, February 1998, pp. 40–7.

6 Gotoda Masaharu, '21 seiki no Nippon no shinro', *Asahi Shimbun*, 25 December 1998.

7 Electoral data at: http://www2.asahi.com/senkyo2005/index.html or, in English, http://en.wikipedia.org/wiki/Results_of_Japan_general_election,_2005. Accessed 3 December 2005.

8 Kamiwaki Hiroshi, 'Kore wa honto ni 'min-i' na no ka', *Sekai*, November 2005, pp. 106–11.

9 Tensei jingo, *Asahi Shimbun*, 26 September 2005.

10 Yamaguchi Jiro and Suzuki Muneo, 'Haisha fukkatsu no seiji o', *Sekai*, February 2006, pp. 47–55 at p. 47.

11 Koizumi elsewhere lists 'Kage Boshi' and X-Japan's 'Forever Love' among his favourites.

12 Nemoto Seiki, 'Kakusa shakai – "futo" ka do ka no sakaime', *Asahi Shimbun*, 22 November 2005.

13 Kamata Satoshi, 'Maru de "Toyota-shiki zetsubo kojo" – karoshi zokushutsu suru yusei kosha', *Shukan Kinyobi*, 17 February 2006, pp. 36–9.

14 OECD, *Economic Surveys, Japan*, July 2006, p. 17.

15 Yumi Wijers-Hasegawa, 'Successor inherits ever unpopular deficit mess,' *Japan Times*, 27 June 2006.

16 National tax office figures indicate a salary reduction of 16 per cent over the preceding ten years for workers in small and medium-sized businesses (with capitalization less than ¥100 million), 9 per cent in businesses with capitalization of up to ¥1 billion, and 1 per cent in those of larger size. Niwa Uichiro, ' "Daini no odoriba" ni kita Nihon no keizai', *Sekai*, March 2006, pp. 96–102, at p. 99.

17 Tsujimoto Kiyomi, 'Nagatacho kokaiki', *Shukan Kinyobi*, 7 July 2006, pp. 54–5.

18 NHK Television, 10pm News, 28 September 2005.

19 'Seikatsu hogosha 104 man setai', *Asahi Shimbun*, 7 October 2006.

20 'Shiawase taikoku o mezashite', *Asahi Shimbun*, 3 April 2005.

21 Sato Yusuke, 'Nihon no soko ga nukehajimeta', *Shukan Kinyobi*, 2 December 2005, pp. 8–12, at p. 8.

22 Nikkeiren (Japan Federation of Employers' Associations), Shin jidai no "Nihonteki keiei", (Tokyo: Nikkeiren 1995).

23 Ibid.

24 For recent discussion, see Hiratate Hideaki, ' "Waking pua" no genjitsu', part 1, *Shukan Kinyobi*, 29 September 2006, pp. 20–2.

25 'Shiawase taikoku o mezashite', *Asahi Shimbun*, 12 June 2005.

26 By 2007, Canon expected to have one-quarter of its domestic production coming from robots. ('Shiawase taikoku o mezashite', no. 11, *Asahi Shimbun*, 12 June 2005).

27 Ouchi Hirokazu, 'Kakusa shakai no kakudai koteika o motarasu kyoiku kihonho kaitei', *Sekai*, November 2006, pp. 48–56, at p. 52.

28 Hiratate, ' "Waking pua" no genjitsu', p. 21.

29 'Frita 417 man nin no shogeki', NHK Special, March 2005. Tachibanaki Toshiaki ('Jakusha no hinkonka ga kakusa o jocho shite iru', *Ronza*, June 2005, pp. 102–7, at p. 106) suggests the figure of 'between 2 and 4 million'. The May 2003 Cabinet Office 'White Paper on National Lifestyle' gives a figure of 1.83 million in 1990, rising to 4.17 million by 2001. (Tetsushi Kajimoto, 'Income disparities rising in Japan', *Japan Times*, 4 January 2006.)

30 '2020s: Dark age of gray-haired freeters', *Daily Yomiuri Online*, 6 June 2005. For a moving documentary on the plight of the freeter, see 'Frita 417 man nin no shogeki', NHK Special, March 2005.

31 Tachibanaki Toshiaki, 'Kakusa kakudai ga yugameru Nihon no jinteki shigen', *Sekai*, March 2006, pp. 103–10, at p. 104.

32 Genda Yuji, 'Wakamono no zasetsu wa "kibo" ga sukuu', *Ekonomisuto*, 20 September 2005.

33 Bungei shunju, ed, *Ronten 2006*, Tokyo, 2005, p. 794.

34 'Shiawase taikoku o mezashite', (4), *Asahi Shimbun*, 24 April 2005.

35 The OECD ('Japan, 2006', p. 115) comments: '. . . strict eligibility conditions and the short duration of benefits in Japan also reduce the number of unemployed receiving benefits to 34% compared to an OECD average of 92%'.

36 Kajimoto, 'Income disparities'.

37 Yamada Masahiro, *Kibo kakusa shakai* (Tokyo: Chikuma 2005), pp. 167–9.

38 'Fueru jisatsusha', *Asahi Shimbun*, 9 January 2005.

39 John Breen, 'Introduction: Death issues in 21st century Japan', *Mortality*, vol. 9, no. 1, February 2004, pp. 1–12, at p. 5.

40 Yamada Masahiro, *Kibo kakusa shakai*, p. 202; *Asahi Shimbun*, 9 January 2005.

41 Breen, 'Introduction: Death issues', p. 5.

42 Uchihashi Katsuto, 'Ushinawareta "ningen no kuni"', *Sekai*, November 2005, p. 36–44, at p. 36. (See translation by Ben Middleton as 'The lost "human country"', *Japan Focus*, http://japanfocus.org/products/details/1801).

43 'Kaisha e no chuseishin Nihon ga sekai saitei', *Asahi Shimbun*, 13 May 2005.

44 Yamada, *Kibo kakusa shakai*, p. 60; Tachibanaki, 'Jakusha no hinkonka . . .' p. 103. The OECD's 'Income Distribution and Poverty in OECD Countries in the Second Half of the 1990s' (March 2005, p. 10) gives the Japan figure as of 2000 at 0.314, already above the OECD average of 0.309. http://www.oecd.org/dataoecd/48/9/34483698.pdf.

45 *Ronza*, December 2004, pp. 8–21.

46 Fifty-three per cent, according to the survey by *Asahi Shimbun*, published 5 September 2005.

47 *Asahi Shimbun*, 29 February 2004.

48 Hayano Toru, 'Koizumi kassai no toki wa sugita', *Ronza*, August 2004, pp. 24–9 at pp. 28–9.

49 Wijers-Hasegawa, op.cit

50 From around ¥540 trillion in March 2001 to ¥780 trillion in March 2005, or over ¥1,000 trillion if all public liabilities are included (Kaneko Masaru, 'Zaisei akaji no sekinin o dare ga toru no ka', *Shukan Kinyobi*, 9 September 2005, pp. 12–13).

51 Otake Fumio and Kohara Miki, 'Shohizei wa honto no gyakushinteki ka', *Ronza*, December 2005, pp. 44–51.

52 Ito Mitsuharu, 'Zozei o shinken ni kangaeyo', *Sekai*, January 2006, pp. 77–95.

53 Jinno Naohiko and Miyamoto Taro, ' "Chisana seifu" ron to shijoshugi no shuen', *Sekai*, May 2006, pp. 96–107, at p. 98.

54 OECD, *Japan 2006*, pp. 108–9.

55 To reach ¥69 trillion. *Asahi Shimbun*, editorial, 10 September 2005.

56 Niki Ryu, 'Koreisha o chokugeki suru, Koizumi seiken saigo no iryohi yokusei seisaku', *Sekai*, December 2005, pp. 20–4, at p. 24.

57 'Futan no nijumu aishutsu kaikaku', *Asahi Shimbun*, 27 June 2006.

58 'Future fiscal plans', *Asahi Shimbun*, 21 August 2006.

59 Kaneko Masaru, 'Zaisei akaji no sekinin wa dare ga toru no ka', *Shukan Kinyobi*, 9 September 2005, pp. 12–13.

60 Ibid.

61 Robin Blackburn, 'Capital and social Europe', *New Left Review* 34 (July–August 2005), pp. 89–114, at p. 89.

62 'Japan now among "oldest" nations in world', *Asahi Shimbun*, 3 June 2006. The UN uses 7 per cent or more as the criterion for 'aging', 14 per cent or more for 'aged', and 20 per cent or more for 'super-aged'. Already 'super-aged', on current trends Japan can expect its over-sixty-five cohort to reach an astonishing 35.7 per cent by mid-century. (Ito Mitsuharu, 'Zosei o shinken ni kangaeyo', *Sekai*, January 2006, pp. 77–95.)

63 Sakaraguchi Chikara, quoted in 'Japanese face extinction due to low birthrate: health minister', *Japan Times*, 22 May 2002.

64 Eric Prideaux, 'Minoru Morita: An "Outsider" speaks out', *Japan Times*, 3 September 2006.

65 OECD, Economic Surveys, *Japan 2006*, p. 15. See also Nicholas Eberstadt,

'Power and population in Asia', *Strategic Asia*, 2003–04, National Bureau of Asian Research, http://www.policyreview.org/feb04/eberstadt_print.html.
66 Prideaux, 'Minoru Morita'.
67 Notably *Kibo kakusa shakai* ('Expectation gap society'), 2004, and *Karyu shakai* ('Lower-class society'), 2005.
68 Tachibana Takashi, *Iraku senso, Nihon no unmei, Koizumi no kakumei* (Tokyo: Kodansha 2004), pp. 62–3.
69 See 'Fact Sheet', Third Report to the Leaders on the US–Japan Regulatory Reform and Competition Policy Initiative, 8 June 2004, http://www.ustr.-gov.
70 Sekioka Hideyuki, 'Ubawareru Nihon – "Nenji kaikaku yobosho" Beikoku no Nihon kaizo keikaku', *Bungei Shunju*, December 2005, pp. 94–108, passim.
71 'US masterminds Japan's postal privatization', *Asahi Shimbun*, 8 April 2005.
72 Okano Kaoru, 'Koizumi, watakushi wa shinsei jiminto wo tsukuru', *Shukan Gendai*, 6 August 2005. See also 'Point of view: US pressure behind postal privatization drive', *Asahi Shimbun*, 18 February 2005, http://www.asahi.-com/english/opinion/TKY200502180155.html. Accessed 18 February 2005.
73 Letter dated 4 October 2004, tabled in the Diet on 2 August 2005. House of Councillors, Special Committee on Postal Privatization, http://kok-kai.ndl.go.jp/SENTAKU/sangiin/162/0087/main.html. Accessed 6 September 2005. See also Tokumoto Eiichiro, 'Takenaka Heizo ga sori daijin ni naru hi', *Bungei Shunju*, December 2005, pp. 110–19, at p. 113.
74 *Wall Street Journal*, 26 August 2006, quoted in Manabu Hara, 'Point of view: Where will the postal funds finally end up?', *Asahi Shimbun*, 14 September 2005.
75 Jetro, 'Japan's $3+ trillion postal privatization to have significant impact on financial markets'.
76 US–Japan Economic Partnership for Growth, *United States–Japan Investment Initiative*, 2006 report, June 2006.
77 *Tokyo Shimbun*, 13 September 2005.
78 'Editorial: Female Candidates', *Asahi Shimbun*, 8 September 2005.
79 LDP member Ota Seiichi in June 2003, in Hosaka Masayasu, *Sengo seijika bogenroku*, (Tokyo: Chuko shinsho rakure, No. 173 2005) p. 236.
80 They must be aware of the fate of Tanaka Makiko, the enormously popular foreign minister in the first Koizumi administration, who was roughly shunted aside in January 2002 when she began to take steps to 'reform' her ministry.
81 Unlike Tony Blair, or even John Howard, Koizumi has suffered no political ill consequences for his unwavering support of Bush's war and occupation. For Koizumi, it was simply a 'righteous cause'.
82 Ito Makoto, 'Nihon keizai no kozoteki konnan', *Sekai*, August 2005, pp. 194–203, at p. 199.
83 Uchihashi, 'Ushinawareta "ningen no kuni"', p. 44.

84 Kunimasa Takeshige, Goto Kenji and Hoshi Hiroshi, 'Kokkai wa shinda no ka', *Sekai,* June 2005, pp. 64–73.

85 Wakamiya Yoshibumi, 'Koizumi-shi no hofuku', *Asahi Shimbun,* 29 August 2004.

86 Quoted in Yokota Hajime, 'Rinen-naki "kaikaku" ha tachi no shotai', *Shukan Kinyobi,* 23 September 2005, pp. 16–19.

87 LDP membership declined from 3.3 million in 1997 to 1.4 million in 2003, and 1.06 million in 2006. Hoshi Toru, 'Jiminto sosaisen e no shiten', part 2, *Asahi Shimbun,* 9 September 2006.

88 'Kamikaze tanomi no ayausa', editorial, *Asahi Shimbun,* 27 June 2006.

89 Nakanishi Terumasa, 'Kono hoshu no satetsu o norikoete tatsu no wa dare ka,' *Seiron,* November 2005, pp. 48–70.

90 Noda Nobuo, 'Kokeisha naki shidosha minshushugi no munashisa', *Chuo Koron,* November 2005, p. 97.

91 Nishio Kanji, 'Haijakku sareta hyoryu kokka, Nippon', *Seiron,* November 2005, pp. 62–70.

92 Union membership, 35 per cent of the work force in 1975, by 2005 had fallen to around 19 per cent. Sasamori Kiyoshi, 'Roso wa gakeppuchi?' *Asahi Shimbun,* 14 October 2005.

93 Terashima Jitsuro, 'Toshi sarariman ga Koizumi jiminto o eranda riyu', *Sekai,* November 2005, pp. 33–5, at p. 35.

94 The outstanding insider trading and corruption scandal of the time, forcing a string of political resignations and criminal trials, beginning in 1989. It caused the ruling LDP first to lose favour and then, in the 1993 election, to lose its parliamentary majority.

95 Okada made a half-hearted attempt to suggest he would withdraw the Self-Defence Forces from Iraq by December if victorious in the election, but failed to pursue the issue convincingly.

4 Japan in Bush's World

1 'Bush lauds strength of Japan–US alliance', *Japan Times,* 4 July 2004.

2 Speech to the Diet, 18 February 2002, http://www.Usembassy-china.org.cn/press/release/2002/0902-gwbjapan.html. Accessed 6 June 2004.

3 Zbigniew Brzezinski, *The Grand Chessboard: American Primacy and its Geostrategic Imperatives* (New York: Basic Books, 1997), p. 40.

4 Ibid., p. 152.

5 Ibid., pp. 63, 198.

6 ' "Kokuren wa sukutte kurenei" shusho ga domei jushi riyu shimesu', *Asahi Shimbun,* 28 January 2004.

7 'Tensei jingo', *Asahi Shimbun,* 17 November 2005.

8 Kishi Nobusuke, prime minister from 1957 to 1960, addressing the lower house of the national Diet on 30 September 1958. (Hayano Toru, 'Kishi

shusho mo idai na hato-ha datta!?' *Asahi Shimbun,* 14 January 2004.)

9 Article 82 of the SDF Law spells out clear requirements for the exercise of force by the SDF, which include immediate threat to life and/or property. Maeda Tetsuo, 'Kaijo keibi kodo "kakusareta ito"', *Sekai,* May 1999, pp. 22–6.

10 Fifty-one per cent found the response 'appropriate under the circumstances', 38 per cent believed it should have been *more* severe, and only 8 per cent found it excessive (*Kyodo Tsushin,* survey of 6 April, 1999).

11 Ministry of Foreign Affairs, Japan, 'Guidelines for Japan–US Defense Cooperation' (New York: Japan, Ministry of Foreign Affairs, 1995). http://www.mofa.go.jp/region/n-america/us/security/guideline2.html.

12 This was the view taken, for example, by LDP elder statesman Gotoda Masaharu. 'Hatashite ampo no wakunai ka', *Ryukyu Shimpo,* 1 February 1999.

13 'News 23', TBS TV, 13 April 1999.

14 Don Oberdorfer, *The Two Koreas: A Contemporary History* (London: Little Brown, 1997), pp. 305–36. See also Gavan McCormack, *Target North Korea: Pushing North Korea to the Brink of Nuclear Catastrophe* (New York: Nation Books, 2004).

15 For a comparison between the provisions of the wartime 'general mobilization' and the Guidelines, see Koketsu Atsushi, 'Kokka sodoinho yori mo kiken na shuhen jitai hoan no "futomeisa"', *Shukan Kinyobi,* 19 March 1999, pp. 24–7.

16 Kang Sangjung and Yoshima Shunya, 'Konseika shakai e no chosen', part 4, 'Kokka no "taijo" to "kajo"', *Sekai,* December 1999, pp. 287–300.

17 Tsurumi Shunsuke, 'Seiki no opera kaimaku, soshite', *Asahi Shimbun,* 18 August 1999.

18 See James J. Przystup, 'US–Japan Relations: Progress towards a mature partnership' (Washington: Institute for National Strategic Studies, June 2005), http://www.ndu.edu/ndu/sr_japan.html.

19 Institute for National Strategic Studies, 'The United States and Japan: Advancing toward a Mature Partnership', Washington, National Defense University, commonly known as the 'Armitage Report' (Washington: National Defense University Press, October 2000).

20 Stephen Clemons, 'Armiteji hokoku no gyokan o yomu', *Sekai,* July 2001, pp. 98–103. English version, 'The Politics of the Armitage Report: Reading between the lines', at http://www.newamerica.net/index.cfm?pg=article&-DocID=417. Accessed 8 December 2006.

21 Ibid.

22 Zalmay Khalilzad et al., 'The United States and Asia: Toward a New US Strategy and Force Posture' (better known as the 'Rand Report'), June 2001, http://www.rand.org/publications/MR/MR1315, p. 15. Accessed 8 December 2006.

23 Armitage to Japanese ambassador in Washington, Yanai Shunji, on 15 September, 'US hopes Japan will send support troops,' *Mainichi Daily*

News, 18 September 2001; and ('head in sand') to *Asahi Shimbun* on 5 October. 'Nihon saidaigen no kanyo o, *Asahi Shimbun*, 6 October, 2001 (evening).

24 The White House, Office of the Press Secretary, 25 September 2001.

25 On the legality, see Geoffrey Robertson, 'Let The Hague Decide', *The Age*, 29 September 2001; the editorials in *The Japan Times* for 23 September, 6 and 10 October, by W. Bradnee Chambers, John Barry Kotch and Myint Zan; Michael Mandel, 'Say what you want, but this war is illegal', *Toronto Globe and Mail*, 9 October 2001, and Kajimura Taiichiro, 'Hofuku senso de wa naku, nikushimi o koete', *Shukan kinyobi*, 28 September 2001, pp. 16–17.

26 Mandel, 'Say what you want, but this war is illegal.' The court rejected the US claim to be acting under Article 51, defending Nicaragua's neighbours.

27 Mandel, 'Say what you want, but this war is illegal'.

28 Gordon Smith (director for the Centre for Global Studies at the University of Victoria and former Canadian deputy minister of foreign affairs and ambassador to Nato), 'We're buddies with a bully', *Toronto Globe and Mail*, 15 May 2001 (reproduced in Nautilus Nuclear Policy Project Special Report, 16 May 2001).

29 Shinohara Hajime, quoted in Toshi Maeda, 'Diet enacts defense bills, but doubts on alliance linger', *Japan Times*, 24 May 1999.

30 Armitage to Japanese ambassador in Washington, Yanai Shunji, on 15 September, and ('head in sand') to *Asahi Shimbun* on 5 October. ('Nihon no zenmen kanyo o motome, jirai tekkyo mo kitai Bei kokumu fuku-chokan', Asahi.com, 6 October (http://www.asahi.com/), and in Toshiaki Miura, 'All or nothing, says U.S.', Asahi.com, 9 October 2001.

31 'New era in defence policy wins praise from the US', *Yomiuri Shimbun*, 11 June 2003, 'Iraq to jieitai, tokuso hoan wa tou', part 1, 'Bei tsuiju to dokujisei no aida de', *Asahi Shimbun*, 25 June 2003.

32 '"Kokuren yori Bei" no meian', *Asahi Shimbun*, 19 March 2004.

33 'US demands Japan send troops to Iraq early', *Kyodo*, 15 September 2003.

34 'Jiki, chiiki de niten santen, taibei kyoryoku o yusen – rikujo jieitai no Iraq haken', *Asahi Shimbun*, 9 October 2003.

35 'Shudanteki jieiken de naikaku hoseikyoku kaishaku o hihan, Beikokumu fukuchokan', *Asahi Shimbun*, 10 September 2003.

36 '"US will assist SDF in Iraq", Armitage pledge to Ishiba', *Japan Times*, 3 February 2004.

37 Quoted in Amaki, 'Jieitai Iraq haken . . .', p. 64.

38 Reiji Yoshida, 'Fukuda refuses to budge on WMD', *Japan Times*, 30 January 2004.

39 Kishi Nobusuke, quoted in Hayano Toru, 'Kishi shusho mo idai na hato-ha data', *Asahi Shimbun*, 13 January 2004.

40 Yoichi Nishimura, 'Armitage expects "generous" Japanese assistance to rebuild Iraq', *Asahi Shimbun*, 26 September 2003.

41 Senate Foreign Affairs Defence and Trade Committee, 'Inquiry into Japan' (Parliament House: Canberra, 1999), http://www.aph.gov.au/hansard. Craig Skehan, 'Downer to tell Japan: get stronger and lead more', *Sydney Morning Herald*, 17 May 2001.

42 Okamoto Susumu, 'Donna kokkai ga haken o shonin shita ka', *Sekai*, April 2004, pp. 20–4, at p. 23.

43 'Ex-posts minister sues over SDF dispatch to Iraq', *Japan Times*, 30 January 2004; Minowa Noboru, 'Koizumi-kun, jieitai ho o benkyo shinasai', *Shukan Kinyobi*, 13 February 2004, p. 15.

44 Amaki Naoto, 'Jieitai Iraq haken . . .', pp. 60–5.

45 Gotoda Masaharu and Kato Shuichi, 'Rekishi ni seitai shinakereba', *Sekai*, August 2005, pp. 48–61, at p. 51.

46 *Asahi Shimbun* polls reported opposition falling to 55 per cent in December, 48 per cent in January when the SDF was dispatched, and 41 (against 42 in favour) in March. Yomiuri found 53 per cent in favour of dispatch by January, and 58 by February. Mainichi found a low of 16 per cent in favour, rising to a high of 50 per cent by March 2004. *Asahi Shimbun*, 23 February and 21 March 2004; *Yomiuri Shimbun*, 27 February 2004; *Mainichi Shimbun*, 8 March 2004.

47 Quoted in Okamoto, 'Donna kokkai . . .', p. 24.

48 See, for example, the analyses by Kang Sangjung, in Kang Sangjung and Kato Shuichi, 'Rekishi no bunkiten ni tatte', *Ronza*, April 2004, pp. 10–23, at p. 11; and by the military affairs specialist Maeda Tetsuo, 'Kyusoku ni rinsen josei totonoeru jieitai', *Sekai*, April 2004, pp. 20–4, at p. 24.

49 Kang Sangjung, 'Rekishi no bunkiten ni tatte', p. 11.

50 J. Sean Curtin, 'Japan's "Fortress of Solitude" in Iraq – plus karaoke', *Asia Times*, 19 February 2004.

51 Nao Shimoyachi, 'SDF vs. NGO – an Iraqi tale of cost effectiveness', *Japan Times*, 16 May 2004.

52 NHK television, 17 June 2004.

53 The UN term *toitsu sareta shiki* was rendered *as togo sareta shireibu*. 'Kokusai koken ga yugande iru', editorial, *Asahi Shimbun*, 18 June 2004.

54 On 28 May, however, two other Japanese journalists were attacked and killed in their car just south of Baghdad.

55 Kumaoka Michiya, 'Hahei hantai messeji', *Shukan Kinyobi*, 16 April 2004, p. 16.

56 In October 2006, the *Lancet* medical journal raised the estimate of civilian deaths as a result of the US-led invasion to 655,000 – around 2.5 per cent of the population (Sarah Boseley, '655,000 Iraqis killed since invasion', *Guardian*, 12 October 2006).

57 'Shusho mizukara "haken kanketsu" ', *Asahi Shimbun*, 20 June 2006.

58 See *Sunday Times*, 1 May 2005.

59 Quoted in Komurata Yoshiyuki and Sato Takeshi, 'Zainichi beigun saihen ga honkakuteki', *Asahi Shimbun*, 19 February 2005.

60 Kato Yoichi, 'Beigun saihen to Nichibei domei – (I), Yuji taio kara yobo-gata e', *Asahi Shimbun*, 28 June 2006.

61 Asai Motofumi, 'Beigun kichi hantai ni okeru shiten tenkan o', *Ryukyu shimpo*, 6 November 2005.

62 'Security Consultative Committee Document, US–Japan Alliance: Trans-formation and Realignment for the Future', Secretary of State Rice, Secretary of Defense Rumsfeld, Minister of Foreign Affairs Machimura and Minister of State for Defense Ohno, Ministry of Foreign Affairs of Japan, 29 October 2005, http://www.mofa.go.jp/region/n-america/us/security/scc/doc0510.html. Accessed 10 December 2006.

63 Editorial, *Japan Times*, 2 May 2006. See also *Asahi Shimbun*, 25 April 2006.

64 Department of State, United States–Japan Roadmap for Realignment Implementation Issued Following 1 May 2006 Meeting of the US–Japan Security Consultative Committee involving Secretary of State Condoleezza Rice, Secretary of Defense Donald Rumsfeld, Japanese Minister of Foreign Affairs Taro Aso, Japanese Minister of State for Defense Fukushi-iro Nukaga, 1 May 2006, http://www.state.gov/r/pa/prs/ps/2006/65517.htm. Accessed 10 December 2006.

65 The details of these plans, discussed in *Asahi Shimbun*, have been kept secret. Honda Masaru, 'Beigun saihen to Nichibei domei (2) Chikyu kibo no seiji domei e', *Asahi Shimbun*, 29 June 2006. On the '5055' plan for Japanese cooperation with US forces in the event of war on the Korean peninsula, see *Asahi Shimbun*, 12 December 2004.

66 Department of Defense, 'Quadrennial Defense Review Report', 6 February 2006, http://www.defenselink.mil/qdr/.

67 Ibid., p. 7.

68 'Coordination with Japan, South Korea', *Japan Times*, 9 March 2006. See also Michael Klare, 'Containing China', *Tom Dispatch*, 19 April 2006, http://www.tomdispatch.com/index.mhtml?pid=78021.

69 Umebayashi Hiromichi, *Beigun saihen*, (Tokyo: Iwanami bukkuretto, No. 676, 2006).

70 Ibid., p. 7.

71 '84%: government had not sufficiently explained the realignment', *Asahi Shimbun*, 23 May 2006.

72 Nonaka Hiromu, 'Kokumin fuzai no giron ni ikari', *Asahi Shimbun*, 29 April 2006.

73 Maeda Tetsuo, quoted in Handa Shigeru, 'San-cho en futan o yobikonda senryaku naki kanryo no daizai', *Shukan Kinyobi*, 19 May 2006, pp. 10–14, at p. 14.

74 Iya Igarashi, 'Armitage says Japan on par with UK', *Yomiuri Daily Online*, 20 March 2006. See also Richard Armitage, 'How the US–Japan alliance will shape Asia', *The Oriental Economist*, March 2006.

75 David Gee, *United States Military and Intelligence Bases in Britain: A Briefing* (Quaker Peace and Social Witness, Peace Campaigning and Networking Group, June 2004), http://nfpb.gn.apc.org/basesu_s.pdf. Accessed 10

December 2006. Also Duncan Campbell, *The Unsinkable Aircraft Carrier: American Military Power in Britain* (London: Michael Joseph, 1984).

76 Campbell, *Unsinkable Aircraft Carrier*, p. 27.

77 Ibid., p. 22.

78 Joint Chiefs of Staff assessment, quoted in Campbell, *Unsinkable Aircraft Carrier*, p. 43.

79 First published in the *Sunday Times*, 1 May 2005. See Mark Danaher, *The Secret Way to War: The Downing Street Memo and the Iraq War's Buried History* (New York: New York Review Books, 2006).

80 Robert Scheer, 'A distinct lack of intelligence', *Nation*, 9 October 2006, http://www.thenation.com/doc/20061009/truthdig. Accessed 12 October 2006.

81 'Yo, Blair', Wikpedia, http://en.wikipedia.org/wiki/Yo,_Blair. Accessed 10 January 2007.

82 'Armitage says Japan on par with UK', *Daily Yomiuri Online*, 20 March 2006. Accessed 12 December 2006.

83 'Japan urged to up defence spending', *Asahi Shimbun*, 17 March 2006.

84 'Rekishijo mottomo seijuku shita nikokukan kankei', Joint Statement, *Asahi Shimbun*, 30 June 2006. The literal equivalent for 'mature' (*seijuku shita*) was rendered in the official English text as 'accomplished', presumably an indicator of bureaucratic discomfort somewhere in the Japanese system at the realization of fulfilment of the long-term American agenda. Ministry of Foreign Affairs, 'Japan–US Summit Meeting, The Japan–US Alliance of the New Century', 29 June 2006, http://www.mofa.go.jp/region/n-america/us/summit0606.html.

85 From 20 March 2003, in a report to the Diet, quoted in Heigo Sato, 'The Koizumi administration and Japan–US Relations', *International Symposium on Security Affairs* (Tokyo: National Institute for Defense Studies, 2005), http://www.nids.go.jp. Accessed 3 March 2006.

86 OECD, *Economic Surveys, Japan*, 2006, p. 60.

87 See Tachibana Takashi, *Horobiyuku kokka – Nihon wa doko e mukau no ka* (Nikkei: BP-sha, 2006), pp. 385–6.

88 From $2.7 trillion in 1989, and heading towards $12.8 trillion by 2016, according to Congressional Budget Office. Girish Mishra, 'American Economy: some worries', Z-Net, 16 August 2006, http://www.zmag.org/content/print_article.cfm?itemID&sectionID=72. The 30 August 2006 figure from Bureau of the Public Debt, US Treasury, http://www.publicdebt.treas.gov/opd/opds082006.htm. Accessed 15 September 2006.

89 Japanese public debt total approximately ¥1 quadrillion: 'Kuni no saimu choka, 20 cho en zo', *Asahi Shimbun*, 26 August 2006. (A lower figure, around ¥850 trillion, is sometimes given, but it does not include liabilities of public instrumentalities.)

90 Philip S. Golub, 'US the world's deepest debtor', *Le Monde Diplomatique*, October 2003.

91 Taggart Murphy, 'East Asia's dollars', *New Left Review* 40, July–August 2006, pp. 39–64.

92 Maeda, 'Kaijo keibi . . .', p. 47.
93 Chalmers Johnson, *The Sorrows of Empire: Militarism, Secrecy and the End of the Republic* (London and New York: Verso, 2004), p. 202.
94 Terashima Jitsuro, '21 seiki Nihon gaiko no kosoryoku Iraq senso o koete', *Ronza,* January 2004, pp. 20–7, at p. 24 puts the figure of ¥10 trillion (ca $90 billion) on Japan's post-9/11 'rear support', but the source of the figure is not clear.
95 'Bei – Iraq shiensaku ni shai', *Asahi Shimbun,* 18 October 2003.
96 Tachibana Takashi, *Iraku senso, Nihon no unmei, Koizumi no unmei* (Tokyo: Kodansha 2004), p. 165.
97 'Japan considers waiving half of Iraq's $7 billion debt', *Kyodo,* 5 March 2004.
98 'Iraku saimu, susumanu sakugen', *Asahi Shimbun,* 11 June 2004.
99 Handa Shigeru, 'Misairu boei tonyu giman o abaku', *Gendai,* March 2004, pp. 70–9, at pp. 73, 77.
100 Michael Swaine, Rachel Swanger, Takashi Kawakami, *Japan and Ballistic Missile Defense* (Santa Monica: Rand Corporation 2001), p. 67.
101 Taoka Shunji, 'Misairu taisaku hi to koka', *Aera,* 24 July 2006, p. 25. 'Ugokidasu BMD' (part 1), *Asahi Shimbun,* 7 October 2006.
102 'Misairu boei e Nihon kasoku', *Asahi Shimbun,* 18 September 2003; and 'North Korean missile threat spurs missile defense action', *Asahi Shimbun,* 20–21 December 2003.
103 Leo Sartori, 'Bush's Missile Defense System: Does it Pass Muster?' (Washington: Center for Arms Control and Non-Proliferation, 3 December, 2003).
104 Oliver Burkeman, '$100 bn later, Star Wars hits its missile', *Guardian,* 2 September 2006.
105 Quoted in 'Ugokidasu BMD', *Asahi Shimbun,* 7 October 2006.
106 Handa, 'San-cho en futan . . .', p. 75.
107 'Kawase kainyu 3 cho 3420 oku en – 2 gatsu', *Asahi Shimbun,* 28 February 2004.
108 Takao Hishinuma and Eiji Hirose, 'US official says Japan "not just some ATM"', *Daily Yomiuri,* 10 October 2003.
109 Hamish McDonald, 'Howard's blank cheque for Washington may come with a hefty surcharge', *Sydney Morning Herald,* 18 September 2001.
110 Wada Haruki, *Tohoku Ajia kyodo no ie* (Tokyo: Heibonsha 2003), p. 166.
111 For 'comprador', see Gavan McCormack, 'Introduction' to second revised edition, *The Emptiness of Japanese Affluence*, p. xx. For 'parasite', see Ishida Hidenari, Ukai Satoshi, Komori Yôichi, Takahashi Tetsuya, '21 seiki no manifesuto – datsu "parasaito nashonarizumu"', *Sekai,* August 2000, pp. 189–208.
112 The short-lived parliamentary vice-minister at the Defence Agency in August 1999 who called for Japan to arm itself with nuclear weapons.
113 Governor of Tokyo from 1999, previously well known author of books such as *The Japan That Can Say No* (New York: Simon & Schuster, 1991).

114 For recent discussion on the theme of reviving nationalism, see Eugene Matthews, 'Japan's New Nationalism', *Foreign Affairs*, November–December 2003, and Steven C. Clemons, 'Nationalism: Old News or New Worry?' *Daily Yomiuri*, 9 December 2003. See my 'New Tunes for an Old Song: Nationalism and Identity in Post-Cold War Japan', in Roy Starrs, ed., *Nations Under Siege: Globalization and Nationalism in Asia* (New York: Palgrave, 2002), pp. 137–67.

115 Hoshi Toru, 'Kita Chosen gaiko', *Asahi Shimbun*, 4 January 2005.

116 The beef matter took up 70 per cent of their short meeting time. Tersahima Jitsuro et al., 'Ogoru na Amerika, me o hiraku Nippon', *Ronza*, January 2005, pp. 34–47.

117 Nishibe Susumu, 'Seiron', *Sankei Shimbun*, 15 September 2006. Nishibe's views are said to be positively regarded by Abe Shinzo, prime minister from September 2006.

5 Japan in Asia

1 See the Defence Plan ('Heisei 17 nendo iko ni kakawaru boei keikaku no taiko ni tsuite') adopted by cabinet on 10 December 2004, http://www.jda.go.jp/j/defense/policy/17taikou/taikou.htm. Accessed 5 July 2005. On the background, see Tanaka Sakai, 'Sensuikan shinnyu mondai to Nichu kankei', *Tanaka News*, 19 November 2004, http://tanakanews.com/e1119japan.htm. Accessed 21 November 2004.

2 'South Korean leader warns Yasukuni is clouding ties', *Japan Times*, 16 August, 2001.

3 Speech of 1 March 2005, *Japan Times*, 2 March 2005.

4 Yoshii Ruri, 'The Special Law on pro-Japanese anti-Korean activities under Japanese Forcible Occupation: Establishment and Historic Origin' (unpublished MA thesis, International Christian University, Tokyo, 2006).

5 *Yomiuri Shimbun* and *Hankook Ilbo* survey, *Yomiuri Daily News*, 10 June 2005; virtually unchanged a year later, at 89 per cent in mid-2006 (*Daily Yomiuri*, 7 August 2006).

6 Quoted in Akasaka Harukazu, 'Chugoku han-Nichi demo no haikei', *Sekai*, June 2005, pp. 21–4.

7 'Dokyumento – Gekido no namboku Chosen', *Sekai*, July 2006, pp. 254–61, at p. 256.

8 'Our very own preemptive option', editorial, *Japan Times*, 18 July 2006.

9 'Ayaui "seigi" no keikaishin', *Asahi Shimbun*, 4 September 2002.

10 Owaku Masashi, '"Kita Chosen no kyoi" no shotai', *Aera*, 14 April 2003, pp. 19–20.

11 Marcus Noland, *Avoiding the Apocalypse: The Future of the Two Koreas* (Washington, DC: Institute for International Economics, 2000), p. 350.

12 Funabashi Yoichi, 'KEDO to iu gaiko tejina', *Asahi Shimbun*, 3 July 2003.

13 For details see Gavan McCormack, *Target North Korea*.

14 Nonaka Hiromu, *Rohei wa shinazu* (Tokyo: Bungei shunju, 2004), p. 295

15 A fact at first denied, but eventually recognized in a cabinet memo of February 2006 in response to a Diet question by Suzuki Muneo. Honshi Nicho mondai shusaihan, 'Nimaishita gaiko ga 'kokueki' o sokonau', *Shukan kinyobi*, 3 March 2006, p. 59.

16 Details in Wada Haruki and Gavan McCormack, 'Forever stepping back: The strange record of 15 years of Negotiations between Japan and North Korea', in John Feffer, ed., *The Future of US–Korea Relations* (London and New York: Routledge, 2006), pp. 81–100.

17 *Asahi Shimbun*, 29 January 2004.

18 *Japan Times*, 2 March 2005.

19 Wada and McCormack, 'Forever stepping back'.

20 'Kin soshoki wa atama no tenkai hayai hito', *Asahi Shimbun*, 28 May 2004.

21 'Rokusha kyogi, Beikoku mo ugoku toki da', editorial, *Asahi Shimbun*, 22 June 2004.

22 Hoshi Toru, 'Kita Chosen gaiko', *Asahi Shimbun*, 4 January 2005.

23 On his departure for Pyongyang, 22 May 2004, NHK TV.

24 'Nicho no kokko seijoka, shusho "ichinen inai ni"', *Asahi Shimbun*, 3 July 2004.

25 Details in Wada and McCormack, 'Forever stepping back'.

26 Fujita Yutaka, 'Zainichi Korian no kodomotachi ni taisuru iyaragase jittai chosa', *Sekai*, October 2003, pp. 248–54.

27 Shin Sugok, 'Ganbare' tte watakushi ni iu anata jishin wa doko ni iru nda?' Keisen jogakuen daigakuin kokusai shimpojiumu jikko iinkai, ed., *Chotto yabai n ja nai? Nashonarisumu* (Tokyo: Kaiho shuppansha, 2006), pp. 61–79, at p. 63.

28 McCormack, *Target North Korea*, p. 122.

29 Yamaguchi Jiro, 'Seiji jihyo', *Shukan Kinyobi*, 21 January 2005, p. 14.

30 For the Japanese government's statement of 24 December, see Nicho kokko sokushin kokumin kyokai, *Nicho kankei to rokusha kyogi* (Tokyo: Sairyusha 2005, pp. 66–9).

31 Ibid., p. 46.

32 'Abe: abducted son looks like Yokota's husband in North', *Asahi Shimbun*, 28 June 2006.

33 David Cyranoski, 'DNA is burning issue as Japan and Korea clash over kidnaps', *Nature*, vol. 433, 3 February 2005, p. 445.

34 Ishiyama Ikuo and Yoshii Tomio, *DNA Kantei Nyumon* (Tokyo: Nanzando, 1998).

35 'Politics versus reality', *Nature*, vol. 434, 17 March 2005, p. 257.

36 Norimitsu Onishi, 'Asia Letter: About a kidnap victim, DNA testing, and doubt', *International Herald Tribune*, 2 June 2005.

37 David Cyranoski, 'Geneticist's new post could stop him testifying about DNA tests', *Nature*, vol. 437, 7 April 2005, p. 685.

38 Machimura, in response to a question in the House of Representatives, 30 March 2005.

39 McCormack, *Target North Korea*, passim.

40 Selig S. Harrison, 'Crafting Intelligence: Iraq, North Korea, and the road to war', *Japan Focus*, 15 March 2005. http://japanfocus.org/products/details/1915.

41 Selig S. Harrison, 'Did North Korea Cheat?', *Foreign Affairs*, January–February 2005, and *Japan Focus*, March 2005 http://japanfocus.org/products/details/2112.

42 Various statements by President Bush, Secretary of State Rice, and Under-Secretary of State for Global Affairs Paula Dobriansky, January–May 2005.

43 Victor Cha's term. Cha was appointed Director for Asian Affairs at the National Security Council in December 2004.

44 Unification Minister Lee Jong-seok, quoted in 'US pressure on N. Korea may not be effective, Seoul', *Reuters*, 3 May 2006.

45 Yang Sung-chul (former Korean ambassador to the US), 'On Korean question: rhetoric and realities', *Korea Herald*, 19 April 2006.

46 Thus the images of North Korea as porcupine and as snail, discussed above, p.94.

47 *Asahi Shimbun*, 22 June 2005.

48 International Crisis Group, 'After North Korea's Missile Launch: Are the Nuclear Talks Dead?' Policy Briefing, Asia Briefing No. 52, Seoul/Brussels, 9 August 2006.

49 Hamish McDonald, 'Pushing the boundaries', *Sydney Morning Herald*, 15 October 2006.

50 Charles L. (Jack) Pritchard, 'Six Party Talks Update: False Start or a Case for Optimism', Conference on 'The Changing Korean Peninsula and the Future of East Asia', sponsored by the Brookings Institution and *Joongang Ilbo*, 1 December 2005.

51 Joseph Kahn and David E. Sanger, 'US–Korean deal on arms leaves key points open', *New York Times*, 20 September 2005.

52 For relevant documents, *Korea and World Affairs*, vol. xxix, 3 (Fall 2005), pp. 445–64.

53 Ibid. p. 458.

54 'US, Partners end N. Korean nuclear project', *Associated Press*, 22 November 2005.

55 *Korea and World Affairs*, pp. 455–64.

56 For fuller discussion of this shift, see Gavan McCormack, 'Criminal States: Soprano vs. Baritone – North Korea and the US', *Korea Observer*, Seoul, vol. 37, No. 3, Autmn 2006, pp. 487–511.

57 Daniel Glaser, deputy assistant secretary for terrorist financing and financial crimes, stated that North Korea 'needs to cease its criminal financial activities'. Quoted in Josh Meyer and Barbara Demick, 'N Korea running counterfeit racket, says US', *Sydney Morning Herald*, 14 December 2005.

58 'US says N. Korea "criminal regime"', BBC News, 17 December 2005.

59 According to a PEW survey, 'American public views north as biggest threat', *Joongang Ilbo*, 19 November 2005.

60 'US accuses North Korea of $100 bill counterfeiting', *Washington Times*, 12 October 2005.

61 Klaus W. Bender, *Moneymakers: The Secret World of Banknote Printing* (Weinheim, Germany: Wiley-VCH Verlag, 2006), pp. 260–6.

62 'Yukizumaru 6-sha kyogi', *Sekai*, May 2006, pp. 258–65, at p. 259.

63 Philippe Pons, 'Les Etats-Unis tentent d'asphyxier financièrement le régime de Pyongyang', *Le Monde*, 26 April 2006.

64 Toshihiko Yada, 'US: DPRK behind "supernotes" ', *Yomiuri Shimbun*, 27 October 2006.

65 United States of America, Department of the Treasury, Financial Crimes Enforcement Network, 'In the Matter of Israel Discount Bank of New York', No. 2006–7 (Assessment of Civil Money Penalty). I am indebted to John McGlynn of Tokyo for this information.

66 When early in 2007, as discussed below, a deal was done in which North Korea made no concession other than to promise that the funds would be used for educational or humanitarian purposes, the sense that the case had been politically inspired in the first place became even stronger.

67 Ogawa Kazuhiko, ' "Teki kichi kogeki-ron" no yojisei', *Shukan Kinyobi*, 21 July 2006, pp. 18–19.

68 UN Security Council, Resolution 1695, 15 July 2006, http://www.un.org/News/Press/docs/2006/sc8778.doc.htm. Accessed 21 July 2006.

69 'Japan's preemptive strike plan lacks sense of history', Hankyoreh Online, (Seoul: Hankyoreh shinmoon, 12 July 2006).

70 'Poll: 92% support sanctions on N. Korea', *Daily Yomiuri*, 8 July 2006.

71 UN Security Council, No. 1718, 14 October 2006, http://www.un.org/News/Press/docs/2006/sc8853.doc.htm. Accessed 21 October 2006.

72 Bilateral trade of ¥120 billion in 1980 reduced to ¥27 billion in 2004, and halved just in the period 2002–04. (Nicho kokko sokushin kokumin kyokai, *Nicho kankei*, pp. 51–5; and n.a. 'Dokyumento – Gekido no namboku Chosen', *Sekai*, August 2006, pp. 266–73, at p. 273.)

73 'Aso: Stage set to help U.S. on ship inspections', *International Herald Tribune*, 16 October 2006, http://www.asahi.com/english/Herald-asahi/TKY200610160115.html. Accessed 16 October 2006.

74 Selig Harrison, 'In a test, reason to talk', *Washington Post*, 10 October 2006.

75 Interview, Ignacio Ramonet, 'Tension en Corée', *Le Monde Diplomatique*, October 2006, p. 1.

76 Harada Takeo, 'Abe Shinzo "hatsu gaiko" yaburetari', *Gendai*, September 2006, pp. 166–72, passim.

77 International Crisis Group, Policy Briefing, Asia Briefing no. 52, 9 August 2006.

78 Gavan McCormack, 'Member of the Axis of Evil No More,' Yale Global Online, 5 March 2007. http://yaleglobal.yale.edu/display.article?id=8865.

79 'North Korea may still be nuclear in 2020: report,' *The Hankyoreh* (Seoul, 18 February 2007).

80 Wada Haruki, 'The North Korean nuclear problem, Japan, and the peace of

Northeast Asia,' *Japan Focus*, 10 March 2007. http://japanfocus.org/products/details/2376

81 Gavan McCormack, 'Community and identity in Northeast Asia: 1930s and Today', *Japan Focus*, posted 15 December 2004. http://japanfocus.org/product/details/1591.

82 Goldman Sachs, Global Economics Working Paper, no. 99, 'Dreaming with the BRICs: The path to 2050', 1 October 2003. See also 'Mei-an Ajia no miraizu', *Asahi Shimbun*, 4 November 2006.

83 Tersahima Jitsuro, round table discussion with Sakakibara Eisuke and Nishibe Susumu, 'Asia o butai ni 21 seiki no gemu ga hajimatte iru', *Ronza*, March 2005, pp. 28–45.

84 East Asian Vision Group Report, 2001, 'Towards an East Asian Community: Region of Peace, Prosperity and Progress', http://www.mofa.co.jp/region/asia-paci/report2001.pdf. See also Wada Haruki, 'From a "Common House of Northeast Asia" to a "Greater East Asian Community"', *Social Science Japan* (March 2004), pp. 19–21.

85 'Higashi Ajia kyodotai koso bunsho zukuri teian e', *Asahi Shimbun*, 26 November 2004.

86 Wada Haruki, *Tohoku Ajia kyodo no ie* (Tokyo: Heibonsha, 2003); Kang Sang-Jung, *Tohoku Ajia kyodo no ie o mezashite* (Tokyo: Heibonsha, 2001).

87 Mori Kazuko, interviewed in *Sight*, Summer 2006, p. 64.

88 Ito Ken'ichi, 'Kasoku suru Higashi Ajia no chiiki togo koso', Seiron, *Sankei Shimbun*, 15 April 2004. English translation at http://www.sankei.co.jp/databox/e_seiron/2004/040415.html.

89 Gregory W. Noble, 'Japanese political economy and Asian economic cooperation', *Social Science Japan* 28 (April 2004): pp. 12–15, at p. 14.

90 Shioya Takafusa, 'The Grand Design for Northeast Asia', (Tokyo: National Institute of Research Advancement, 2004). http://www.nira.go.jp. Accessed 3 August 2005.

91 Interview, *Asahi Shimbun*, 1 May 2005.

6 The constitution and the Fundamental Law of Education

1 Details in Glenn D. Hook and Gavan McCormack, *Japan's Contested constitution* (London and New York: Routledge, 2001).

2 Matsuzawa Tessei, 'Yon-ju nendai no kuhaku – Osutoraria ni yoru tenno senpanron o chushin ni', *Shiron*, (Tokyo: Tokyo Joshi Daigaku, 2005 vol. 56, no. 1, and vol. 58).

3 Paragraph 1 of the secret memo of 3 February 1946, headed 'Copy of penciled Notes of C-in-C handed to me on Sunday 3 February 1946 to be basis of draft constitution', now held in the library of University of Maryland, College Park, Md, begins 'Emperor is at the head of the state . . .'

4 On 27 February 1946, via Prince Higashikuni (Umaru Yoichi, '"Tai-I" yureta tenno', *Asahi Shimbun*, 13 July 2006).

5 Fujiwara Akira, Ito Satoru, Yoshida Yutaka, and Kunugi Toshihiro, *Tenno no showashi*, (Tokyo: Shin Nihon shinsho, no. 346: 1984), pp. 109-110.

6 John Dower, *Embracing Defeat: Japan in the Wake of World War II* (New York and London: WW Norton & Company, The New Press, 1999).

7 Harry Harootunian and Naoki Sakai, 'Dialogue – Japan studies and cultural studies', *positions*, vol. 7, no. 2, Fall 1999, pp. 593–647, at p. 604. See also Sakai's *Shisan sareru Nihongo, Nihonjin* (Tokyo: Shinyosha, 1996).

8 Terashima Jitsuro, 'Chugoku o kyoi to suru mae ni', *Sekai*, March 2006, pp. 41–3.

9 Article 3 of the Self-Defence Law, 1954.

10 Hook and McCormack, *Japan's Contested constitution*.

11 Yasuoka Okiharu, interviewed by Takahashi Tetsuya, 'Kempo Gekiron (2) Jiminto', *Shukan Kinyobi*, 25 June 2004, pp 14–17. See also Takahashi Tetsuya, *Kyoiku to kokka*, (Tojyo: Kodansha gendai shinsho, no. 1742: 2004), p. 95.

12 Kishi Nobusuke, prime minister 1957–60, addressing the lower house of the national Diet on 30 September 1958. Hayano Toru, 'Kishi shusho mo idai na hato-ha datta!?' *Asahi Shimbun*, 14 January 2004.

13 Prime minister Sato Eisuke, in 1970, quoted in 'Report of the Senate Standing Committee on Foreign Affairs and Defense', Canberra, AGPS, 1973, p. 23.

14 Yet Japan's defence throughout the Cold War (and beyond) rested on the US nuclear deterrent, on which see Chapter 7.

15 'Armitage: Article 9 hinders Japan's alliance with US', *Asahi Shimbun*, 23 July 2004.

16 'State Department Roundtable with Japanese Journalists', August 2004, http://www.state.gov/secretary/fomer/Powell/remarks/35204.htm.

17 The 'Armitage Report' offered the special relationship between the US and Great Britain as a model for the relationship with Japan.

18 'Shusho, TV bangumi de "jieitai o kokugun to aratameta ho ga ii"', *Yomiuri Shimbun*, 2 November 2003.

19 'Critics slam Koizumi's take on constitution', *Japan Times*, 13 December 2003.

20 Quoted by Maeda Tetsuo, Maeda et al., 'Tohoku Ajia no anzen hosho to kempo 9-jo', *Sekai*, October 2003, pp. 44–64, at p. 46.

21 Koizumi speaking on 23 October 2001, quoted in Amaki Naoto, 'Jieitai hitei wa higenjitsuteki gomakashi wa genkai da', *Ronza*, February 2004, pp. 28–33, at p. 31.

22 Quoted in *Asahi Shimbun*, 22 February 2004.

23 See LDP web page: http://www.jimin.jp/jimin/shin_kenpou/; and for the October 2005 draft, the web page of the LDP's Center to Promote Enactment of a New constitution: http://www.jimin.jp/jimin/shin_kenpou/shiryou/pdf/051122_a.pdf. Accessed 10 January 2006.

24 This term is also variously translated as 'the scope of socially acceptable protocol' or 'ethno-cultural practices'.

25 Colin Powell told Japanese journalists in August 2004 that Japan would have to revise Article 9 if it wished to be considered for a permanent seat on the Security Council. 'State Department Roundtable with Japanese Journalists', http://www.state.gov/secretary/fomer/Powell/remarks/35204. htm. Accessed 3 October 2004.

26 Tetsushi Kajimoto, 'Nakasone hits Koizumi populism, Yasukuni visits', *Japan Times*, 23 November 2005.

27 See the *Yomiuri Shimbun* proposals, Hook and McCormack, *Japan's Contested constitution*, pp. 55–91.

28 'Nihon wa sekai o do koken suru ka', Ozawa Ichiro interviewed by Hayano Toru, *Asahi Shimbun*, 1 November 2001.

29 Yamaguchi Jiro and Kato Koichi, 'Seiji ga komyuniti o kowashite wa naranai', *Sekai*, March 2006, pp. 44–51.

30 Nakasone Yasuhiro, *Japan: A State Strategy for the Twenty-first Century*, translated by Lesley Connors and Christopher P. Hood (London and New York: RoutledgeCurzon, 2002), p. 1.

31 Ezra Bowen, 'Nakasone's World-Class Blunder – Japan's leader stirs a tempest by linking race to intellect', *Time*, 6 October 1986.

32 Toru Hayano, 'Interpretational constitutional Revision – Protecting or Revising the constitution?' *Asahi Shimbun*, 19 November 2004, http://www.asahi.com/column/hayano/eng/TKY200411190180.html. Accessed 19 November 2004.

33 Tetsushi Kajimoto, 'Nakasone hits Koizumi populism, Yasukuni visits', *Japan Times*, 23 November 2005.

34 Nakasone Yasuhiro, 'Watakushi no kempo kaisei shian', *Voice*, April 2005.

35 Draft revised Preamble, by Nakasone Yasuhiro, 7 July 2005. Jiyu minshuto, 'Shin kempo kiso iinkai, yoko, dai ichiji soan', http://www.jimin.jp/jimin/shin_kenpou/. Accessed 6 October 2005.

36 Yasuoka Okiharu, interviewed by Takahashi Tetsuya, 'Kempo Gekiron (2) Jiminto', *Shukan Kinyobi*, 25 June 2004, pp 14–17.

37 See Utsumi Aiko, Takahashi Tetsuya and So Kyungsik, eds, *Ishihara tochiji 'Sankokujin' hatsugen no nani ga mondai no ka* (Tokyo: Kage shobo, 2000).

38 See discussion in Koseki Shoichi, 'The case for Japanese constitutional revision assessed', translated Rihard H. Minear, *Japan Focus*, 12 December 2006. http://japanfocus.org/products/details/2289.

39 Kato Koichi, interviewed by Yamaguchi Jiro, 'Seiji ga komyuniti o kowashite wa naranai', *Sekai*, March 2006, pp 44–51, at p. 50.

40 *Asahi Shimbun*, 1 May 2004.

41 Fujimori Ken, in Katsura Keiichi et al, 'Kaiken choryu no naka no media', *Sekai*, 2005, pp. 239–52, at p.243.

42 'Editorial: People are calling for constitutional revision,' *Daily Yomiuri*, 2 April 2004.

43 Quoted Koseki, 'The case for Japanese constitutional revision assessed'.

44 Material taken from May 2005 and 2006 issues of *Asahi Shimbun* and *Yomiuri Shimbun*.

45 *Asahi Shimbun*, 1 May 2004.
46 *Asahi Shimbun*, 1 May 2004.
47 *Asahi Shimbun*, 1 October 2001.
48 *Tokyo Shimbun*, 3 October 2001.
49 *Mainichi Shimbun*, 27 September 2001.
50 Shimin rikken foramu, 'Shimin rikken o togi suru ni atatte', http://www.citizens-i.org/kenpo/paper050401.html. Accessed 6 June 2006.
51 See Hook and McCormack, *Japan's Contested constitution*, pp. 92ff for details and criticism of this proposal.
52 Wada Haruki, Yamaguchi Jiro, Maeda Tetsuo, and Koseki Shoichi, 'Kempo 9-jo iji no moto de, ikanaru anzen hosho seisaku ga dekiru ka', *Sekai*, June 2005, pp. 92–109.
53 'SDF activities are unconstitutional', *Asahi Shimbun*, 2 April 2006, http://www.asahi.com/english/Herald-asahi/TKY200602040128.html. Accessed 4 April 2006.
54 John Junkerman, Gavan McCormack and David McNeill, 'Japan's political and constitutional crossroads', *Japan Focus*, August 2006. http://japanfocus.org/products/details/2175
55 This and the preceding figure are both from the 2002 survey conducted by Nihon Seishonen Kyokai.
56 UN Information Service, Geneva, 'Committee on Rights of Child Concludes Eighteenth Session, Geneva 18 May to 5 June'. Press Release HR/4366, 8 June 1998.
57 In a January 2000 interview, *Nihon kyoiku shimbun*, 7 January 2000, quoted in Yakura Hisayasu, 'Naze kyoiku kihonho o kaitei shitai no ka', *Nihon no shinro*, November 2000, http://www.kokuminrengo.net/2000/200011-dm-ygr.htm. Accessed 25 November 2006. See also Yasuhiro Nakasone, *Japan: A State Strategy for the Twenty-first Century*, translated by Lesley Connors and Christopher P. Hood (London and New York: RoutledgeCurzon, 2002), p. 144.
58 *Yomiuri Shimbun*, 21 April 1997, quoted Takashima, p. 14.
59 'Fiscal health "will need 27 trillion yen in cuts"', *Daily Yomiuri*, 26 March 2006.
60 Nakasone, *A State Strategy*, p. 218.
61 Quoted in Ouchi Hirokazu and Takahashi Tetsuya, *Kyoiku kihonho 'kaisei' o tou* (Tokyo: Hakutakusha and Gendai shokan, 2006), p. 8.
62 Quoted in Takahashi, *Kyoiku to kokka*, pp. 135–6.
63 Umehara Takeshi, 'Nihon no dento to wa nanika?' *Asahi Shimbun*, evening edition, 17 May 2005. English translation, 'What is the Japanese tradition?' by Ota Yusei and Gavan McCormack, *Japan Focus*, 12 July 2005, http://japanfocus.org/products/details/2128. See also Umehara's 'Yasukuni wa Nihon no dento o itsudatsu shite iru', *Sekai*, September 2004, pp. 72–8.
64 Norma Field, 'The child as laborer and consumer: The disappearance of childhood in contemporary Japan', Sharon Stephens, ed., *Childhood and the Politics of Culture* (Princeton: Princeton UP, 1995), pp. 51–78, at p. 67.

65 Shoko Yoneyama, *The Japanese High School: Silence and Resistance* (London and New York: Routledge, 1999), pp. 123–9.

66 CEBc (Citizens Educational Board for Children), ' "Kokoro no noto" ni tsuite', 2003?, http://www.cebc.jp/s-eduad/kokoro/index.html. Accessed 6 July 2006.

67 For details, see Gavan McCormack, *The Emptiness of Japanese Affluence*, Chapter 6.

68 In November 2004. 'Japan ready to distort history education again?' *The Hankyoreh*, 6 December 2004.

69 See the web page of the Kodomo to kyokasho zenkoku Netto 21 (Children and Textbooks Japan Network 21), http://www.ne.jp/asahi/kyokasho/net21/top_f.htm (accessed 22 December 2006); and Tawara Yoshifumi, '05 nendo koko kyokasho no kentei kekka', *Shukan kinyobi*, 21 April 2006, pp. 12–13.

70 Tawara Yoshifumi, 'Atarashii kyokasho o tsukurukai' naibu koso no shinso', *Ronza*, June 2006, pp. 228–35. See also Kato Yusuke, 'Shin, Atarashii rekishi kyokasho tanjo no uchimaku', *Aera*, 3 July 2006, pp. 4–5.

71 Teruoka Yasutaka, *Hinomaru kimigayo no naritachi* (Tokyo: Iwanami Bukkuretto, no. 187, 1997), p. 6.

72 Tamaru Hisae, ' "Hiroshima no ko" to shite mananda koto', *Sekai*, June 2000, pp. 182–7.

73 Takahashi, *Kyoiku to kokka*, p. 159.

74 Aoto Yasushi, Ikezoe Noriaki and Mochizuki Yoshitaka, *Hinomaru, Kimigayo to kodomotachi* (Tokyo: Iwanami Bukkuretto, no. 517, September 2000), passim.

75 Takahashi, *Kyoiku to kokka*, p. 146.

76 Ogi Naoki and Nishihara Hiroshi, 'Kore wa "kyoiku no kudeta" da', *Sekai*, July 2006, pp. 89–99, at p. 90. The measurement of voice volume was reported from Fukuoka – see Takahashi, *Kyoiku to kokka*, p. 146.

77 Tanaka Nobumasa, ' "Kimigayo" kyosei o kempo ni tou "kokoro saiban" ', part 1, *Shukan Kinyobi*, 25 February 2000, pp. 52–5; part 2, 3 March 2000, pp. 30–3.

78 Quoted in Takashima Nobuyoshi, 'Yoto-an minshuto-an no kore dake no mondaiten', in Takashima Nobuyoshi, Takahashi Tetsuya, Sataka Makoto and Tawara Yoshifumi, *Kyoiku kihonho no kore ga mondai* (Tokyo: Kinyobi 2006), pp. 3–36, at p. 25.

79 Kashida, ' "Hinomaru, kimigayo" sotsugyoshiki sorezore no arasoi', *Shukan Kinyobi*, 17 March 2006, pp. 8–11, at p. 10.

80 Ibid.

81 'Hinomaru kimigayo sosho hanketsu riyu', *Asahi Shimbun*, 22 September 2006; Jun Hongo, ' "Kimigayo" directive violates freedom of thought, court rules', *Japan Times*, 22 September 2006. 'City Hall to appeal "Kimigayo" ruling', *Japan Times*, 23 September 2006.

82 Gavan McCormack, 'The Japanese Movement to "Correct" History', in

Laura Hein and Mark Selden, eds, *Censoring History: Citizenship and Memory in Japan, Germany and the United States* (New York: M. E. Sharpe, 2000), pp. 55–73.

83 See Nishizawa Junichi, *Kyoiku kihonho muttsu no teigen* (Tokyo: Shogakukan bunko, 2000).

84 Mori Yoshiro, interviewed in *Asahi Shimbun*, 11 May 2006.

85 Takahashi, *Kyoiku to kokka*, p. 10–11.

86 Quoted in Shoko Yoneyama, 'Japanese "Educational Reform": The Plan for the Twenty-First Century', in Javed Maswood, Jeff Graham, and Hideaki Miyajima, (eds), *Japan: Change and Continuity* (London: Curzon Press), 2002, p. 197.

87 Yoneyama, 'Japanese "Educational Reform"'.

88 Saito Takao, *Kikai fubyodo* (Tokyo: Bungei shunju, 2000), pp. 40–1.

89 Quoted in Takahashi Shiro, 'Kihonho ni aikokushin meiki o', *Sankei Shimbun*, 20 March 2006.

90 Chuo kyoiku shingikai, 'Atarashii jidai ni fusawashii kyoiku kihonho to kyoiku shinko keikaku no arikata ni tsuite (toshin)', 20 March 2003, http://www.mext.go.jp/b_menu/shingi/chukyo/chukyo0/toushin/030301.htm

91 Akemi Nakamura and Hiroko Nakata, 'Diet handed "patriotic" education bill,' *Japan Times*, 29 April 2006.

92 Miyake Shoko, 'Japan's education law reforms and the hearts of children'.

93 Ibid.

94 *Nihon Keizai Shimbun* (28 November) found a majority (55 per cent) saying there was no need to rush the issue. Another survey found only 4 per cent of people who thought education would become better, 28 per cent saying that it would become worse, and 46 per cent that the new law would make no difference. *Asahi Shimbun*, 27 November 2006.

95 Tawara Yoshifumi, 'Tandoku saiketsu wa aseri no araware', *Shukan Kinyobi*, 24 December 2006, pp. 8–9.

96 *Yomiuri Shimbun*, 14 November 2006.

97 'Yarase shitsumon wa 15 kai, 6 wari no TM de hatsugen irai', *Tokyo Shimbun*, 20 December 2006.

98 Mishima Yukio, 'Aikokushin: kansei no iya na kotoba', *Asahi Shimbun*, 8 January 1968.

99 Ouchi Hirokazu and Takahashi Tetsuya, *Kyoiku kihonho 'kaisei' o tou* (Tokyo: Hakutakusha and Gendai shorin, 2006), pp. 37–49, at pp. 40–4.

100 'Kyoiku kihonho, chakuchiten miezu', *Asahi Shimbun*, 25 June 2006.

101 Quoted in Saito, *Kikai fubyodo*. See also Ouchi Hirokazu, *Kyoiku kihonho kaiseiron hihan* (Tokyo: Hakuhatsusha and Gendai shokan, 2003), p. 78.

102 Ouchi, *Kyoiku kihonho kaiseiron hihan*, p. 119.

103 Okudaira Yasushi, 'Now is the time for a national debate on the monarchy itself', *Japan Focus*, 13 June 2006, http://japanfocus.org/products/details/2168.

104 Historian Irokawa Daikichi, quoted in Hook and McCormack, *Japan's Contested constitution*, p. 35.

105 Tsujimoto Kiyomi, with Sataka Makoto, 'Nihonkoku kempo no gyakushu', *Sekai*, October 2000, pp. 44–52, at p. 51.

7   Okinawa: Disposal and Resistance

1 George H. Kerr, *Okinawa: The History of an Island People* (New York: Tuttle, 1958), p. 10.

2 Ota Masahide is the preeminent historian of the Battle of Okinawa. See, for example, *This was the Battle of Okinawa* (Haebaru, Okinawa: Naha Publishing Company, 1981), and 'Reexamining the history of the battle of Okinawa', in Chalmers Johnson, ed., *Okinawa: Cold War Island* (Cardiff, CA: Japan Policy Research Institute, 1999), pp. 13–37.

3 John W. Dower, 'Peace and democracy in two systems', in Andrew Gordon, ed., *Postwar Japan as History* (Berkeley, CA: University of California Press, 1993), p. 11.

4 Herbert P. Bix, *Hirohito and the Making of Modern Japan* (New York: Harpercollins, 2000), pp. 488–90.

5 The letter was penned by Hirohito's close aide, Terasaki Hidenari, but was understood on all sides to come from the emperor. Shindo Eiichi, 'Bunkatsu sareta ryodo', *Sekai*, April 1979, pp. 31–51, at pp. 45–50. See also Bix, *Hirohito*, pp. 626–7.

6 Chalmers Johnson, *The Sorrows of Empire: Militarism and the End of the Republic* (London and New York: Verso, 2004), p. 201.

7 Arasaki Moriteru, *Okinawa gendaishi* (Tokyo: Iwanami shinsho, no. 986, 2005). See also Arasaki interview in *Shukan Kinyobi*, 12 May 2006, pp. 34–5.

8 A protest meeting in Yogi Park on 15 May 1972 drew 30,000 people. Fukushi Hiroaki, 'Okinawa no "Nihon fukki"', *Shukan Kinyobi*, 12 May 2006, pp. 30–3.

9 Arasaki, *Okinawa gendaishi*, pp. 29–30.

10 Asle Sveen, Ivar Libaek and Oivind Stenersen, *The Nobel Peace Prize: 100 Years for Peace* (Oslo: Cappelen, 2001). See also ' "Sato moto shusho no heiwasho wa gimon" Noberu sho iinkai ga kinenshi ni kijutsu', *Asahi Shimbun*, 5 September 2001.

11 See discussion of the reversion in Jon Halliday and Gavan McCormack, *Japanese Imperialism Today: 'Co-Prosperity in Greater East Asia'* (London: Pelican Original, 1973), pp. 195–209, and the text of the 1969 Sato-Nixon Communiqué at ibid. pp. 241–4.

12 Gabe Masaaki, *Okinawa henkan to wa nan datta no ka* (Tokyo: NHK Bukkusu, 2000), pp. 190–206.

13 $300 million as a grant in the form of goods and services, and $200 in yen credits in annual installments, over ten years from 1965.

14 Boei shisetsucho (Defense Facilities Administration Agency), 'Zainichi Beigun churyuhi futan no sui-i', 1979–2005, http://www.dfaa.go.jp/US_-keihi/suii_img.html. Accessed 20 October 2006.

15 'Omoiyari yosan', Wikipedia, accessed 20 October 2006.

16 'Ex-official admits Okinawan "secret pact" ', *Yomiuri Shimbun*, 12 February 2006.

17 Nishiyama Takichi, ' "Mitsuyaku' ga ima no Nichibei kankei no kiten datta', *Sekai*, May 2006, pp. 40–51.

18 On 10 February 2006. Yamaguchi Masanori, ' "Seifu no uso" yurusanai tsuikyu hodo o', *Shukan Kinyobi*, 3 March 2006, p. 26.

19 Ota Masahide, 'Beyond hondo: devolution and Okinawa', in Glenn D. Hook and Richard Siddle, eds, *Japan and Okinawa: Structure and Subjectivity* (London and New York: RoutledgeCurzon, 2003), pp. 114–139, at pp. 122–3. See also Koji Taira, 'Okinawa's choice: independence or subordination', in Chalmers Johnson, ed., *Okinawa: Cold War Island*, pp. 171–84, at pp. 175-6.

20 Ota Masahide, lecture, International Christian University, Tokyo, 14 November 2005.

21 Details in Gavan McCormack, 'Okinawa and the structure of dependence', in Glenn D. Hook and Richard Siddle, eds, *Japan and Okinawa*, pp. 93-113.

22 Ota Masahide, *Okinawa: kichinaki shma e no michishirube* (Tokyo: Shueisha, 2000), pp. 60–3.

23 Details in McCormack, 'Okinawa and the structure of dependence'.

24 Ota, *Okinawa: kichinaki shma e no michishirube.*

25 Ota, 'Beond hondo', pp. 123–4.

26 Chalmers Johnson, 'Okinawa between the United States and Japan', Japan Policy Research Institute, JPRI Occasional paper no. 24, January 2002.

27 See McCormack, 'Okinawa and the structure of dependence', pp. 93-113.

28 Hideki Yoshikawa, 'Elections in Okinawa and the US: Widening the Okinawan struggle', *Japan Focus*, 5 January 2007, http://japanfocus.org/products/details/2314. See also Makishi Yoshikazu's blog ('Maxi's blog'): http://blogs.yahoo.co.jp/okinawa_maxi/folder/268483.html. Accessed 30 January 2007.

29 Article 31 requires the publication of a document explaining the methods to be used and a process of review by the Ministry of the Environment and other relevant ministries or agencies before commencement of any environmental impact assessment activities.

30 Urashima Etsuko – a local activist, author, and environmentalist – has written a powerful chronicle of the local movement: *Henoko: umi no tatakai* (Tokyo: Impakuto shupankai, 2005). Events since 2006 are covered in her columns in the journal *Shinshu Jichiken.*

31 Kanako Takahara, 'Japan, US agree on a new Futenma site', *Japan Times*, 27 October 2005.

32 Ministry of Foreign Affairs, Tokyo, Security Consultative Committee Document, *US–Japan Alliance: Transformation and Realignment for the Future*, 29 October 2005, by Secretary of State Rice, Secretary of Defense Rumsfeld, Minister of Foreign Affairs Machimura, and Minister of State for

Defense Ohno, http://www.mofa.go.jp/region/n-america/us/security/scc/doc0510.html. Japanese text in *Asahi Shimbun*, 30 Otober 2005.

33 'Beigun 66 nen ni no keikaku', *Asahi Shimbun*, 4 November 2005. Okinawan architect and activist Makishi Koichi has posted key US archival documents on this plan on his blog. See also Makishi's 'US Dream Come True? The New Henoko Sea Base and Okinawan Resistance', *Japan Focus*, 12 February 2006. http://japanfocus.org/article.asp?id=522.

34 Interview, Nago City, 5 November 2005. See also Miyagi Yasuhiro, 'Okinawa: Rising Magma', *Japan Focus*, no 464, posted 4 December 2005, http://japanfocus.org/article.asp?id=464.

35 *Asahi Shimbun*, 9 November 2005.

36 Opinion surveys, *Okinawa Times*, 14 September 2004; *Ryukyu shimpo*, 22 June 2005; and *Okinawa Times*, 5 November 2005.

37 *Okinawa Times*, 19 April 2006.

38 Ryukyu Shimpo, 14 April 2006.

39 Hiyane Teruo, 'Kawaru kokka zo – Okinawa no kiki', *Ryukyu Shimpo*, 7 & 8 November 2005.

40 'Kyoken – Okinawa neraiuchi/hanron fusatsu ni tsuyoi ikari', *Okinawa Times*, 27 October 2005.

41 Hiyane, 'Kawaru kokka zo . . .'.

42 Tatsuya Fukumoto and Takashi Imai, 'Okinawa torn over base plan', *Yomiuri Shimbun*, 10 April 2006.

43 *Japan Times*, 5 May 2006.

44 'Futenma plan "may be accepted,"' *Daily Yomiuri*, 14 April 2006.

45 'Kiwamete ikan', *Asahi Shimbun*, 30 May 2006.

46 By 50 per cent, according to Ginowan mayor Iha Yoichi, addressing a meeting at Meiji University on 2 July 2006.

47 Quoted in *Mainichi Shimbun*, 3 August 1998 (BBC, *Summary of World Broadcasts*, Part 3, Asia-Pacific, August 1998, FE/3298/E1).

48 ' Kyoken', *Okinawa Times*, 27 October 2005.

49 Specifically by trying to revive the idea of a small-scale 'heliport'. Takashi Imai, 'Uncertainty surrounds base relocation', *Daily Yomiuri*, 29 August 2006.

50 Shimoji Mikio, 'Koizumi sori no "kakusa" to Inamine chiji no "kakusa" no chigai', Inamine kensei 8 nenkan no kensho, part 8, 13 December 2006, http://www.mikio.gr.jp/s_voice177.html. On debt (bond) dependence levels, see also his part 5 in the same series, 'Okinawa ken to shi-cho-son no zaisei wa aka shingo', 21 December 2006, http://www.mikio.gr.jp/s_voice179.html. Accessed 21 December 2006.

51 'Patoriotto, 31 shucho, haibi hantai', *Ryukyu Shimpo*, 7 October 2006.

52 '"Senryoka to kawarazu" chubu shucho issai ni hanpatsu', *Ryukyu Shimpo*, 12 October 2006.

53 *Ryukyu Shimpo*, 21 November 2006.

54 Gavan McCormack, Sato Manabu and Urashima Etsuko, 'The Nago mayoral election and Okinawa's search for a way beyond bases and

dependence', *Japan Focus*, 16 February 2006, http://japanfocus.org/products/details/1592.

55 Ota, 'Beyond hondo', p. 127.

56 Hamazato Masashi, Sato Manabu and Shimabukuro Jun, *Okinawa jichishu – anata wa do kangaeru?* (Naha: Okinawa jichi kenkyukai, 2005).

57 Oyama Chojo, former mayor of Koza City (now Okinawa City), *Okinawa dokuritsu sengen* (Declaration of Okinawan Independence) (Okinawa: Gendai shoin, 1997), p. 6 – quoted in Ota, 'Beyond hondo', p. 126.

58 Medoruma Shun, *Okinawa sengo zero nen* (Tokyo: NHK seikatsu shinsho, 2005), p. 189.

59 John Pilger, 'Diego Garcia: paradise cleansed', *Guardian*, 4 October 2004; see also his *Freedom Next Time*, (London: Bantam Press, 2006).

60 Yoko Sellek, 'Migration and the nation-state: structural explanations for emigration from Okinawa', in Hook and Siddle, *Japan and Okinawa*, pp. 74–92. See also Kozy Amemiya, 'The Bolivian connection: US bases and Okinawan emigration', in Chalmers Johnson, ed., *Okinawa: Cold War Island*, pp. 149–70.

61 Keiichi Inamine, 'Okinawa as a Pacific crossroads', *Japan Quarterly*, July–September 2000, pp. 10–16, at p. 14.

8   Japan as a Nuclear State

1 To quote only from the October 2005 statement, 'US strike capabilities and the nuclear deterrence provided by the US remain an essential component to Japan's defense capabilities . . .', Ministry of Foreign Affairs of Japan, Security Consultative Committee Document, 'US–Japan Alliance: Transformation and Realignment for the Future', 29 October 2005, http://www.mofa.go.jp/region/n-america/us/security/scc/doc0510.html. Accessed 20 December 2006.

2 Morton Halperin, 'The nuclear dimension of the US–Japan alliance', Nautilus Institute, 1999, http://www.nautilus.org/archives/library/security/papers/US-Japan-4.html (accessed 20 May 2006); 'Secret files expose Tokyo's double standard on nuclear policy', *Asahi Evening News*, 25 August 1999.

3 Conplan refers to the global strike plans under which Stratcom (Strategic Command, Omaha) deals with 'imminent' threats from countries such as North Korea or Iran by both conventional and nuclear 'full-spectrum' options, under President Bush's January 2003 classified directive. William Arkin, 'Not Just A Last Resort? A Global Strike Plan, With a Nuclear Option', *Washington Post*, Sunday, May 15, 2005.

4 Mohammed ElBaradei, 'Saving ourselves from self-destruction', *New York Times*, 12 February 2004.

5 '60 nendai, 2 shusho ga "kaku busoron" Bei kobunsho de akiraka ni', *Asahi Shimbun*, 1 August 2005.

6 Andrew Mack, 'Japan and the Bomb: a cause for concern?' *Asia-Pacific Magazine*, no. 3 June 1996, pp. 5–9.

7 Statement of 3 March 1999, quoted in Taoka Shunji, 'Shuhen yuji no "kyoryoku" sukeru', *Asahi Shimbun*, 3 March 1999.

8 'Nishimura quits over nuclear arms remarks', *Daily Yomiuri*, 21 October 1999.

9 Yoshida Tsukasa, ' "Kishi Nobusuke" o uketsugu "Abe Shinzo" no ayui chisei', *Gendai*, September 2006, pp. 116–29, at p. 127.

10 Dan Plesch, 'Without the UN safety net, even Japan may go nuclear', *Guardian*, 28 April 2003.

11 Jimmy Carter, 'Saving nonproliferation', *Washington Post*, 28 March 2005.

12 William Arkin, 'Not just a last resort: A global plan with a nuclear option', *Washington Post*, 15 May 2005.

13 *Chosun ilbo*, (Seoul: Chosun ilbo), 6 June 2005.

14 Ted Daley, 'America and Iran: Three nuclear ironies', *Truthdig*, 7 July 2006, http://www.truthdig.com/report/item/20060707_three_nuclear_-ironies. Accessed 25 July 2006.

15 Robert McNamara, 'Apocalypse Soon', *Foreign Policy*, May–June 2005, reproduced in *Japan Focus*, 8 May 2005, http://japanfocus.org/products/details/1671.

16 'Government to ok India as N-state', *Yomiuri Shimbun*, 10 January 2007.

17 For outlines of a 'Northeast Asian Nuclear Weapon-Free Zone', see Hiromichi Umebayashi, 'A Northeast Asian Nuclear Weapon-Free Zone', Northeast Asia Peace and Security Network, Special Report, 11 August 2005, http://www.nautilus.org/napsnet/sr/2005/0566NEANWFZ.html (accessed 23 October 2005); and Umebayashi Hiromichi, 'Nihon dokuji no hokatsuteki kaku gunshuku teian o', *Ronza*, June 2005, pp. 188–93.

18 Paul Rogers, 'Britain's nuclear weapon fix', and 'Nuclear weapons: the oxygen of debate', Open Democracy, 29 June and 29 December 2006, http://www.opendemocracy.net. Accessed 10 January 2007.

19 Rogers, 'Nuclear weapons: the oxygen of debate'.

20 Citizens' Nuclear Information Center (CNIC), 'Cost of Nuclear Power in Japan', Tokyo, 2006, http://cnic.jp/english/newsletter/nit113/nit113articles/nit113cost.html. Accessed 10 January 2007.

21 'Nuclear power for civilian and military use', *Le Monde Diplomatique, Planet in Peril* (Arendal, Norway: UNEP/GRID-Arendal, 2006), p.16.

22 'Genpatsu no seisui wakareme', *Asahi Shimbun*, 6 June 2006.

23 Michael Meacher, 'Limited Reactions', *Guardian Weekly*, 21–27 July 2006, p. 17.

24 Quoted in 'Genpatsu no seisui wakareme', *Asahi Shimbun*, 6 June 2006.

25 Tsukasa Kamata, 'Huge tract for ITER sits vacant', *Japan Times*, 25 November 2006.

26 Iida Tetsuya, 'Shizen enerugii fukyu o', *Asahi Shimbun*, 8 June 2004.

27 Many have been constructed on active tectonic faultlines where major earthquakes occur frequently. Leuren Moret, 'Japan's deadly game of nuclear roulette', *Japan Times*, 23 May 2004, revised version at *Japan Focus*, 29 November 2005. http://japanfocus.org/products/details/2013

28 According to the 'New National Energy Strategy' published by the Ministry of Economics, Trade and Industry. Keizai sangyosho, *Shin Kokka Enerugii Senryaku*, May 2006, http://kakujoho.net/blog/archives/000046.html. Accessed 30 November 2006.

29 'Safe storage of nuclear waste', editorial, *Japan Times*, 25 July 2006.

30 Sogo shigen enerugii chosakai, denki jigyo bunkakai, genshiryoku bukai (Subcommittee on Nuclear Energy Policy, Advisory Committee on Energy Policy, Ministry of Economy, Trade and Industry (METI); *Genshiryoku rikkoku keikaku* (Report on Plan to Build a Nuclear Energy Based Nation), draft, 8 August 2006. http://www.meti.go.jp/committee/materials/downloadfiles/g60815a05j.pdf.

31 Frank Barnaby and Shaun Burnie, *Thinking the Unthinkable: Japanese Nuclear Power and Proliferation in East Asia* (Oxford and Tokyo: Oxford Research Group and Citizens' Nuclear Information Center, 2005), p. 17. Around three-quarters of that is presently being processed in Britain's Sellafield, and will be returned to Japan in due course. Eric Johnston, 'Nuclear foes want Rokkasho and Monju on UN nonproliferation agenda', *Japan Times*, 2 April 2005.

32 'Nuclear power for civil and military use', *Le Monde Diplomatique*, p. 17.

33 Barnaby and Burnie, *Thinking the Unthinkable*, p. 8.

34 Ibid., p. 8.

35 Mohammed ElBaradei, 'Seven steps to raise world security', *Financial Times*, 2 February 2005.

36 Suzuki Manami, *Kaku taikokuka suru Nihon* (Tokyo: Heibonsha shinsho, 2006), p. 214.

37 Director General, IAEA, 'Implementation of the NPT Safeguards Agreement in the Republic of Korea,' 11 November 2004 (Geneva: IAEA), http://www.iaea.org/documentgov/2004/84. Accessed 15 March 2007.

38 Yoshioka Hitoshi, 'Genpatsu wa "kaiko" ni atai suru no ka', *Asahi Shimbun*, 21 November 2005.

39 Such cost would amount to between one-half and two-thirds of the costs of reprocessing. Yoshioka, 'Genpatsu wa "kaiko" . . .'.

40 Shaun Burnie, 'Proliferation Report: sensitive nuclear technology and plutonium technologies in the Republic of Korea and Japan, international collaboration and the need for a comprehensive fissile material treaty', paper presented to the International Conference on Proliferation Challenges in East Asia, National Assembly, Seoul, 28 April 2005, p. 18.

41 Estimate by Shaun Burnie, Greenpeace International, personal communication, 4 September 2006. For table showing projected spent fuel waste accumulation to 2050, see Tatsujiro Suzuki, 'Global Nuclear Future: A Japanese Perspective' (Melbourne: Nautilus Institute at RMIT University,

September 2006), http://www.nautilus.org/~rmit/lectures/0601t-suzuki/index.html. Accessed 15 October 2006.

42 Michael Casey, 'Asia embraces nuclear power, *Seattle Times*, 28 July 2006. US stocks of spent nuclear fuel amounted to 53,000 metric tonnes as of December 2005, projected to rise by 2010 to between 100,000 and 1,400,000 (*sic*). (US Department of Energy, May 2006). http://www.gnep.energy.gov.

43 Monju experimental fast breeder was shut down from 1995 after leakage of a tonne of liquid sodium from the cooling system. Two workers were killed, and hundreds exposed to radiation, in a 1999 accident at Tokaimura fuel processing plant when workers carelessly mixed materials in a bucket, causing criticality and near catastrophe. Five more were killed when sprayed with superheated steam from a corroded cooling system pipe in a 2004 accident at Mihama.

44 Plans for large-scale plutonium use in the form of mixed oxide fuel (MOX) collapsed in 1999–2001, when it was revealed by Japanese environmental groups that vital quality control data for fuel delivered to Kansai Electric by British Nuclear Fuels had been deliberately falsified. The effect of this was to galvanize opposition in three prefectures selected for MOX fuel use – Fukui, Fukushima and Niigata.

45 Burnie, 'Proliferation Report', p. 19.

46 Takubo Masafumi, 'Kadai wa New York de wa naku, Nihon ni aru', *Sekai*, June 2005, pp. 142–51, at p. 151.

47 H. A. Feiveson, Princeton University, statement at UN meeting, 24 May 2005, http://kakujoho.net/e/feiveson.html. Accessed 12 July 2006.

48 Eric Johnston, 'Nuclear fuel plant not biz a usual', *Japan Times*, 10 August 2004.

49 *Scientific American* (Digital), May 1994. http://www.sciamdigital.com. Accessed 3 December 2006.

50 Yoshida Yoshihiko, 'NPT o ketsuretsu saseta no wa Beikoku no tandoku kodoshugi', *Ronza*, August 2005, pp. 154–9.

51 CNIC, 'Statement by CNIC and Greenaction about GNEP', 11 July 2006.

52 Ibid.

53 Eric Johnston, 'Safety concerns remain: one decade after accident, Monju may be reborn', *Japan Times*, 9 December 2005.

54 'New fast-breeder reactor to replace prototype Monju', *Asahi Shimbun*, 27 December 2005.

55 'Editorial: Pluthermal project', *Asahi Shimbun*, 16 February 2006.

56 Suzuki, p. 214. Plutonium stocks will reach sixty tonnes by 2010, and remain thereafter at above 50 tonnes.

57 Hirata Tsuyoshi, 'Shinso no kaku haikibutsu', *Shukan Kinyobi*, 25 May 2003, pp. 38–41.

58 Although such discharge only began in March 2006, seawater levels of radioactivity soon rose, sparking protests from the governor of Iwate prefecture (into which the currents from Rokkasho flow) and local fish-

ermen. CNIC, 'Active tests at the Rokkasho Reprocessing plant', June 2006, http://www.cnic.jp/english/newsletter/nit113/nit113articles/nit113Rokkasho.html, and Koyama Hideyuki, 'Sanriku no umi ni hoshano hoshutsu nodo wa genpatsu no 2700 bai', *Shukan Kinyobi*, 19 May 2006, p. 5.

59 George Monbiot, 'Dirty bombs waiting for a detonator', *Guardian*, 11 June 2002.

60 Jim Giles, 'Nuclear power: Chernobyl and the future: when the price is right', *Nature*, no. 440, 20 April 2006, pp. 984–6.

61 Sato Eisaku, 'Tachidomari kokuminteki giron o', *Asahi Shimbun*, 24 May 2003.

62 Barnaby and Burnie, *Thinking the Unthinkable*, p. 9.

63 Umebayashi, 'Nihon dokuji no', p. 193.

64 US Department of Energy, 'The Global Nuclear Energy Partnership', updated July 2006, http://www.gnep.energy.gov.

65 Geoff Elliott, 'US backs Howard's nuclear vision', *The Australian*, 17 August 2006.

66 Paul Sheehan, 'A thirsty world running dry', *Sydney Morning Herald*, 31 July 2006.

67 Anthony Albanese, 'Twenty years on: lest we forget the lessons of Chernobyl', *Sydney Morning Herald*, 26 April 2006.

68 Citizens Nuclear Information Center (CNIC) and Green Action, 'Japan should withdraw its opportunistic, cynical and impractical offer to cooperate with the US Global Nuclear Energy Partnership', statement, 10 July 2006, http://www.greenaction-japan.org. Accessed 1 October 2006.

69 US Department of Energy, 'The Global Nuclear Partnership', p. v.

70 'Kaku gijutsu kaihatsu, Bei "saidai 4 cho 7000 oku en"', Bei chokan kenkai, Nihon nado no kyoryoku kitai', *Chugoku Shimbun*, 17 February 2006.

71 CNIC and Green Action, 'Japan should withdraw . . .'.

72 Michael Meacher, 'Limited Reactions', *Guardian Weekly*, 21–27 July 2006, p. 17.

73 John Busby, 'Why nuclear power is not the answer to global warming', *Power Switch*, 25 May 2005, http://www.powerswitch.org.uk/portal/index.php?option=content&task=view&id=805. Accessed 26 September 2006.

9　The Schizophrenic State?

1 Tsurumi Yoshiharu, 'Saigo made shippo o furutta pochi', *Shukan kinyobi*, 7 July 2006, pp. 20–1.

2 'Press conference by Prime Minister Junichiro Koizumi following the G-8 Summit', 17 July 2006, http://www.kantei.go.jp/foreign/Koizumispeech/2006/07/17press_e.html.

3 Geoffrey Hodgson, 'Yo, Blair', Open Democracy, 19 July 2006, http://www.opendemocracy.net.

4 According to former Japanese diplomat Amaki Naoto, quoted in Tachibana

Takashi, *Iraku senso, Nihon no unmei, Koizumi no kakumei*, Kodansha, 2004, p. 362.

5 See above, p.85.

6 See above, p.3.

7 'Koizumi naikaku heikin 50% no koshijiritsu', *Asahi Shimbun*, 28 August 2006.

8 Wieland Wagner, 'Pilgrimages to the shrine', *Spiegel* International Online, 6   September   2006,   http://www.spiegel.de/international/spiegel/ 0,1518,435377,00.html. Accessed 10 September 2006.

9 *Asahi Shimbun*, 23 August 2006.

10 'Next leader should shun shrine: US lawmakers', *Japan Times*, 16 September 2006. See also 'Beikoku kara no toikake', editorial, *Asahi Shimbun*, 17 September 2006.

11 *Asahi Shimbun*, 30 August 2006.

12 For a subtle portrait of Abe and his grandfather's influence on him, see Hara Yoshihisa, 'Kishi Nobusuke to Abe Shinzo', *Sekai*, November 2006, pp. 80–90.

13 *Asahi Shimbun*, 13 December 2006.

14 Quoted in Nemoto Seiki', Abe seiken no shiten', part 1, *Asahi Shimbun*, 22 September 2006.

15 Miyake Shoko, 'Japan's education law reforms and the hearts of children'.

16 Tachibana Takeshi, 'Mijuku na Abe naikaku ga yurushita kiken na kanryo boso no jidai', Media Online Politics, No 92, 27 December 2006, http:// www.nikkeibp.co.jp/style/biz/feature/tachibana/media/061227_kanryou/ index.html. Accessed 15 January 2007.

17 'Govt to seek public opinion on what makes a "beautiful country"', *Yomiuri Shimbun*, 31 December 2006.

18 Published in 1937 by the Ministry of Education, later translated as *Kokutai no hongi: Cardinal principles of the national entity of Japan* (Cambridge MA: Harvard University Press, 1949).

19 Wada Haruki, 'Abe Shinzo shi no rekishi nishiki o tou', *Sekai*, October 2006, pp. 57–65, at p. 58.

20 'Kibo no kuni, Nihon', *Nihon Keidanren*, 1 January 2007, http://www.kei-danren.or.jp/japanese/policy/207/vision.html. Accessed 15 January 2007.

21 Jürgen Habermas, 'Why Europe needs a constitution', *New Left Review* 11, September–October 2001, pp. 5–26, at p. 21.

22 Edward Said, *Culture and Imperialism* (New York: Vintage, 1993), p. xxix.

23 For general discussion of the Ikeda-Robertson Agreement, see John Dower, *Empire and Aftermath: Yoshida Shigeru and the Japanese Experience, 1878–1954* (Cambridge, MA and London: Harvard University Press, 1979), pp. 451–63. For the text of the communiqué quoted here, see Ouchi and Takahashi, *Kyoiku kihonho 'kaisei' o tou*, pp. 62–3.

24 Quoted in Debito Arudou, 'Righting a wrong', *Japan Times*, 27 June 2006. For the résumé of the Diene Report, see Doudou Diene, 'Report of the Special Rapporteur on contemporary forms of racism, racial discrimination,

xenophobia and related intolerance, Addendum, Mission to Japan', January 2006, reproduced at http://www.debito.org/UNdienereport012406.html.

25 Kato Koichi, Komori Yoichi, Suzuki Kunio, Sataka Makoto and Hayano Toru, 'Ima genron no jiyu o kangaeru', *Sekai*, January 2007, pp. 128–38, at p. 133.

26 Sir Nicholas Stern, 'Stern Review on the Economics of Climate Change', London, HM Treasury and Cabinet Office, 30 October 2006, http://www.hm-treasury.gov.uk/independent_reviews/stern_review_economics_climate_change/sternreview_index.cfm.

27 McCormack, *The Emptiness of Japanese Affluence*, p. 66.

Index